"Five Mile River, Rowayton c. 1920" by the noted marine artist
John Stobart. Oil on canvas: 20" x 36": circa 1986.

Rowayton on the half shell

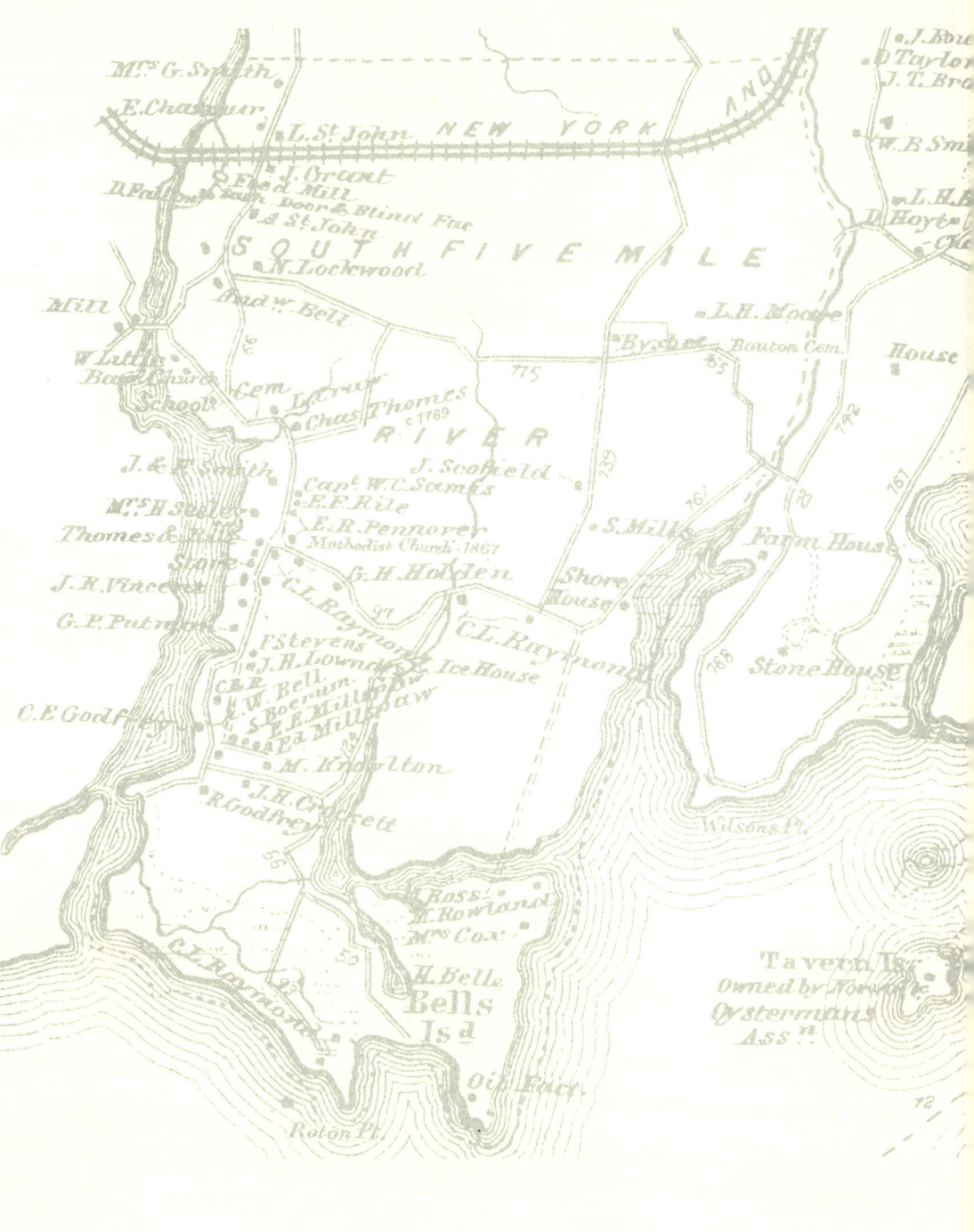

Rowayton on the half shell

the history of a Connecticut coastal village

by
Frank E. Raymond

Published for
The Rowayton Historical Society, Inc.

by
PHOENIX PUBLISHING
West Kennebunk, Maine

Library of Congress Cataloging-in-Publication Data

Raymond, Frank E., 1916–
  Rowayton on the half shell: the history of a Connect-
icut coastal village/by Frank E. Raymond.
    p. cm.
  Includes bibliographical references.
  Includes index.
  ISBN 0-914659-48-0 : $20.00
  1. Rowayton (Conn.)—History. I. Title
  F104.R76R39   1990
  974.6'9—dc20   90-7392
                                                         CIP

Printed in the United States of America

To all the members
of the Rowayton Historical Society, past and present,
whose constant dedication and generosity
has resulted in a most worthy collection
of local memorabilia,
this book is respectfully
and appreciatively dedicated.

CONTENTS

FOREWORD

THE HISTORY OF ROWAYTON has been long in the making. A cattle-grazing range in the 1650s . . . an active fighting front during the Revolutionary War . . . an oyster capital of the world—Rowayton has always been a distinctive, contributive community on the historically evolving landscape of New England. Some call Rowayton's identity a special charm, some refer to it as ambience, some label it contrariness—all call it unique.

Virtually all of Rowayton's history has been amassed and absorbed—and some of it even participated in—by the author of this work, Frank E. Raymond. In addition to being an observant and knowledgeable historian, Frank has served his "home" community in numerous public capacities, with sagacity and skill, unfailing good humor and a sincere appreciation of this "unique" history of which all Rowaytonites are part.

For many years Rowayton's history has been stored in the records of the Rowayton Historical Society and in Frank Raymond's head. At least two generations of Rowaytonites have been urging him to get it down on paper. That he has now done, with commendable clarity and comprehension.

As you will find noted elsewhere on these pages, Rowayton is the only place in the world which bears that name. But Rowayton's uniqueness is not limited to this geographical identity alone. Rowayton has another singular, almost mystical quality: it is the place that has been wise enough to wait this long, long time to carefully select the proper spokesman for its unique history.

John W. Bender
President,
The Rowayton Historical Society

ACKNOWLEDGMENTS

This book is a distillation from many sources, (some secondary-a few original) and from many people. To a large extent I have relied upon the research of others. In the text and in the notes I have tried to give credit where credit is due. When citing those who have contributed, one thing is certain, someone is sure to be unintentionally overlooked. To them I offer my sincere apologies.

In particular I would especially like to thank Jack Bender, president of the Rowayton Historical Society when much of the writing was being done, and later as chairman of the book advisory committee. A retired editor, Jack read the manuscript and has given unstintingly of his skill and knowledge. Also, my gratitude to Mrs. Thomas Cohn, Dudley D. Hoyt, Dorothy E. Johnson, Emily Stevens Merriman, and Harold Martin, all of whom read the manuscript and made many valuable suggestions.

If it were not for the diligence and talent of Mrs. Louise McLean of the Darien Historical Society, the chapters treating the Revolutionary War would have been far less complete and interesting. Doctors Deborah Ray and Gloria Stewart graciously granted permission to quote extensively from their definitive history Norwalk, *published some ten years ago by the Norwalk Historical Society.*

Especially helpful also were Norwalk Historian Ralph Bloom, Rowayton Librarian Mrs. Bonnie Flowers, Joseph Cheh, Mauro Bossone, and Malcolm P. Hunt, historian and cartographer, for permitting use of his maps, and for his advice and encouragement. I am indebted also to Mr. and Mrs. William J. Robinson for making their extensive collection of Rowayton pictures available, and to Nina Pallesen Craig for use of her delightful sketches.

I am also indebted to Mrs. Robert J. Pettus for her patience and accuracy while translating my scrawly notes and typing the original draft with all its faults. The publishers, A. A. Paradis, editor, and A. L. Morris, the designer of the book, have been exceptionally helpful and a pleasure to work with.

And to my wife, Esther, my special thanks for being supportive and allowing the maintenance of the household to deteriorate alarmingly, with only a minimum of complaint.

F.E.R.

Rowayton, Connecticut
January 1990

INTRODUCTION

IT CAN FAIRLY BE SAID that Rowayton is in my blood. My ancestors were among the first to push down into this section of the "Towne of Norwake"—as early as the 1660s. Norwalk was purchased from various local Indians in 1640 by Roger Ludlow and Daniel Partrick (or Patrick), but wasn't settled by the white man until some eleven years later in 1651. Two years later in 1653 one Richard Raymond moved to Norwalk, with wife Judith and son John, from Saybrook, Connecticut. He and two brothers were the first of the family line in this country, his name appearing in the records of Salem, Massachusetts, as a freeman, May 14, 1634.

Richard was a mariner by profession, owner, or possibly part owner, of a sailing packet, *Hopewell*, engaged in coastal trading. His trading carried him ever westward eventually into Long Island Sound, making him one of the very first commercial watermen on the Sound. His grandson, John, was born in Norwalk, September 9, 1665, the first Raymond to be born in America. We've been stuck in the mud around here almost without interruption ever since, mine being the eleventh generation.

I was born in Rowayton, September 9, 1916, in my grandmother's house at 128 Rowayton Avenue. From the time I was a small boy, I have been exposed to Rowayton's past. My father, also a mariner, after finishing a stint in command of a navy tug during World War I (picking up decorations from the French and Italian governments along the way), went to sea. Consequently he was seldom home during my early years. As a result, my grandmother's three brothers, one of whom lived next door, and the two others nearby, became my surrogate fathers. Their tales of their times and what they heard from their elders in turn reached back almost to the founding of the Republic. Too bad for all of our generation that so little was ever committed to paper at that time.

If it had been, much of what follows might have been written by someone far better qualified than I: Edgar D. Lynch, Oscar Mills, S. Edward Dibble, Edwin L. Stevens, Harry S. Street, or Wilbur Smith. All were well-steeped and rooted in the Rowayton story. Any one of them could have, perhaps should have, written it, but, unfortunately, never got around to doing it.

"Fools rush in where angels fear to tread." Much of what follows is oral history, word-of-mouth, hand-me-down information, reminiscences, all subject to the vagaries of the human memory. I would like to think I usually listened rather intently to grandmother's generation, and to the others who should have written this, but who knows what tricks memory will play? Any and all errors of fact and judgment that crop up in the manuscript cannot be blamed on others. I assume full responsibility.

Frank E. Raymond

Rowayton, Connecticut
February 15, 1990

Rowayton on the half shell

First Contact

*N*O TREATMENT of local history in New England can commence without reference to the Indians. Indian artifacts, oyster shell piles, and archeological digs all testify to the presence of the Red Man in the Rowayton area for hundreds of years prior to the coming of the White Man. It so happens that Norwalk has more traces of Indian habitation than any other part of Fairfield County. Outlines of a village complete with burial site have been unearthed at Belden's Point, now Wilson Point. At the time of the first settlement, "contact time" in historical parlance, the Indians in this immediate vicinity were of the Siwanoy tribe, or Sachendom, encompassing an area roughly from the Bronx River to the Five Mile River. Further east, the Tankiteke Sachendom extended on to Fairfield, and northerly inland to the Danbury area.[1]

The Siwanoys were of the Algonquian linguistic group, part of the loosely affiliated Wappingers Confederation covering the lands from the Hudson River, between Manhattan Island and Poughkeepsie, to the lower Connecticut River valley. Mohawks were to the north and west, Pequots to the east, both war-like tribes far from friendly to the whites. After a series of retaliatory killings on both sides, organized warfare erupted between the Pequots and the English settlers in 1637, to go down in history as the Pequot Indian War.

The decisive fight of the Pequot War (and, as it turned out, the final one) took place July 30, 1637, in an area known as Great Swamp, near where the Boston Post Road now crosses the Westport-Fairfield town line. The significant result of the Pequot War to Rowayton was that both Roger Ludlow and Daniel Partrick* came into this area of the state for the first time. Both were officers in the "Great Swamp Fight"—Partrick as a major, and Ludlow, the only lawyer in the Connecticut Colony at the time, almost certainly also in command of troops. The two officers must have been favorably impressed with what they saw here, as both were to return three years later to quickly acquire as much real estate hereabouts as they could lay their hands on.

That turned out to be considerable. Between the two of them—they had negotiated with the Indians separately—they purchased title to all the land which now comprises Norwalk, as well as huge tracks that are now parts of Westport, Wilton, Darien, New Canaan, and Ridgefield! Three months after his acquisitions here, Major Partrick showed up a few miles west, where for next to nothing he picked up a deed for most of Greenwich.

Roger Ludlow was probably the most prominent man in the Connecticut Colony in 1640 when he purchased Norwalk. Many historians have concluded he was the principal draftsman of "The Fundamental Orders of Connecticut" adopted the previous year by the General "Corte." The orders were the forerunner of the Connecticut Charter, the world's first written constitution. Ludlow, historians maintain, was the only man in Connecticut at the time with sufficient training to provide the final polished legal phraseology of the fundamental orders. Born in Wiltshire about 1590, he matriculated at Oxford in 1610 and was elected as an assistant to the Massachusetts Bay Company in 1629 and sailed to New England with the Winthrop fleet when he was forty years old. His wife, Mary Endecott, was a sister of the governor of the Massachusetts Colony.

In 1634 he became the deputy governor of that colony. In 1636 he was in Connecticut and presided over the first meeting of the Massachusetts Bay Commission and continued to serve as the presiding officer throughout the commission's existence. He also presided over the first session of the Connecticut General Corte in May 1637. In the fall of that year, together with John Hayes, he signed the peace treaty with the Pequots. Ludlow was a controversial figure in both colonies. He was stern, passionate, and demanding of his peers as well as subordinates. He was quick tempered with a sharp tongue, but his religious convictions were sincere and fervent. In 1639 he had had five years' experience in colonial government in the Bay, another in Connecticut on the Bay Commission, and still another on the General Corte.[2]

Fourteen years after the Norwalk purchase, distraught and humiliated, he left the Connecticut Colony under a cloud. He had been reprimanded by the

*Also spelled Patrick in some records.

Rowayton on the half shell

General Corte for this warlike attitude toward the Dutch, and was facing a suit for slander by an irate husband whose wife he had called a witch and a liar. Before going, however, he signed the following document: "Memorandum, That the sayed Rodge Ludlowe, both by these presentes, assigne and sett over unto Nathaniel Eli and the rest of the Inhabitants of Norwalke, all my title, interest, claims and demands whatsoever, to the plantation of Norwalke and every part thereof, and doe acknowledge myself satisfied for the same, Witness my hand the day and year above, April 13, 1654." No doubt, a document that is unique in Colonial history.[3]

The Indian concept of the right to property and transfer of land differed widely from that of the colonists attuned to English common law. When the Indians assigned a white man's deed they possibly thought they were granting hunting and occupation rights. They probably had no idea they were signing a conveyance of real estate ownership, or that they might be excluded forever from the very land they had always roamed at will. Exclusive ownership of the land was alien to their thought processes. Consequently they made their signature marks freely and uncoerced in the blissful ignorance of not knowing what they were signing.

Although the local Siwanoys may have had no idea of deed conditions or land values, they had their virtues. Unlike the Pequots, they were friendly, unwarlike semi-nomads. They favored the shore during the warm months and retired back into the country during the winter. Each tribe had its own territory, roughly defined areas of fixed habitation. While here they planted maize (corn), pumpkins and squash, and hunted for turkey, and what other game there was to be had. They fished as well as hunted and were interested here primarily to live off the fat of the Sound. Fin fish and especially shellfish abounded hereabout. Clams, oysters, mussels, and scallops were plentiful and easy to gather, open, and eat; even succulent, once you acquired the taste. It is conceivable they also managed to get their hands on a lobster or two occasionally. They also caught a variety of crabs—soft-shell, blue, horseshoe, and fiddler.

Among Norwalk's traces of Indian habitation are several Indian burial grounds and the remains of an Indian village, Naramake. Some claim the name of the town of Norwalk is derived from the name of the village. This village was located on Wilson Point. Its outlines were long visible. Wigwams were laid out in regular lines like houses on a city street. Graves in the adjoining cemetery were in the same order, all facing east, a custom of the Mohawks. Opinion prevails that Naramake was originally a Mohawk settlement. Implements taken from the graves are of a superior sort, said to be evidence of Mohawk origin. In the Indian cemetery which lay between Washington and

First Contact

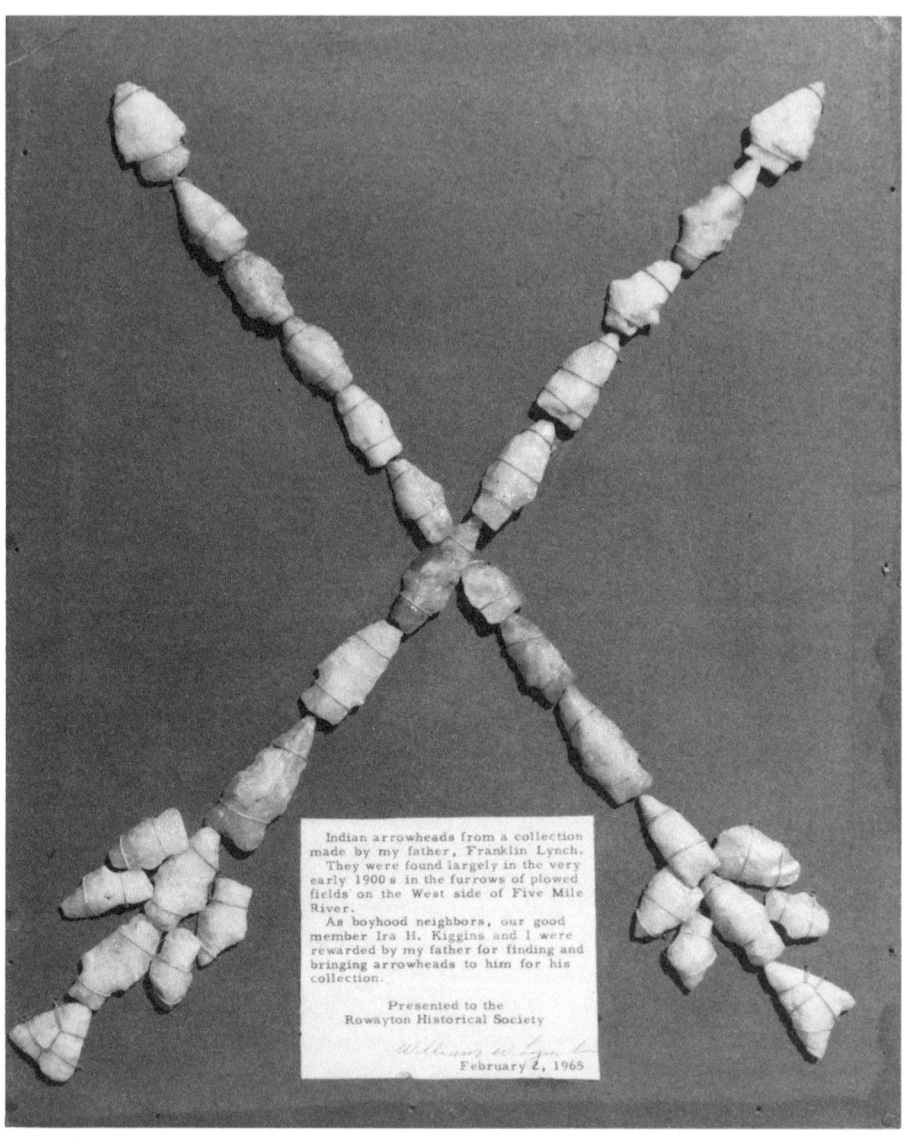

Indian arrowheads from a collection
made by my father, Franklin Lynch.
 They were found largely in the very
early 1900 s in the furrows of plowed
fields on the West side of Five Mile
River.
 As boyhood neighbors, our good
member Ira H. Kiggins and I were
rewarded by my father for finding and
bringing arrowheads to him for his
collection.

 Presented to the
Rowayton Historical Society

February 2, 1965

Proof of the Indian presence. Arrowheads collected mainly from the west side of the Five Mile River.

Rowayton on the half shell

Concord Streets in South Norwalk, mutilated bones were intermingled with shells in a fashion which indicated the practice of cannibalism,[4] wholly uncharacteristic of Siwanoys.

Piles of oyster shells have been uncovered on Wilson Point, along the creek on the north end near the Nash Engineering plant, and on the eastern Norwalk harbor shore, as well as at the burial sites; solid evidence of a substantial Indian presence here, as well as of their hearty appetites. Small shells of various kinds were in demand for use as wampum, or siwan, but it is doubtful local Indians developed the skill required to reduce large shells into valuable trinkets in large quantities. If they had, there was enough raw material here for them to have become very wealthy indeed.

Although the local Indians were not a physical threat to the whites, friction sparked between them as it has between neighbors since time began. Indians could be, and often were, a bother and a nuisance, and kept getting in the way. The Ludlow Code of Laws, as the Fundamental Orders were commonly called, adopted in 1639, protected both English and Indians alike. Indians were forbidden to trespass on the English plantations. English were forbidden to sell or trade cider or gunpowder with Indians, or settle among them.[5] But the Indians were neither by training nor instinct strict observers of the fine points of English law. Ownership of land, boundaries, or property rights meant little or nothing to them. They tended to plant their maize, pumpkins, or squash wherever they pleased and to wander about as they always had.

At the Norwalk town meeting held April 18, 1655, it was "voted and ordered Lieftenant Olmsted and Thos. Fitch . . . to take of and look after the Indians . . . and also that no Indian sett★ within a quarter mile of the towne."[6] In an effort to keep the Indians farther away, on December 12, 1687, the town allocated three acres on the west side of the Norwalk River to the Indians and "sequestered" three score (sixty) acres of pasturage exclusviely for Indian usage.[7] This latter acreage, possibly one of the earliest Indian reservations in the colonies, was atop Rhotan Hill running northerly from a point approximately where Witch Lane intersects Highland Avenue.

It is easy to imagine an area the size of Connecticut sustaining a large Indian population with thickly clustered encampments all within a few miles of each other, much like our cities and towns are today. But such was not the case. Generally accepted estimates of the entire Indian population of the Connecticut Colony at any one time place it between only 1800 and 2000 souls.★ The total Indian head count in Norwalk probably never exceeded

★The exact word is obliterated in the town records.
★Some estimates range as high as 20,000, however.

First Contact

three hundred at any one time. Mrs. Dannenberg in her book, *Romance of Norwalk*, places it at not over two hundred. It is doubtful if the Rowayton area ever held more than half that number at any one time.[8]

Some have estimated the Indian population of Wilson Point alone to have exceeded these figures based on the oyster shell piles and a number of Indian burials uncovered there. In all probability it was the principal camp site of the Naramake tribe especially during the warm months.[9] That the entire tribe ever reached that size is subject to question. The limited number of unearthed graves, the size of the shell piles and their scarcity, the paucity of other evidence (arrow heads, etc.), all argue against it.

The west side of Five Mile River was well known to the Indians. Relics found on Butler's Island add credence to the belief that Chief Runckinheague of later mention himself camped there at length. A sizeable number of arrow heads and other stone artifacts have been turned up over the years in the Tokeneke section as the surface was plowed, graded, or spaded.[10] Similar findings have occurred along Rowayton Avenue above Cudlipp Street and in other parts of Rowayton. But, again, as to how many Indians actually were here, is a classical matter of some conjecture.

In any event, less than fifty years after the white man came to stay, the red man had virtually disappeared from Norwalk. After centuries of abiding here unmolested, the Indians wandered off on their own, never to return. They became nomads in the end. They withdrew from this area to Ridgefield and eventually to a reservation in Kent, Connecticut, where some are said to have lived down into modern times. Some went over into New York State, farther westward, and into Canada. Very few stragglers were left behind.[11]

In another fifty years, the Connecticut census of 1756 recorded no Indians at all in Norwalk, nor any in Fairfield County for that matter. A more careful count, however, did turn up five Indian females and four Indian males for the 1774 census. The first federal census was conducted in 1790, when the number of Indians here was considered to be so negligible that they were not enumerated separately. "They seemed to have melted away unnoticed."[12]

Unnoticed then, but noted today. They left their mark upon us, especially in place names, many of which were names of their sachems or sagamores. "Rowayton" is clearly of Indian derivation, "Roton," "Tokeneke," "Cockenoe" (pronounced Cock-kay-nee), "Naramake," "Chimmons" (from Mamachimmens), "Sasqua," "Saugatuck," "Ponus," "Winnepauk," etc., add pepper and salt to local language.

The very earliest records of this area refer to it in a manner closely resembling the present day spelling of "Rowayton." "Noewanton" appears in the

Daniel Partrick deed dated 20 April, 1960; "Rooaton" in the deed from Runc-kinheage of 15 February 1651; and "Rowerton" in the Winnepauk deed to "his beloved friend Thomas Hanford" dated 2 December, 1690, giving him title to Sheffield Island. "Noroton" could have been derived from Noewanton and his local connotation. The outermost tip of Bell Island appears today on official U.S. Government navigation charts as "Noroton Point," as it has for years past. In the Partrick deed "Noewanton" could have referred to either the land mass of what we know of as Rowayton, or to Five Mile River itself which seems more likely. Indian land descriptions often mention water courses where applicable.

There can be no doubt as to "Rooaton" and "Rowerton" being in Roway-ton's direct lineage. Colonial spelling left a lot to be desired especially when translated from the local dialect of Algonquian, not to mention English. With due allowance for the spelling of the day, the family strain is obvious. "Ro-ton," on the other hand had more varied and imaginative spellings than Rowayton. Perhaps because it was shorter. "Rhootan," "Rooton," "Rho-ton," "Roaton," "Rottan," etc. At one time the flagship of the original Rowayton Yacht Club (of more later), owned by then Commodore S. Edward Dibble, was named *Ro-ah-wah-ha*. He told the writer the name had passed down through his family as that of a local sachem. Perhaps so; it does have a nice rhythm, but I have yet to see a written reference.

Whatever its antecedents may have been, "Rowayton" has a distinction that is unique. It is the only place in the United States, or the world I dare say, bearing the name. There is no other such listing in the United States Postal Register. Rowayton is one of a kind.

First Contact

To Reach The Salt Lick

*N*ORWALK'S EARLIEST settlement was on the east side of the Norwalk River, along lower East Avenue in the vicinity of present day Fort Point Street, Osborne Avenue, Fitch Street, etc. The white man spread out rapidly. He soon had crossed the river and was firmly ensconced on the river's west bank soon to be called "Old Well" and later "South Norwalk."[1] Of necessity they lived off the land, subsistence farming at its purest and simplest. In order to better their existence it was essential to acquire more and more land suitable for tilling and/or grazing. As their tools improved and their herds grew, they utilized larger tracts especially for grazing, and preferably along the shore line. Shore line grasses being heavily salted are especially desirable for hay. "The salt lick" was known even in the early days to contain therapeutic qualities beneficial to cattle.

It was this seeking for additional pasture land, reaching out for more of the salt lick, that pushed the first white man over the ridges west of Old Well into the Rowayton area with its fringe of small islets skirting the shore. It was a long walk back to Old Well, so they soon began to stake Rowayton out. As far as they knew, it was all part of Norwalk.

The first white men to come into this area, whether as land speculators or as settlers, to their everlasting credit, formally purchased the land from the Indians. Deeds describing boundaries and conditions were carefully drafted in legalistic form, all properly signed, witnessed, sealed, and all left to posterity to be interpreted as best they could. Such proceedings were not to become the norm wherever the white man settled. Almost the opposite, "commandeered" is a more apt word to describe the takeover of Indian lands nationwide. Upon presentation of the impressive legal papers it was apparently little or no problem to have the local braves readily sign on the dotted line. Piamikin, one of the Five Mile River valley sachems, it seems, was willing to sign with no hesitation whatever.

The deed dated the 20th of April, 1640, to Daniell Patricke pertaining to the purchase of the western section of Norwalk described the boundaries "on the west side with 'noewanton,' on the east side to the middle of the River of Norwake." Quite simple phraseology, but, as it turned out, sufficiently vague to cause later lawyers to rub their heads as well as their hands, and to create real animosity between Norwalk and its neighbor town Stamford for years to come. The question was: does "Noewanton" refer to what we know as Rowayton or to Noroton?

Another purchase from the Indians was consummated February 15, 1651, complete with formal deed duly witnessed and signed by no less than a full dozen Indian sachems, sagamores, chieftans and/or braves. This came to be known as the Runckinheage deed as he was the first to sign, probably because he was either the highest ranking Indian present or ruler of the major part of the tract, or both. The second Indian to sign, and therefore second in importance, was Piamikin. No doubt the multitude assembled that historic day were well intentioned and sincere, including Piamikin, but they succeeded in establishing a western boundary which was destined to become even more obscure than "noewanton." The tract involved was spelled out as "all their (Indian) lands called and known by the names Ruckinheage, Rooaton, or by whatever name or names the same is called or known, lying and bounded on the east upon ye land purchased of Captain Patriarke, so called, on the west by the Brook called Pampaskeshanke, which such Brook and passage, the Bounds West, extendeth up into the country by marked trees; . . . and the aforesaid land bounded with the Brook called as aforesaid Pampaskeshanke . . . down along to the Sea." All fairly clear and simple so long as they knew where Pampaskeshanke Brook was.

Of course there were no ancient maps available for ready reference. Local opinion was, as might be expected, widely split. Some living on the east side of Five Mile River contended Pampaskeshanke was the Indian name for "Pine Brook" which is known today as the Good Wives' River emptying into Noroton Bay via Gorham's Pond. Those residing on the west side of the river tended to believe that the Five Mile River itself was the boundary brook. As late as 1896 Reverend Selleck thought it was the brook that empties into the head of Wilson Cove, a mile to the east.[2] It was not a matter that was taken lightly.

As indicated, the grazing of cattle by the Norwalkers extended down into

To Reach the Salt Lick

the Five Mile River valley areas of Brookside and Rowayton from the earliest years of settlement. Minutes of the town meeting of May 30, 1655, agreed that the dry cattle shall be herded together on the "other side" of the Norwalk River. This was nothing more than formal approval of what had already been going on. The meeting held the previous week noted "the dry herd had been driven out to Rooaton by three men each to be allowed 6d a turne." Rooaton was used here to probably mean the flat lands atop the ridge west of the Flax Hill which Highland Avenue bisects for its full length. This ridge appears on old maps as Rhoton and later Roton Hill. The Five Mile River Valley is just beyond, slightly farther west.

When the Norwalk herd was found to be grazing on the west side of Five Mile River a hot boundary dispute was on. There the embattled farmers stood. Tensions grew with the usual accompanying personal bitterness. Eventually hay was burned and the cattle guarded. Only a handful of people were involved, it is true, but they were the entire white population of the disputed area. At the Norwalk town meeting held August 26, 1666, it was voted and agreed "that such men of our inhabitants as doe goe to cutt hay on the other side of five mile river, the towne will stand by them in the action to defend them, and to beare an equal proportion of the damage they shall sustaine upon that account; and if they shall be affronted by Stamford men, the towne will take as speedy a course as they can to prosecute them by law, to recover their just rights touching the lands in controversy; and also they have chosen and deputed Mr. Thomas Fitch to goe with the sayed men when they goe to cutt or fetch away, to make answer for and in be halfe of the towne, and the rest be silent." The Runckinheage deed had been solemnized en masse hardly ten years before, but no one could definitely establish which was the Pampaskeshanke Brook. Piamikin apparently was not available for consultation. It was to be left to the courts.

The resolve and support of the town meeting may have had a quieting effect in the form of a temporary truce, but probably not, human nature being what it is, and was. If there was a truce it was short lived. A mere two years later, September 30, 1668, the town meeting voted and ordered "that the deputies that are chosen to goe to court in October next, shall doe thier best indevor that the diference between Stamford and Norwalk may be brought to an issue . . . and that it shall be left to the towns men to send a letter to Stamford to signifie the towns intension about the difference of Bounds." The matter was at long last in the hands of the General Court.

After another two years of festering sores Norwalk made a further attempt at conciliation. A committee of three was dispatched to go to Stamford "to see if they and we can come to a loving and neighborly issue and agreement."[3]

Rowayton on the half shell

Looking south along Five Mile River Road, c. 1870. The John Selleck homestead is at left center. The house and barns on the right are still standing.

But to no avail. The matter had to be adjudicated. Three years later the court got around to acting. In 1673 it fixed the town line as follows: "That the five mile brook between Stamford and from the mouth thereof until it meets with the cross path that now is where the country road crosses the said River, shall be the bounds, and from there to run up into the country until the twelve miles be expired."[4] Thus the court avoided defining the whereabouts of the Pampaskeshanke Brook and decided to use the Five Mile River instead. At least there was some agreement as to where that was.

This decision was undoubtedly based upon the disclosure of a deed the same sachem Piamikin had signed back as early as March 24, 1645.[5] In that deed he had, the court held, sold the same land to Andrew Ward and Richard Law, both of Stamford, that he later signed away to Richard Web, Nathaniel Eli, et al., of Norwalk on February 15, 1661. The Stamford claim being prior was upheld and the western boundary of Norwalk more clearly defined by the court. It is interesting to ponder, however, had Piamikin been called and available to testify, would the court have acted differently? He would at the very least have been able to give his version of where Pampaskeshanke Brook was, thus eliminating the uncertainty which persists to our day, and may have radically changed the map of present-day Darien. In all fairness to Piamikin, who can say he acted knowingly? After all, sixteen years is a long time between deeds.

To Reach the Salt Lick

Another consideration which was well known may have influenced the court. The Samuel Selleck family of Tokeneke was possibly the first to take up permanent residence along the western shore of Five Mile River in the Middlesex Parish of Stamford. The Sellecks were soon to be the largest land-holders in the neighborhood with approximately 580 acres comprising all the shore property between the river and the Good Wives' River - all of Tokeneke, Butler's, Contentment and the Fish Islands, Scott's Cove, Great and Hay Islands, plus all of Long Neck Point![6] It is readily apparent they had an avid interest in the court's decision. Had their sympathies been with Norwalk during the grazing war, perhaps it would have been a consideration of the court. In any event, any claim to all or part of this now highly valuable tract between the Five Mile and Good Wives' rivers was lost to Norwalk forevermore.

The Stamford forces were still not satisfied, however. The Norwalk-Stamford boundary was a bone of contention as late as 1715. In that year the Superior Court, with a Norwalk judge presiding, Captain Joseph Platt, sustained Norwalk's right to grant land *east* of the Perambulation Line established in 1673[7]; that is, on the Rowayton side of the river. Apparently the Stamford boys, having gained so much the first time around, sought to have a second try. Perhaps they were hoping the court would place Pampaskeshanke Brook at the head of Wilson Cove where Ely Brook now empties. Be that as it may, land in the Rowayton area at long last could be acquired with a clear title, and much of it was included in subsequent grants of Norwalk town land.

In order to effect a systematic expansion, colonial towns allocated land generally in two ways. First, newcomers to town who were accepted were granted home lots; and secondly by divisions of unallocated land, commonage, among the inhabitants on a most undemocratic basis of individual net worth. Grants of land were also given from time to time in recognition for outstanding service to the town and later to veterans of King Philips War. A variable formula was agreed upon at town meetings setting the apportionment of acres per hundred pounds of assets, much as corporate boards of directors today set the dividend amount to be paid to stockholders. Norwalk, it seems, was niggardly in comparison to other Connecticut Colony towns in this respect, but by 1687 the allotment had increased from three to twenty acres per hundred pounds possessed.[8]

Those qualified to share land drew lots at town meetings, the area to be divided having been previously surveyed and the lots numbered. The lots were then laid out in size equal to that owner's proportionate share.

Since the original settlers were clustered on the opposite side of the Norwalk River along lower East Avenue, there was little interest in land so far removed as Rowayton. To go up to where the Norwalk River was crossable and then trudge down to Rhotan Hill or Five Mile River and back in one day was a long tiresome trek. Consequently, the outlying areas developed very slowly during the early decades.

At the time of the land division of 1687, John Raymond, son of Captain Richard, for instance, had assets listed at two hundred pounds entitling him to a forty-acre share, some of which may have been allotted in Rowayton.[9] The first recorded land division of "Rowayton and the Islands" in the Norwalk Town Proceedings took place in 1705. Seventeen acres were then allocated to John Raymond, nine acres (more or less) south of the stone wall which now separates the post office parking lot and the fire house, and eight acres, more or less, north of that same sturdy stone wall. These tracts are sometimes referred to in the Norwalk Land Records as "Raymond's Lower Field" and "Raymond's Upper Field." The upper field was bounded northerly by Witch Lane and westerly by Witch Lane (where it runs north and south) and by present-day Crest Road. The easterly boundaries were vague, possibly Farm Creek and the brook that empties into it.

Malcolm Hunt, a talented and experienced historian and professional title searcher who worked for many years in Norwalk while living in Rowayton, has left detailed records of his Rowayton findings in the archives of The Norwalk Museum, Lockwood House, East Avenue, Norwalk. In them he states the Raymond fields were probably granted prior to 1687. Other grants of land in the area were recorded at about this time, prior to the land division of 1705, the first to include Rowayton property. The 1686/87 grants were recorded to the Betts brothers, John, Thomas, and Daniel, and to a James Jupp for certain "meadow land fresh and salt at Roaton about the Islands or adjacent thereto," indicating the value of the salt lick. On August 1, 1678, the town deeded to Marke Sension (probably of French Huguenot extraction later Anglicized to St. John) a large tract south of Wilson Avenue between Farm Brook and Wilson Cove. This property became known as the St. John farm, hence "Farm Creek" was named.[10]

The Brookside area immediately to the north of Rowayton aroused the interest of the earliest settlers. Not only was it on the path to Stamford, but there was rapid water where the path crossed the Five Mile River—just above the present-day Flax Hill Road-Old King's Highway bridge. At the town meeting of November 9, 1677, they granted unto Richard Holms "liberty to erect, set up, and improve a sawmill upon five mile river, and liberty for timber one mile on this side of ye said river; onlly the sayd Richard is not to pass over ye sayd grant to any but such as the town shall approve of; this

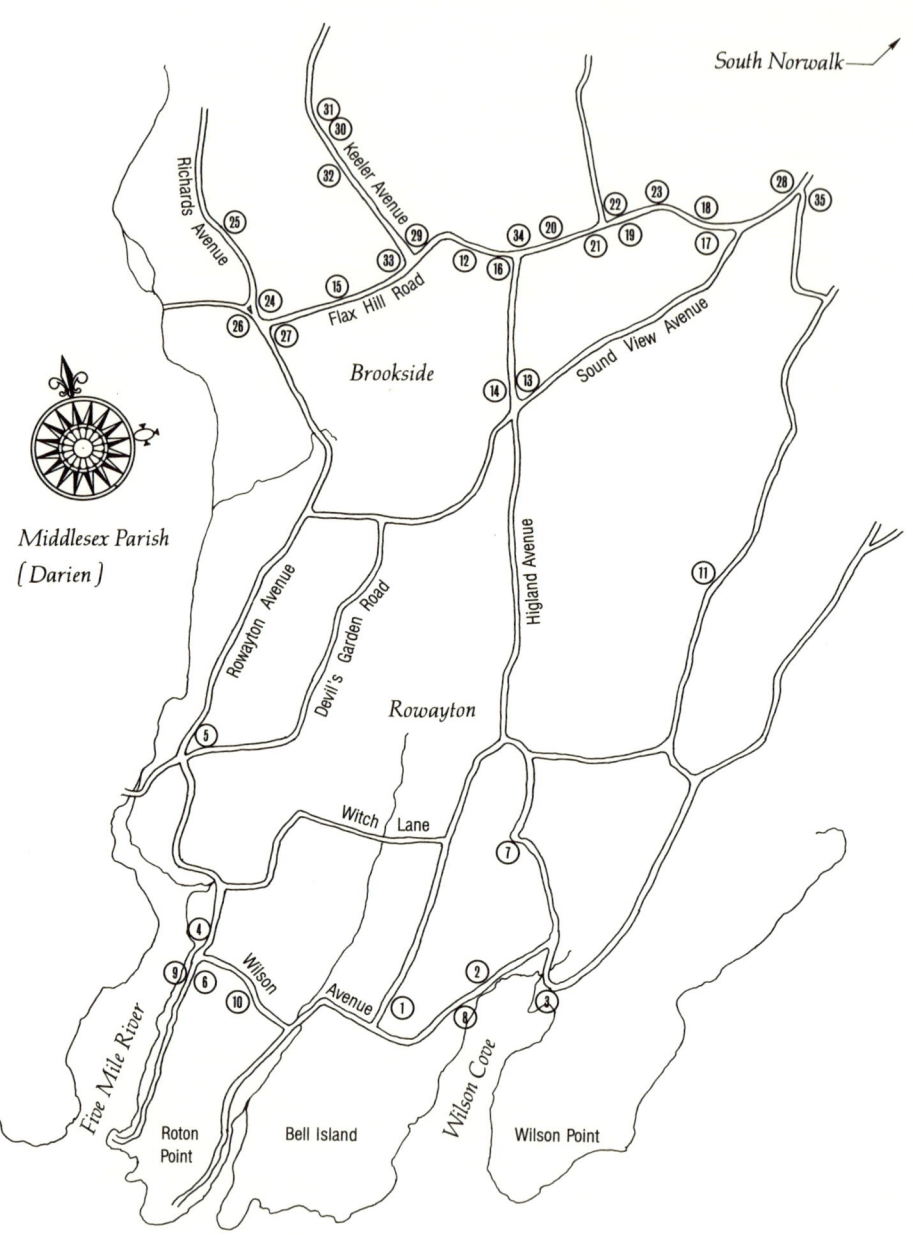

South Norwalk

Richards Avenue

Keeler Avenue

Flax Hill Road

Brookside

Sound View Avenue

Middlesex Parish
(Darien)

Rowayton Avenue

Devil's Garden Road

Higland Avenue

Rowayton

Witch Lane

Wilson Avenue

Five Mile River

Wilson Cove

Roton Point

Bell Island

Wilson Point

Long Island Sound

Rowayton on the half shell

Compiled from four maps dated 1740, 1760,
1776, and 1780 researched and drawn by
Malcolm P. Hunt between 1963 and 1966.

Key to locations

As of 1740
1) John Waring
2) Jeremiah Wantwood
3) Samuel Seward
4) (Richard's) Shipyard

Additions and changes as of 1760
5) Nathaniel Selleck
6) Gershom Raymond
7) Esaias Bouton
8) Joshua Chase
9) Richard's Store
   Belden replaced
   Seward (3)

Additions and changes as of 1776
10) Paul Raymond
11) Sands Raymond
12) Joseph Waring
13) Joseph Waring, Jr.
14) Eliakim Waring
15) Nathan Waring
16) Edmond & Enoch
    Waring
17) Moses Byxbee
18) William Raymond
19) Daniel Raymond
20) Thomas Hanford
21) Nehemiah Hanford
22) John Smith
23) John Hoyt
24) Eli Reed
25) Benjamin Reed
26) David Seward
27) Solomon Whitmore
28) Daniel Hoyt
29) Samuel Richards

30) Nathaniel Richards
31) John Richards
32) Gersham Richards
33) Daniel Richards
34) Jesse Raymond
35) Samuel Raymond
    Gilbert Wolsey replaced
    Nathaniel Selleck (5)
    Jedediah Raymond re-
    placed Jeremiah Want-
    wood (2)

Changes as of 1780
Heirs of John Waring re-
placed John Waring (1)

Note: As drawn, the Hunt maps of 1740, 1760,
& 1780 did not include Brookside, Upper
Highland Avenue, and Flax Hill Road areas and
it is certain some of those listed on the 1776 map
(#10 through #35) predated 1776.

---

saw mill is to be set up and finished within two years after this date, or else
it is forfit; and the sayd Richard is to sell his boards and planks to the townsmen as the(y) doe at other towns to their neighbors, and whear their are saw
mills."[11]

By 1692/93 John Reed and his son were granted the right to erect a sawmill "at the head of the salt on Five Mile River, with timber rights in the adjacent area." The Reeds were the first family to build homes in Brookside,
but exactly where they built the sawmill is a question. Rather than "at the
mouth of the salt," it was probably built in their own back yard as several
of their neighbors held shares in a mill located there years later.[12] The mill
was also operated by Nathan Bouton.

To Reach the Salt Lick

A rather common misconception today is the theory that the original name of Five Mile River was Five Mill River. It is true that as the name first appears in the Norwalk Town Proceedings, April 30, 1656, it is spelled "five mill river." This is undoubtedly a spelling error. There were no mills on the river at that early date. The only mill then in existence in Norwalk was in the Cranbury area owned by a Jonathan Marsh for grinding corn and grain. This mill was sold in 1664 to Nathaniel Richards. The next year the town voted permission to Henry Whitney to build a second "corne mill, and that at the mouth of the Norwake River by the falles." If the town scribe had difficulty spelling such words as "corn," "Norwalk," and "falls" correctly by our standards, it is conceivable he had equal trouble spelling "mile." In the Town Proceedings for the meeting of August 26, 1666, the scribe was an excellent speller for he wrote "five mile river" in reference to the boundary dispute.[13]

Other mills were erected along the river, but it is doubtful there were ever as many as five at any time. In later years a mill for grinding corn and grain was built "at the head of the salt." It was in operation for the better part of a century and burned as recently as 1908, leaving evidences to this day. The mill was situated on the west bank of the river just north of the intersection of Raymond Street and Tokeneke Road at the "White Bridge." Remains of a rugged stone dam one hundred feet or so upstream of the bridge, and of a millrace that paralleled the west bank were still visible until recently. For many years the mill was owned and operated by the Stephen Raymond family of Five Mile River Road. A photograph showing both the mill and the bridge is in the archives of the Rowayton Historical Society.

Notable among John Reed's neighbors in Brookside, on the Norwalk side of the river, were Captain Samuel Richards and his brother, Captain James Richards. The brothers were partners in the overseas shipping trade and had prospered. They were the first known owners of the Seeley-Dibble-Pinkney Park property. In the swale at the south end of the property they established a slipway for boat building and repair in the early 1700s, Rowayton's earliest boatyard, by far. In 1753 they opened a general store on the bank of the river, the primary purpose of which must have been to warehouse produce in transit, as there were hardly enough souls in the entire area to support a store. Although settled nearly a hundred years, the Rowayton-Brookside area was still very sparsely populated in the mid-1700s.

Life Style Of The Out-Livers

*O*NE OF THE BETTER treatments of the life-style of those generations immediately following the first settlers is found in Lynn W. Wilson's *History of Fairfield County*, upon which much of this chapter is based.[1] By the time the early settlers decided to leave the comforts of the inner town and risk living in the surrounding areas, the first dwellings, of hewn logs with clay chinked between and thatched roofs, had been replaced by frame houses. Sawmills, the first structures to be erected beyond the confines of the compound, had been erected where water power was sufficient and thus made sawn timber, lumber, shingles, and lath available.

The frame houses were often built one and one-half and two stories high with back roofs slanting and low, and hinged windows with panes frequently of diamond shaped glass. The roofs were almost certainly shingled with siding of either clapboard or shingles. The center of the house was occupied by a great stone chimney with a vast fireplace opening into the kitchen. The kitchen was the chief living room in which the family gathered during cold weather. An iron crane was suspended within the fireplace on which cooking vessels and utensils could be swung over the log fire. Walls were lathed and plastered, plaster having been available for a long time.

In 1653 a resolution was adopted by the freemen of Norwalk instructing Ralph Keeler and Walter Haite (Hoyt) "to fell all the timber, hew and frame it, raise the house, make it tight, and hange the shinckles and pinnes." This was the Reverend Thomas Hanford's house. It was to be thirty-one feet long and eighteen feet wide. Forty years later Mr. Hanford died and a new house was built to accommodate (and attract) a new minister. Mr. Stephen Buck-

Five Mile River Road residence of John Selleck (1706–1788).

ingham was eventually hired, and it was agreed to build the new house forty feet long and twenty-two feet wide, two stories high with double chim-
neys, a comely porch, a stone cellar in one end, all to be decently finished
at the town's expense. It was also voted to pay Mr. Buckingham eighty
pounds a year. His salary was to be paid in winter wheat at five shillings a
bushel, Indian corn at two shillings and sixpence, rye at four shillings, pork
at threepence farthing a pound, beef at two pence per pound, and no one was
to pay above one third part in rye (grain, that is).

After building shelter for his family and his animals, the early out-liver
turned his attention to the land. Most of the land in the Rowayton peninsula
was ledge rock or rocky outcropping which the glaciers during the ice age
eons before had deposited in ridges and rills. Much of the land had to be
cleared of stones to be made tillable, hence the miles of stone walls piled without end across all of New England. Areas a mile or two inland from the sound
were left comparatively cleared of stone by the glaciers which would account
for the fact that the Brookside area was more densely settled than Rowayton proper in the earliest times. There was more acreage inland ready for the
plow. In the beginning all were farmers, and for generations after, subsistence farming was the full-time occupation of the large majority of all
colonists.

Rowayton on the half shell

Williamson residence on Old Farm Road in Tokeneke typifies local homes of the Colonial period. This was taken in 1900 after wing on right had been added.

As Lynn Wilson points out, the minister and the magistrate did not hesitate to cultivate the soil. There were few instruments to facilitate tilling. It was many years before iron plows were common, and heavy wooden ones were inferior to those the Romans brought to Britain centuries before. The first crop was Indian corn or maize, planted in the native fashion in hills. The same hills were used year after year and were fertilized with fish. Beans, peas, and pumpkins were grown in the same field as the corn, the seeds sometimes being planted in the same hill. One of the most colorful agrarian scenes of the day was the golden pumpkin growing amidst the waving corn.

The settlers brought from England the original herds and flocks. They had cattle, horses, sheep, and swine. Some towns were known to purchase a bull with public funds to attempt to improve the quality of the milk and the beef herd. For many years the quality of the cattle deteriorated caused by poor pasturage, inferior grasses, and lack of fresh stock for breeding. It took decades to bring in the English grasses and obtain a supply of good hay. It was because of this that the lowlands abutting the high salt content marsh grass became more and more attractive. It might be possible, after all, to survive in the rock infested area near the Rowayton shore.

Life Style of the Out-Livers

Kitchen fireplace of Elias Pennoyer home, 168 Rowayton Avenue.
The plates on mantel are pewter. The cast iron oven door probably
dates to the early nineteenth century.

The settlers suffered losses through the depredation of wolves and other animals. Wolves were the most destructive, and wolf pits were standard fixtures in every town. Bounties were paid for destroying the creatures. Blackbirds were destructive of corn, and pigeons were said to cross in such numbers as to darken the sky, and were responsible for much damage. Blights appeared and took the entire crop occasionally, whereupon days of fasting would be established when prayer was offered for the removal of these impediments. A vote of the town meeting in Newtown in 1712 indicates how slowly the English grasses were brought in. It was then that Stephen Pamerly had permission to use the acre and a half of land "which is the burying place provided he clear the bushes and fence it and sow it with English grass seed."

Fruit trees were brought to New England very early. By 1670 apple, quince, cherry, and plum trees were common. Gardens grew cabbage, carrots, beets, red currents, cucumbers, melons, and many familiar herbs, vegetables or berries. The strawberry grew wild in great abundance. Before 1650 it was required that each family plant at least one spoonful of hemp seed, or a quantity of flax. Tobacco was raised, but of a much inferior quality by to-

Early Brookside home with well and outbuildings nearby.

day's standards. The life of the outlander was, to put it mildly, laborious.

Each household was self-contained. Only in the homes of a very few wealthy families might be found most of the luxuries obtainable in England: tapestries, carpets, silver, elegant furniture, and other fine things. The women made their own yarns and wove their own cloth from the wool of their own sheep. They made their own clothing, though in time there were tailors and shoemakers who went from house to house, in season, doing this type of work. There were periods of scarcity when crops were poor and winters unusually severe, but the table was usually abundantly supplied. Wood was the universal fuel. Game was plentiful. Fish were easy to take, clams and oysters abundant, especially here.

Furniture and utensils were made by the men, the clothing by the women. The garments of both were of homespun, but they often had more fashionable apparel for special occasions. Fashions changed as governments changed in England. When Charles II came to the throne wigs were the style. Knee breeches, a three cornered hat and a powdered wig were then the usual thing. There were no carpets, no clocks, and little china. Sundials were common. Dishes were of wood and pewter.

Beer for a period was the chief drink, but when the orchards began to produce, cider became the common beverage. It was no disgrace to trade in rum. Rum was sold freely and used in every home by all classes, except, of course,

Life Style of the Out-Livers

the Indians. Strong drink was a race poison to the Indians, and almost immediately laws were enacted forbidding its sale to them. Bootlegging was as tempting then as later, so these laws were more honored in the breach than in the observance. Many historians maintain intemperance of the natives did more to destroy the race than anything else. The health of the colonial family was the concern of the housewife, who knew the medical herbs, grew them in her garden, and administered them when the occasion demanded.

Marriages were early and families were large. A household without a woman was in a difficult way, so second and third marriages were relatively more numerous than now. The women carried on such essential duties as baking, brewing, spinning, and weaving without interruption until the day set for a wedding. Banns were read in the church. The neighbors frequently marched to the home of the bride in a body where the feast equalled or surpassed Thanksgiving dinner. Large families were the rule rather than the exception. There was work for everyone to do, even small children. There was some play, but no organized games. Sports common in England were adopted here, such as quarter shaft, single stick, wrestling, cock fighting and dog fighting. There was the great life of the outdoors. Hunting, fishing, and trapping were sports, but they might also be industries and means of supporting the household. Everyone, including the young, knew how to use firearms and many were good marksmen. Also everybody was a horseman and women rode proficiently.

There were neighborhood gatherings in which work and play were combined as when a house was raised, sheep were sheared, corn husked, and sugar made. Strong drink was freely used upon such occasions, but "with effects less disastrous on bodies inured to exercise, employed in the hardest kinds of work and able healthily to consume great quantities of food." There would be exhibitions of skill in running, jumping, wrestling, fencing, backsword, and cudgel. Election day, too, was devoted to pleasure making. Women came to town riding behind their husbands, bought the goods they needed, and learned about the latest fashions, but Thanksgiving Day was the great festivity. It was celebrated with a profusion of hospitality, and the dinner was the finest the housewife could provide.

Children worked at a younger age and harder than they do now, but they were full of life and energy and inclined to get into mischief. Also they were not decorous in church, and the townsmen appointed those whose duty it was to keep the young people in order. The Norwalk townsmen in 1681 appointed Thomas Barnum to oversee and keep good decorum amongst the young "on the sabbath and other publique meetings; and the town doth empower him if he see any disorderly, for to keep a small stick to correct it with."

Rowayton on the half shell

Deed of August 26, 1816 transferring land with buildings thereon at Five Mile River from Gershom Raymond to Mary Raymond.

Life Style of the Out-Livers

Home at 2 Wilson Avenue built by Gershom Raymond c. 1790, for his son Gershom, Jr. It is still standing.

He also had the authority to keep nodding adults in church at attention which he did with a light tap of a rod. Every church had such an officer!

Stray horses and cattle were arrested for the profit of the town. A part of the sale price was given to the person who brought them in. Animals that were found without earmarks were deemed stray. Earmarks were carefully registered, each farmer having his own mark; the earliest branding. In 1679 Zerubabell Haite (a variation of Hoyt) undertook to beat the drum for public meetings. For that and for stray horses brought in to be sold, he was to have fourteen shillings from the town of Norwalk and ten pence for each horse. The whipping posts and stocks were sources of excitement on dull days. Offenders were whipped or pilloried for small offenses, or for mere differences of opinion regarding religion or public policy.

Development of the outlands surrounding the towns in the entire Connecticut Colony was a slow process. Fortunately the Indians were not hostile, but there were virtually no roads for decades after first settlement and few draft animals. Rapid population growth outside the settlements was severely hindered by the major role religion played in the daily lives of the times. There was a strong reluctance on the part of the devout, God-fearing first settlers to detach themselves from their places of worship and from their minister. It took a great deal of pluck and individuality to decide to leave the security, cohesiveness, and camaraderie of the center of life and move to the outskirts. In 1705 one hundred and fifteen years after first settlement, the population of Connecticut Colony stood at a mere 70,000 souls.

The settlers of the Rowayton area and eastern Middlesex Parish had to face the anguish of having their church and ministers far afield in Norwalk

Rowayton on the half shell

Home at 200 Rowayton Avenue built by Gershom Raymond for son Edward, c. 1798. Also still standing.

and Stamford. It was a long tedious journey to either town. When the minister of the Norwalk Congregational Church was dismissed for conduct unbecoming a wearer of the cloth in 1727, a number of the outlanders in this area saw it as an opportunity. Being supporters of the minister, they sought designation as a separate parish with the thought to hire him to continue to administer to their needs. A petition was signed by some fourteen of the faithful and presented to the elders for consideration.[3] The petition was denied. Rightly so. In those days separation from a parish meant political separation as well, necessitating creation of another township. There were far too few souls in Rowayton, Brookside, West Norwalk, and along the west side of the river in Middlesex to justify another parish, let alone another township. Here, then, is the first recorded attempt of the residents of Rowayton to secede from Norwalk, a sentiment that has proven a hardy perennial flowering periodically to this day.

It was some hundred and thirty years later before either Rowayton or Brookside had a church they could call their own. Other parishes bordering Norwalk and Stamford splintered off in due time, New Canaan in 1801, Wilton 1802, and Darien 1820. Rowayton, West Norwalk, and Brookside east of the Five Mile River remain within the Town of Norwalk. Because of its harbor and later its railroad station and post office, Rowayton developed into a village, not to be confused with a township. So it is to this day, a village within the Town of Norwalk.

The earliest residential map of Rowayton now available is that of 1740, drawn by Malcolm Hunt in 1953. It shows but two dwellings in Rowayton proper, that of John Waring located on the east side of Highland Avenue near

Life Style of the Out-Livers

the intersection of Wilson Avenue, and that of Jeremiah Wantwood near the foot of the hill at the head of Wilson Cove. Hunt drew a progression of maps on a twenty-year basis. They show with graphic clarity the slow pace of the settlement of Rowayton. Only four more houses appear on the map of 1760: that of Nathaniel Selleck on the northeast corner of Main Street (Rowayton Avenue) and Hunt Street; Gershom Raymond has built down the street a half mile just south of Wilson Avenue where the post office block now stands; Esais Bouton is on Witch Lane, just up from Wilson Cove; and his neighbor Mr. Wantwood has built a new residence close by his former location, which is now occupied by Joshua Chase. Both the store and the boatyard of the Richards Brothers on the east bank of the Five Mile River are shown.

As of 1780 John Waring has died, his property listed in the possession of his heirs; Nathaniel Selleck's home has been transferred to the heirs of Gilbert Wolsey; Jedediah Raymond now occupies the original Wantwood house at the head of the cove; and Gershom Raymond has built a house for his son, Paul, on top of Wilson Avenue hill,★ the only new construction in twenty years! Paul at the time is serving as a sergeant of rebels in the American Revolution.

★Currently the home and office of Dr. Abraham Levine, 26 Wilson Avenue.

Rowayton on the half shell

A Frontier Of The Revolutionary War

*T*HERE HAD BEEN five major intercolonial wars prior to the Revolutionary War: King Philip's, 1675–76; King William's, 1689–97; Queen Anne's, 1700–13; King George's, 1718–29; and the French and Indian War, 1755–63. The war records show Norwalk men were involved, but very few whose names match the handful of residents of the Rowayton area.[1] It is conceivable the few Rowaytonites may have not even known some of these wars were going on, or when one stopped and another began until the French and Indian War. During that conflict, a friend, neighbor, and relative of many of the early families, Thomas Fitch, great grandson of the original settler, was governor of the Connecticut Colony, having been elected in 1754. Everyone knew him, or of him. Defeated for election to a third term as governor mainly by resentment to the Stamp Act, which ironically he had opposed but felt duty-bound as chief magistrate to enforce when it became law, he returned to the private practice of law in Norwalk in 1766. His successor, Jonathan Trumbull, thereby became the war governor for the duration and, of course, the one history remembers.

As astonishing as it may seem, Rowayton was on one of the fighting frontiers during much of the Revolutionary War. There was a surprising amount of military activity in and about Rowayton and vicinity—Brookside, Darien, Noroton, as well as along the shores and among the coves east and west of Five Mile River, especially after the British occupied Long Island. Here, where the Sound is narrow, the North Shore towns of Fairfield and Westchester Counties—directly opposite the territory occupied by the British—were under constant harassment by foraging parties of marauders who raided the farms and stores for food and other valuables, killing and taking prisoners as the situation dictated. For a thorough and well written account of this action, see *Brothers At War*, Darien Historical Society Annual for 1976, Bicentennial Edition, by Louise H. McLean, from which much of this chapter is taken with her gracious permission.

> At this time much of the area of Rowayton was part of Middlesex Parish (Darien) for religious purposes. The numerous Reed, Waring, Raymond and Richards families owned much of the land, and although they attended the one church in the parish at Brookside Road and Old King's Highway, they were residents of the town of Norwalk. None of the people of Middlesex Parish on either side of the river were wealthy. They were hard working farmers or fishermen for the most part. A few were blacksmiths, shoemakers, millers, carpenters and weavers. All had large families—it was the rule in the 18th century. By 1775 the parish was overrun with young people in their early teens and twenties. Intermarriage had bound neighbors into one loose family group to be torn and deeply divided between Patriots and Tories when the war came. Many families had lost their taste for the strict puritanical doctrine of their fathers, and in recent years had become devoted Anglicans. The influence of the Church of England was strong in western Connecticut, and in Middlesex Parish at least a third of the residents had become Episcopalian churchmen. Their allegiance to the King of England as head of their church usually determined their political sentiments. When the time came to choose sides in 1775, nearly all Anglicans in Connecticut remained loyal to the King despite their dissatisfaction with royal policies.[2]
>
> There were at least 67 Anglican families (i.e., married men) living in Middlesex Parish out of an approximate total of 214 families. A good number of these people lived in the Rowayton section of the Parish, and attended St. Paul's Church in Norwalk. On the Stamford side of the river the Anglicans were members of St. John's Episcopal Church in Stamford. Only 86 families can be counted as members of the traditional religious group, the Middlesex Society, Congregationalists, and a third group of about 62 families not registered members of either church, although by law they paid their annual taxes for the support of Dr. Moses Mather, the Middlesex minister. Dr. Mather was an ardent patriot, as were many Congregationalists, whom he constantly tried to persuade to support the cause of liberty. He, more than any other man in Middlesex, led the fight for freedom.

The rebels, too, did their share of raiding. To quote Mrs. McLean further,

> there came a day in November of 1775 when a colorful procession of horsemen rode down the Country Road [Flax Hill Road—Old King's Highway] through Middlesex. It was a raiding party headed by the rabble-rouser Isaac Sears, sometimes called "Captain," sometimes "King" Sears. He was a popular leader of the stringent group

Rowayton on the half shell

called "The Sons of Liberty," which had seized power in New York. Sears had gone
to New Haven where he collected for his venture "sixteen respectable inhabitants of the
town." They left New Haven on November 20th and were "on the way joined by Captains Richards, Selleck and Mead with 80 men." It is reasonable to suppose that all
three Captains and their friends lived in the Norwalk-Stamford area. Sears was a native of Norwalk and must certainly have been well acquainted there. Also there were
at least three Rowayton men who were called "Captain" Richards. All three were members of the Middlesex Society. There was also a Captain Mead living in Norwalk. As
for Captain Selleck who reputedly joined the raiding party, there were probably only
two with that title, Captain Simeon and Captain Abraham Selleck. Abraham deserted to the Loyalist side, but Captain Simeon Selleck had earlier demonstrated his loyalty
to the patriot cause by capturing King's stores with his Middlesex sloop in the lower
East River in New York City.

   The party rode down the main Country Road through Stamford to Westchester, where
the men seized three eminent outspoken Tories, burned a small British sloop at Mamaro-
neck, and then rode on to New York City. "With bayonets fixed" they approached the
printing house of James Rivington and carried off the press and lead type. Rivington's
newspaper "The Royal Gazette" was known for its Loyalist sympathies. "A great crowd
at the Coffee House cheered." The return to New Haven was a leisurely five-day proces-
sion. With printing press and prisoners, the vandals (what else could they be called?)
made their way through the shore towns cheered by admiring spectators. One wonders
about their reception in Middlesex as they rode down the Country Road singing "Yankee Doodle," the new ballad that was sweeping the country.

   In March of 1776, the British were forced to evacuate Boston and began to trans-
port their troops by ship to New York. They landed in Brooklyn and spread eastward
deep into Long Island.★ By fall of the year the British had defeated the Rebels in Brooklyn
and driven them from Manhattan Island. Several immediate problems arose in Fairfield County after the British captured New York City. Thousands of defeated militia-
men came straggling back to Connecticut on foot, many wounded and many sick with
"camp fever." Governor Trumbull ordered hospitals set up in each shore town. Each
community did its best as the sick men poured in. By November the Stamford hospitals
were reported to be caring for 121 soldiers, and Norwalk claimed to have 400–500 sick
soldiers billeted in vacant houses.

   An equally pressing problem was the need for housing to accommodate the patriot
refugees who were fleeing from Long Island to Connecticut now that Long Island was
under British control.

   The third problem facing the county residents was soon to develop into a six-year
nightmare. British cruisers had begun in earnest to patrol the western end of Long Is-

---

★Nathan Hale sailed from Norwalk to spy against the British on Long Island that summer.[3]
For more on Hale's capture see appendices.

land Sound. They were seizing market boats and plundering the coastal farms in an effort to feed the thousands of British troops on Long Island and in New York. Ships cruising outside of Norwalk harbor were reported to have landed their men to rob the farms near the shore. The Connecticut Tories who had fled to Long Island for safety joined in these raids, being familiar with the coastline and the homes of their former neighbors. Before long it was these "refugee" Tories with their own sloops and whaleboats, rather than the British Navy, who took over the foraging and plundering. The patriots responded in kind on Long Island; and so developed the bitter guerrilla warfare on both sides of the Sound, which increased in violence as the years went on.

There developed a clandestine "illicit trade" between the Long Island Tories who had access to British imports in New York, and their friends and relatives in Connecticut, many of them in Middlesex Parish. For two years or more they had been harassed, even persecuted, when they refused to take the oath to support the Colonies and to sign the so-called "Articles of Association." Even before the signing of the Declaration of Independence in July of 1776, a number of Loyalists had been convicted and imprisoned. Now, after the fall of New York, the residents of the County were more than ever gripped by panic at the thought of these Loyalists living in their midst. In October the Norwalk Committee of Inspection imprisoned 36 men whom it suspected might cause trouble. Two years later the Committee petitioned the General Assembly for reimbursement for expenditures in that proceeding. The Clerk of the Committee was Captain Jesse Raymond (1729–1805), who is of particular interest. He was a younger brother of Gershom Raymond who remained loyal and was a son-in-law of Dr. Moses Mather. Jesse lived in the Flax Hill section of South Norwalk within the bound of Middlesex Parish. He and his wife, Hannah, would later suffer at the hands of Tory vandals. It is also interesting to observe that in spite of the overwhelming fears of the time, the good people of Norwalk were unwilling to make any financial contribution toward their own safety. They expected the State to repay them for their costs in the affair.

Information about deserters from the ranks can be found in the newspapers of the day. The "Connecticut Journal" for July 22, 1777, listed Abraham Raymond of Norwalk as a deserter from Captain John Mills Company, and in a few brief words described him as "5' high, fair complexion, black hair tied behind. Suit of cotton clothes, ribbed linen stockings." This picture almost brings to life the typical youth of the period, but in some ways Abraham Raymond was not typical. He must have deserted for reasons other than loyalty, because two years later he "enlisted in the Continental Army for the war" under Colonel Zebulon Butler.

In March, 1777, the parish was electrified to learn of the daring enemy raid on the house of Captain Samuel Richards in Rowayton [Brookside]. Captain Richards lived on the east side of Five Mile River on the Country Road [Flax Hill Road-Old King's Highway]. On the night of March 7th, Stephen Hoit of Norwalk and a gang of 25 Tories, who had crossed from Long Island, broke into Captain Richard's house, caused

Rowayton on the half shell

a lot of damage, and carried off the Captain, against whom they were to have had a particular grudge. With him, they captured 14 other men who had taken refuge there out of the rain. Three of them were soldiers on leave from duty in Stamford, but the rest were members of the guard assigned to duty that night at Five Mile River.

Captain Richards, an elderly man of sixty, was taken to New York and confined in one of the notoriously filthy prisons maintained for American prisoners of war, until exchange of prisoners could be arranged. Conditions in those prisons were so barbaric that twenty or thirty men are reported to have died daily at times from hunger and disease. When he was released four months later, Captain Richards was a very sick man and died shortly after his return home.

His loss was deeply felt for he had been a leading citizen for thirty years in the Rowayton community. He and his brother, James, owned a store and boatyard and carried on trade with the West Indies. He had also been a member of the Middlesex Society, a Selectman in Norwalk for several terms, and a Captain of militia in his younger days. After Captain Richard's death, the administrators of his estate, a brother James and a son Samuel, petitioned the Connecticut Assembly to reimburse the estate for losses "sustained from the raid of the enemy led by Stephen Hoit in March 1777, when Samuel Richards was made prisoner and died from the effects."

Louise McLean quotes Walter Bates (1760–1842), a member of a large family of Episcopalians who lived on upper Brookside Road. Many years later Bates wrote a book called *Kingston and the Loyalists of 1783* in which he included his own war time experiences in Middlesex. In it he states:

After Congress declared Independency in July 1776, the British fortified Lloyd's Neck (Long Island) with a garrison, opposite the islands and coves lying between the churches of Norwalk and Stamford, whose inhabitants were wealthy farmers - Churchmen and Quakers - all loyalists and afforded a complete asylum and safe passage, by which my three brothers and hundreds of others passed by night almost continually to the British garrison.

"At length the thing I greatly feared came upon me. A small boat was discovered by the American guard in one of these coves, by night, in which they suspected that one of my brothers with some others had come from the British. They supposed them concealed in the neighborhood, and that I must be acquainted with it. At this time I had just entered my sixteenth year. I was taken and confined at the guard house; next day examined by a Committee and threatened with sundry deaths if I did not confess what I knew not of. They threatened among other things to confine me at low water and let the tide drown me if I did not expose these honest farmers." [He meant, of course, the farmers living by the coves in Rowayton and Tokeneke and on Long Neck.]

The Committee proposed many means to extort confessions from me, the most ter-

A Frontier of the Revolutionary War

rifying was that of confining me to a log on the carriage in the saw mill, and let the saw cut me in two, if I did not expose "those Tories."

The next day Walter was brought before Colonel Davenport in his capacity as a judge. The colonel said severely to him, "I think you could have exposed those Tories." Walter answered, "You might rather think I would have exposed my own father sooner than suffer what I have suffered." Walter was discharged after the third day, and fled to the "mountains." Later he joined other Loyalists on Long Island.

On April 12, 1777, 2,000 British regulars landed on Compo Beach in Westport, under command of Major Tryon (who two years later would return to burn Fairfield and Norwalk), and marched to Danbury, raided the town capturing military stores and ammunition. Returning soundward they were met by an American force under Major General Benedict Arnold in a skirmish called the Battle of Ridgefield. Following constant harassment by patriots from there to the Sound, they disembarked from Compo where their transports awaited them and returned to Long Island. Tryon's raid on Danbury did not subdue the countryside, but it had demonstrated how unprotected the towns on the Connecticut shore really were against a large force of the enemy. Dr. Cogswell wrote that there were so few men left in Stamford that the enemy could walk in at any time from New York. In desperation, the town appealed on May 2nd for more state troops as guards. The Tories, however, continued at night to slip into unguarded inlets and through pasture gates to drive off cattle for the New York market. Often the raiders beached their boats on the shore and met secret collaborators who had rounded up farm animals for them.

In October 1777 some sixty-seven male residents of Norwalk petitioned the General Assembly sitting at Hartford to provide for an armed sloop of six or eight guns to cruise the western shores of the state to protect against further whaleboat depredations.[4]

To quote Mrs. McLean further,

"Five Mile River Harbor was a favorite rendezvous for these raiders. A Loyalist family named Selleck lived there at the head of navigation near the "White Bridge" and Tokeneke Road of today. There were four Selleck brothers, Seymour, Daniel, Kilbourne and Thomas, who were sons of John Selleck (1706–1788), the man whose homestead lands stretched along the heights on the west side of the river from above Tokeneke Road south to Butler's Island. Some years earlier this protected Five Mile River inlet had been swarming with young Sellecks, many of whom were baptised Episcopalians. The four brothers were members of a family of fourteen children, their Uncle, Nathaniel

Rowayton on the half shell

Selleck, had eight children, and their uncle, David, who also lived nearby had eleven young ones. By 1775 most of them had grown up, and many had emigrated to upper Connecticut or to Duchess County over the line into New York State where there was more available and tillable land.

Several times in 1777, Seymour Selleck and his brothers made the local headlines. The first time Seymour was the injured party. He was plundered of 24 sheep on June 3rd, for which he later sought reimbursement from the State. Then on June 9th, Seymour, his brother Daniel and a Tokeneke cousin, Edward Selleck, son of Nathan, were accused of "sickedly, falsely, feloniously and traitorously taking and driving a large number of fatted cattle belonging to diverse inhabitants of Stamford (Middlesex Parish) down to the Harbor adjoining to the Southeasterly part of said Stamford with intent . . . to supply the subject of the King of Great Britain then and still at open war . . . with the United States of America with provisions . . . that Edward Selleck delivered the cattle to the officers and Sea Men belonging to the British armed vessel of War commonly called the Halifax brig, then lying in said Harbour in an Hostile and Warlike manner to annoy the inhabitants of said States."

What consternation and alarm when a British ship of war anchored openly in Five Mile River Harbor!

More than a year later in August, 1778, the case against the Sellecks was disposed of in Fairfield County Court. No evidence was found "to support this indictment" against Edward Selleck, and Daniel was also cleared. Seymour, however, was convicted of this charge and also of another. He was found guilty of having kidnapped David Lockwood on June 18th, the day preceeding the cattle roundup of 1777, and "putting him aboard the British sloop of War "Kitty" then being off Stamford in a warlike and hostile manner, in order to force Lockwood to serve against the United States."

General Tryon continued his strategy of harassing the people of coastal Connecticut. On the fifth of July, 1779, he and 3,000 men, carried by a fleet of some 26 sail, moved up the sound to New Haven. After pilliaging and burning that town, on their return to New York they landed at Fairfield on the 7th, where they burned nearly every house to the ground, plundering on all sides as they went.

On the night of the 10th, they landed 2,600 men at Norwalk where they repeated the same tactics on the following day, Sunday, July 11, 1779, but the homes of the outlivers in Silvermine, Five Mile River and Wilton were spared.[5] Here in Norwalk the Redcoats met with more opposition for the militia had had time to rally. Local history is full of details about the skirmishes which began on the eastern slope of Flax Hill, only a short walk from the Five Mile River in Middlesex.[6] However there is never a word about the Middlesex militia and any part which they played in the resistance in Norwalk. None of their men who applied for pensions later were mentioned as being present on that day.

Although Middlesex and Stamford escaped General Tryon's attention, the night raids

A Frontier of the Revolutionary War

34

by small bands of 'Refugees' increased in ferocity that summer. Now, in addition to seizing livestock and household loot, the Loyalists increasingly made it a habit to kidnap their former neighbors and to hold them as hostages to be exchanged for British or Loyalist prisoners of equal rank who had been captured by Connecticut Privateers. On August 3rd eight Tories, five of whom were Dr. Mather's former parishioners, broke into the parsonage on Brookside Road and captured him and his four sons. The Mathers were imprisoned in New York City until five weeks later when Dr. Mather and two of his sons were released. A third son, nineteen year old Moses, died in prison on September 22nd. His body was brought back to Middlesex for burial in the Brookside Cemetery on Rowayton Avenue. In spite of his deep sorrow, the resolute minister is reported to have said, "I had rather see him a corpse than to have him join the enemies of his country!"

The winter of 1779–1780 was the severest ever known in the United States. Amazingly enough, Long Island Sound was covered with ice so thick a man could walk across it from Norwalk to Long Island. Winter weather brought at least a temporary lull in the war between the Refugees and the Patriots; but with the coming of spring the raids began once more. On the morning of April 9th, as reported in the Connecticut Journal of April 12, 1789, "three boats from Long Island took out of a river between Norwalk and Stamford three small eastern vessels." This indicates the tendency of the press to exaggerate even in that day for the accounts of three local men agree that there were only two vessels involved, not six. A small sloop or schooner owned by a Loyalist named Talcott was lying at Gorham's Mill, or Rings End, at the dock. A Refugee whale boat over from Long Island cut her out and put White Raymond and Raymond Selleck (i.e., Refugees) on board with Talcott to take her to Long Island. Raymond and Selleck made the fatal mistake of letting Talcott take the tiller and steer. Talcott knocked Raymond down with the tiller while Selleck was below drawing brandy. Raymond surrendered. Talcott then offered Selleck quarter, but he undertook to jump out of the hold, whereupon Talcott knocked him down dead with the tiller, and brought the vessel to Norwalk. Raymond afterwards went to Nova Scotia.

On August 28th, 1780, marauders struck at two places at once, with such disastrous consequences that Captain John Bell and Captain Nathaniel Slason wrote to Colonel John Mead on August 30th, as follows:

"On the night before the 29th instant, a party of the enemy in a hostile, violent manner entered the house of Jesse Raymond of Middlesex, and robbed and plundered him to the value of 150 pounds in silver money besides breaking doors, windows, desks, cases of drawers, and the like, carrying off the best cloaths, stripped his house of the greater part of his household utensils, etc.

"The same night a party of the enemy from Long Island drew near Gorum's Mill in sd Middlesex, where they had lately been plundering sundry times; being hailed by the small guard there stationed for the night, the enemy being greatly superior to the guard in numbers, fired on them, whereby one of the guards unfortunately was killed

Rowayton on the half shell

by them and two others of sd Guard were wounded.

"Inasmuch as this particular place is so infested, we desire and request that some way may speedily be devised for our relief, and that a company may be granted to us as guard on each on each side of Five Mile River, which might be a help to each other. The above request is on behalf of ourselves and the rest of the inhabitants."[7]

An active patriot, Jesse Raymond was fortunate to escape with his life that night. His own petition to the General Assembly described his experience in more detail. He added that "your Memorialist very nearly escaping them who had threatened to burn sd house if they could not find your Memorialist, who providentially escaped the misfortune of falling into their hands, and prays that the State and other rates and taxes due . . . to the amount of 155:8 pounds aforesaid may be abated."[8]

On the night of November 30th, the enemy landed at the Rhoton Islands in Middlesex Parish near the mouth of the Five Mile River and marched north in the dark as far as the Country Road. Apparently there was no guard to oppose them. They collected 39 "horned cattle" and five horses from several farms, drove them to their waiting boats, and were soon off again to Long Island. Solomon Whitmore and his son-in-law, Richard Youngs, lost nearly 40 pounds worth of "creatures" from their farm on the Country Road where Rowayton Avenue meets Old King's Highway today. Eli Reed, former militia Captain and their neighbor across the road, had many windows broken in his new house; Nathan Waring lost one horse, and Obadiah Wheeler, living nearby, was robbed of clothing and bed linen."

By far the most famous local raid took place on Sunday, July 22, 1781, when a band of refugees from Long Island under Captain William Frost surrounded the Middlesex Congregational Church during afternoon services, capturing all forty-eight male worshippers, including the minister, Dr. Moses Mather, their outspoken leader in political as well as religious thought. Since the establishment of the church in 1744 the parish line had been set across the town line to include those families living west of the parting brook (Ely Brook)—those of Rhotan Hill, much of the Flax Hill Road area, Rowayton, Brookside and West Norwalk. It was the only Congregational Church between Norwalk and Stamford. Frost was a shoemaker who had moved to Middlesex, married a local girl, and an ardent Loyalist who refugeed to Long Island. A number of the men he commanded that day were also former Middlesex Parish residents well familiar with the area.

Mrs. McLean's account continues:

Frost and his party landed at night on the east side of Scotch (Scott's) Cove, marched through the woods, and concealed themselves near the church. They learned from a lookout who knew all of the congregation personally that three persons who were particularly

A Frontier of the Revolutionary War

*obnoxious to them—Captain Gershom Richards, Josiah Hoyt and Nathaniel Waring—
were not present in church that morning, so the attack was deferred until the afternoon
service. Soon after the afternoon service had commenced, Frost and his men advanced
from the wood unnoticed until they jumped the road fence near the church.*

*Reverend Mather was in the pulpit, and as recalled by four different eye witnesses
years later,[9] Frost said "Come down here, old Mather, I want to use [see?] you." Four
or five members of the congregation managed to escape by leaping from a window and
running, including two sons of Dr. Mather. At least one child is cited as hiding under
a woman' dress, and one man was wounded in the leg while crossing the fence. The
prisoners numbering 48 according to church records were tied two and two and marched
to the islands at the mouth of the Five Mile River [the Fish Islands]. Jonathan Bates
said it was low water and that the men crossed to the inner island. High tide on that
memorable Sunday so long ago was at 10:24 a.m., and sunset at 8 P.M.*

*Frost placed the captives on the outer island with ten guards to watch them, and turned
to defend the inner island against attack by the patriots under Major Davenport. Because of the size of the islands, Davenport was forced to exercise extreme care while at-
tacking so as not to kill and wound prisoners they hoped to free.★ But the fight was surprisingly brisk. Davenport's party continued to fire to the extent that a buttonwood tree
which grew upon the island was filled with bullets.*

*The Loyalists had a galley (sloop) armed with swivels which kept the Rebels off and
swept the bar with grape-shot. The Refugees and prisoners were taken aboard the galley. They had also with them a larger brig, probably the "Halifax," which could not
approach because of the state of the tide, so the Refugees swam their horses off to her,
where they were taken on board, some 36 horses and 36 pillions [saddles]. It was as
late as ten at night when they all re-embarked.*

*The prisoners were all transported to New York City for confinement in various pris-
ons where most languished for five months or more before being exchanged.[10] Moses
Mather and the last of the prisoners returned home on December 27th, several of them
too ill to walk. Captain Richards and Nathan Waring never returned having died in
prison. Josiah Hoyt was returned in a very weak and sickly condition. Young James
Bell, sadly enough, died on the way home.*

★Davenport was later criticized for being too timid. Some men who were present felt Frost
could have been taken, "The men raving to attack, the tide being down, the British vessels aground unable to bring their guns to bear."

Rowayton on the half shell

Whaleboat Marauders

*A*S THE NUMBER and toll of the whaleboat marauders increased in intensity so did the defenses. Early in the conflict, the English and their sympathizers raided and returned unmolested. As the coast guard strengthened, the raiders were more frequently and effectively challenged. Most of the raids were of course amphibious in nature, but a number were strictly naval - whaleboat vs. whaleboat.

The particular design of the boats used by both raiders and defenders caused them to be universally called "whaleboats" although few if any ever chased a whale. Built to support the larger privateers, they were sharp at each end, sheathed with thin planking only one-half inch thick to keep them light so as to be carried on the shoulders. Some were as long as thirty-two feet, manned by from four to ten pairs of oars. Smaller craft ranged from eighteen feet or so up. They could be rowed quietly in calm waters when pursuit by sail was impossible especially under cover of night. They had the capacity to accelerate rapidly leaving pursuers behind.

Ten and sometimes as many as twelve rebel whaleboats went out of Stamford. They did not all belong there but made Stamford their headquarters. Captain Samuel Hawley of Bridgeport was sometimes at that post with his boat. Captain Samuel Lockwood of Greenwich, in the Continental service and in command of Long Island Sound whaleboats, was with him, and also the whaleboat of Captain John Scranton of New London, as well as other vessels.[1]

Many of the marauders were refugees from Long Island living on the Connecticut shore who had commissions from the governors of New York and/or Connecticut to cruise the Sound against British vessels. It required no great

Whaleboat similar in design and construction to those used locally during the Revolutionary War for night raids.

stretch of conscience to go on land and plunder indiscriminately, but there were few records of landings on the Long Island side. The north shore of the island was even more sparsely populated than the Connecticut shore, and was already picked clean by the occupying troops. There is reference to one widow Chichester's tavern, however, near a place called "the cedars" on Huntington Bay. It seems she was a staunch Loyalist called "Widow Chich," and her tavern a "nest of all the Tories."

In 1846 an historian of the Revolution, a Mr. MacDonald, interviewed a number of whaleboat warfare veterans. Henry Chichester of Old Well, presumably no relation of the widow's, when interviewed November 4, 1846, recalled

> *The Coast Guard in Norwalk was commanded by Captain Samuel Keeler and under him was Daniel Jackson, a Lieutenant, who also commanded sometimes. Colonel St. John had the general command, and Keeler was the principal acting man under him. The Coast Guards were state troops and enlisted for periods of one, two or three months at a time. They were called 'state guards.'*
>
> *I was taken [by the refugees from Connecticut to Long Island] at the Norwalk Islands returning from a whaleboat cruise. Captain Quintard commanded our boat. Some Tory had probably informed on us, for on passing the narrow passage called Comstock Island gut (Manresa Island) we found a whaleboat lying in wait on each side of the gut. They both fired upon us, mortally wounding one of our crew named Conklin. We then surrendered and were taken to Lloyd's Neck and to New York, and put aboard the old Jersey prison ship from which I afterwards escaped. It was in the Sugar House Prison in Liberty Street, adjacent to the Mid Dutch Church where Paulding and I were confined in 1780. He escaped with my assistance . . .*

By 1781 the refugee raiders were crossing the sound practically every night the weather permitted. The situation became so tense by mid–summer that Abraham Davenport commanding in Stamford wrote as follows to General Washington on August 10th: "Your excellency has undoubtedly been in-

Rowayton on the half shell

formed of the exposed situation of this part of the country and of the frequent incursions by the enemy. Several inhabitants have been killed and wounded, and nearly sixty within a short time carried into confinement and robbed of their property, and unless some protection is afforded, those who are of ability and inclination will retire into the country and others will make their peace. The ardor of the people (which is to be lamented) has abated in consequence of their distresses, so that very little opposition is to be expected from them." He hoped "guards" from the army may be sent for their protection. "General Parsons will inform Your Excellency of the designs of the enemy against this town."

Thaddeus Bell was one of those captured by the British, confined and later paroled.[2] When interviewed by MacDonald on November 8, 1846, Bell, aged eighty-eight, recalled that

On the 2nd of August, 1781, Major Hubbell landed on the point of Rhoton Neck (east of the Rhotan River/Five Mile River) marched north and east two or three miles and collected cattle. Lieutenant Nathan Howe of the Coast Guard waylaid them on their return at the (Brookside) School house on the Turnpike Road. The school house now stands on the same place it did then. Howe took post on the south side of the Post Road and just on the east side of the road leading to the point where the Refugees were going.

He had little time to form for the Refugees were coming. He engaged the advance party returning from above with cattle, etc. Hubbell then came down, also returning from above, and marching in rear of the advance guard for the east. He instantly took post on the American right behind a stone wall which ran north and south, and so raked the Americans, killing two and wounding several. If Howe had posted his party on the west side of road leading to the Point (where the Refugees were going), it was generally thought afterwards that he probably would have turned the scale. Howe was a good officer, and was overpowered by numbers. The Refugees were most numerous. The spot where this happened is about three-quarters of a mile east of Roton River.

The British landed once at Raymond's Point in 1781, on the east side of the mouth of the Five Mile River, and collected cattle, etc. They got cattle on board, but when they were getting up anchor and getting under sail, the Americans had collected and fired from the shore killing eight of the enemy. I was told of this by an Englishman while I was in prison in New York. This Englishman was with the Refugees involuntarily having come to Lloyd's Neck to claim his vessel, just as they were sailing with her on a cruise.

Bell went on to recall that

On the 27th of April, 1781, Captain Hubbell and others landed on the west side

Whaleboat Marauders

of Norwalk Harbor, near or at Raymond's or Belden's Neck and marched through the woods to the house of one Saunders, a Loyalist. Here they got the information they wanted. One of the party had lived in Colonel St. John's house, and knew a door that was not closed at night, so they got into Col. St. John's bedroom without any alarm, and took him, his son, and Mr. Isaacs, the father of Benjamin and Charles, prisoner.[3]

Surrender of the British at Yorktown, October 19, 1781, did not result in the immediate cessation of marauder raids. One of the most celebrated and bloody of the naval fights occurred off the Norwalk Islands on the morning of December 5, 1782 [1781?]. The patriot vessels were commanded by Captain Brewster and the Tory whaleboats by Captain Joseph Hoyt. We rely again on the memory of Henry Chichester.

Brewster's was an eight oared boat, Ryder's was ten oared and Hoyt's was eight oared. They carried two in addition to the oarsmen, one at the helm and one at the bow. Brewster's number two boat, commanded by Valentine Ryder, carried a swivel gun on the bow. I don't know if the others carried swivels.

Ryder engaged the five oared boat, took her, took out her sails and oars, and bore down to Brewster's assistance who was about equally matched with Hoyt. They had boarded each other several times and had been beaten off. Brewster was wounded and probably could not have taken Hoyt but for Ryder's help. They clenched each other and fought with the breach of their muskets, bayonets, swords, etc. Brewster and Hoyt were bitterly hostile. Ryder came down and fired his swivel at Hoyt's boat, which killed two of his men and decided the engagement. Brewster had ordered the swivel to be fired when they came near, and called to the bowman to know why he did not discharge it. "It is no—is in—isn't—my—my-right" said the bowman, and then fired the decisive shot. The poor fellow had an impediment in his speech and stuttered badly.

Hoyt told me he would have taken Brewster if Ryder had not come up, that he had the advantage of him, and was at the point of capturing his boat, but that when Ryder approached he found it necessary to surrender. Almost every man in the two hostile boats was wounded. Brewster was badly wounded in the breast. Hoyt and Brewster had fought hand-to-hand, clenched each other, etc. They were both very athletic men. In fact, the crew of both boats were very select and powerful men. Whaleboat crews were generally ten or twelve in number. We with four whaleboats once attacked three vessels, one large and two smaller. It turned out the large one had twenty-five marines concealed on board, and as we came up, they fired upon our leading boat and killed or wounded all on board except the helmsman and bowman. Six were killed and wounded. This didn't deter us, but we went on with the attack, ran the armed vessel on shore and took the two others into Norwalk.

Rowayton on the half shell

One of the last and most poignant raids may be dated from the death of Selleck Reed. He was a grandson of Nathan and Catherine Selleck of Old Farm Road, Middlesex, and lived within the parish far out on West Norwalk Road. Jonathan Bates, who was a boy of ten at that time, probably knew Selleck Reed as an older boy who lived nearby. Jonathan later recalled how

a party of refugees once landed on the east side of Five Mile River [November 4, 1782!], and moved up. Their landing was observed by Captain Slosson of the Coast Guard who happened to be near them. Slosson watched them from the west side of the river, unseen by the refugees. He advanced opposite them until they arrived at a large rock near the bridge (the present "White Bridge") south of the highway where a sentry was posted who belonged to the Coast Guards. The sentry, Selleck Reed, hailed the refugees who instantly fired and killed him. Slosson and some men with him attacked the Loyalists and a skirmish ensued. Having several men wounded, Slosson retreated with his party. Reed had travelled four or more miles by foot or horse to volunteer to meet his death. He was nineteen.

Reed's funeral sermon was preached by Dr. Mather, who took his text from I Kings XXII:34. "And a certain man drew a bow at a venture, and smote the King of Israel between the joints of the harness; wherefore he said unto the driver of his chariott, 'Turn thy hand and carry me out of the host; for I am wounded,'" Through the efforts of the Village Green (Norwalk) Chapter of the Daughters of the American Revolution, the graves of many of the soldiers and participants interred in local cemeteries have been identified. In the Brookside and Raymond family cemeteries are: Moses Webb, private; John Richards, householder keeping watch; Stephen Raymond, private; Eli Reed, lieutenant and captain; Jesse Reed, householder keeping watch; Gershom Raymond, committee of safety, county congress, and householder keeping watch; Paul Raymond, (his son), clerk and sergeant; Rev. Moses Mather, D.D., patriot pastor taken by the British and in New York prison ship for six months; John Mather, private.[4]

No account of Rowayton during the Revolution would be complete without stressing the role of Captain Esaias Bouton (1730–1821) who lived on Witch Lane at the head of Wilson Cove. An ardent Loyalist, Captain Bouton is said to have made more money from the war than anyone in Norwalk.[5] He was a staunch Episcopalian, a founder of St. Paul's Episcopal Church, Norwalk, and close friend of the Reverend Jeremiah Leaming, the minister. Leaming was accused by some as a rabid Tory. He left town with Tryon after the burning in 1779 either voluntarily or, as others deduce, a prisoner.[6]

Bouton's home was so situated at the head of Wilson's Cove that a fire in the fireplace was visible the full length of the cove as well as far out into the Sound. When the coast was clear for British whaleboats to land, Bouton

Whaleboat Marauders

would build a roaring fire as a signal favorable to landing, meet the raiders and "drive sharp and profitable bargains for produce and cattle." When there was no fire in the fireplace, there was no raid. "The usual place of shipment" is believed to have been on the eastern shore of the cove. So many cattle were butchered there before being loaded aboard the whaleboats that the feeding brook and adjacent pond were known for years afterward as "Hoof and Horn Creek."

It is puzzling that Captain Bouton's name does not appear on the list of those known, or judged to be, "inimical and dangerous" filed with the town clerk. A pillar of St. Paul's Episcopal Church, Norwalk, he lived a long life after the war in peace with his neighbors, and was buried in the Bouton-Hoyt family cemetery close by the homestead on Witch Lane, Rowayton, in 1821. Ironically, at the seventy-fifth anniversary of the Revolution in 1851, his grandson, Nathaniel Bouton, was invited to deliver the principal address.[8]

Rowayton on the half shell

Watermen From The Start

*D*URING THE PERIOD immediately following the Revolution,
Rowayton, and indeed Norwalk
itself, failed to grow appreciably. One of the principal impediments to growth
was the deplorable condition of the roads and bridges. Travel within and between towns was an ordeal to be avoided if at all possible. Transfer of goods
and persons by road and highway for any distance was almost nil. The main
road between Norwalk and Stamford,—known as the "Boston Post Road,"
after Benjamin Franklin organized the postal service—was what we now
know as Old King's Highway in Darien, then, (east bound) Flax Hill Road
after crossing the Five Mile River in Brookside, then West Street (in those
days) in South Norwalk, to the foot of West Avenue, thence north to the Wall
Street Bridge over the Norwalk River. These roads are basically the same
today.

Since this route neatly by-passed Rowayton proper, as we know it, this
area was even slower to develop. As Drs. Ray and Stewart state,

*Norwalk never seemed to work out a plan to provide decent in-town roads and inter-
town highways. Under one early eighteenth century policy the town was divided into
eight districts, each district maintaining its own roads out of its portion of highway taxes. This did little to comfort the traveller in sparsely-settled districts. Dusty or mud mired
roads remained the rule.*[1]

Rowayton did experience some growth, however, albeit on a small scale.
As animosities gradually diminished and war memories faded, the area experienced the first of a series of growing pains that were to erupt thereafter

WPA mural depicting packet sloop "Chief" loading produce for the New York market in the

following each of the country's major wars. New homes were necessary to accommodate the few returning veterans and numerous siblings who were not veterans, so their elders set about filling the need. A few of the houses they built during that period survive to this day. The first house in from Rowayton Avenue (then Main Street) to the right on Wilson Avenue (then North Street) is one, also 26 Wilson Avenue, and the dwelling on the northeast corner of Rowayton Avenue and Witch Lane (200 Rowayton Avenue) another. A home since moved to Contentment Island, Tokeneke, which stood near Main Street at 137 Rowayton Avenue, are all from that era. They were built by Gershom Raymond for some of his children during the 1790s.

Hauling goods and passengers any distance was obviously done mainly by boat. At sea, and occasionally not so far off-shore, impressment of American seamen and harassment of shipping by the British and French became so rampant during the Napoleonic wars that the United States passed the Embargo Act of 1807 forbidding any American ship to sail to any foreign port. After that act was repealed the Non-Intercourse Act permitted trade with countries except England and France.

War with England came in 1812 and lasted for three years. It was extremely unpopular in Connecticut and throughout New England, but Norwalk ran contrary to the trend and supported the war policies of Presidents Jefferson

Rowayton on the half shell

Five Mile River. Painted by Rowayton artist George Avison c. 1934

and Madison. The governor of Connecticut refused to send the militia (in which some one hundred and thirty-five Norwalk men had enlisted) beyond the borders of the state. The assembly had declared the war unnecessary! The effect of the war, if any, upon the few Rowayton area residents is difficult to determine. The overseas and coastal operation of the Richards Brothers had apparently ceased upon their deaths. Alfred Seeley of New Canaan was yet to move down into the area.

Fortunately Rowayton had a cozy harbor—its one great natural asset—which no doubt attracted Alfred Seeley. The two wars had given impetus to great strides in ship and boat building. New designs, lighter construction, simplified sail plans and rigging contributed to greater speed and reliability. Coastal trading became faster and more dependable. The packet boats, both sloop and schooner-rigged, flourished in the passenger and produce trade along the coasts north and south, in the Sound, and in Five Mile River.

Seeley moved to Rowayton around 1820, purchased the site of Richards Brothers shipyard and store, and proceeded to build a rather large comfortable house on the high river bank we now call Pinkney Park. By 1825 he was owner and operator of the sloop rigged packet *Enterprise* sailing regularly from a dock just south of his home to the New York market and points between. His ledger records that in the same year one Nelson Smith signed

Watermen from the Start

Alphonso and Hannah Seeley Dibble, daughter of Alfred Seeley.

Rowayton on the half shell

The Seeley-Dibble house at 177 Rowayton Avenue c. 1870. Note the oyster boats anchored in the river at left.

on the *Enterprise* as of the first day of April, joined by (or replaced by?) Stephen Hoyt on April 9th. The following year H. Marvin "began" on June 3rd, Israel (no surname) on July 29th, and "later L. Cooke."[2]

The *Enterprise* drew too much water to be suited for the shallow Five Mile River. Eleven years later in 1836 Seeley ordered a new sloop to be built by John I. Felter of Nyack, New York, for two thousand dollars, to be named *Julia* for a Seeley daughter. The ledger shows an additional $877.09 was spent for fitting out, including sails and rigging, cable and anchor, cabin stove and utensils, compass and marlinspike, and $1.00 for a copy of the Holy Bible!

From an enrollment certificate dated April 12, 1836, then required of "all vessels to be employed in the Coastal Trade or Fisheries," we know the *Julia*'s vital statistics: "length Fifty-five feet four inches, breadth Twenty-feet eight inches, depth four feet eight inches, measuring Forty-three and 55/95 tons, having one deck and one mast. Sylvanus S. Raymond, master."

Several years later in 1851 Captain Stephen Raymond from the Middlesex side of the river, now Darien, registered a similar packet sloop which he immodestly and unimaginatively named *Stephen Raymond*. She was fifty-six feet six-inches long, Twenty feet nine-inches wide, drew four feet nine-inches of water and measured forty-four and 62/95 tons.[3] He also built a wharf at the head of the salt.

A number of other packets were well known along the Rowayton water-

Watermen from the Start

ENROLLMENT.

PERMANENT.

Seeley

IN conformity to an Act of the Congress of the UNITED STATES of America, entitled "An Act for Enrolling and Licensing Ships or Vessels to be employed in the Coasting Trade or Fisheries, and for regulating the same," *Alfred Seeley of Norwalk County of Fairfield and State of Connecticut*

have taken or subscribed the _____ required by the said Act, and having _____ that _____

_____ a citizen of the United States, sole owner of the ship or vessel called the *Julia*

Sylvanus Raymond

of *Norwalk* whereof *Sylvanus S. Raymond* is at present master, and as he hath _____ is a citizen of the United States, and that the said ship or vessel was built at *State of New York County of Rockland* as appears by the Master Carpenter Certificate under whose direction she was built —

and *Peter Smith Surveyor* having certified that the said ship or vessel has one deck, and _____ mast and that her length is *Fifty five feet four inches* her breadth *Twenty feet Eight inches* her depth *Eight feet Eight inches* and that she measures *Forty* tons; and that she is a square sterned *Sloop* has _____ no galleries, and _____ head; and the said *Alfred Seeley* having agreed to the description and admeasurement, above specified, and sufficient security having been given, according to the said act, the said *Sloop* has been duly enrolled at the Port of Fairfield.

Given under my hand and seal, at the Port of Fairfield, this *12th* day of *April* in the year one thousand eight hundred and thirty *six*

Certificate of Enrollment of the coastal packet sloop "Julia" dated April 12, 1836. Alfred Seeley was the owner; Sylvanus Raymond the master.

Rowayton on the half shell

Crew of the local coastal schooner "Mary E. Cuff," Charles W. Conklin owner and master, in the 1880s.

front: the *Chief, Joseph Gorham,* and *Sentinel,* the latter owned by Elisha Seeley of New Canaan.

The ports of eastern Connecticut with easy access to the ocean traded afar
to the West Indies and to Europe. Conversely those in western Connecticut
concentrated on the markets of New York City and the thriving Hudson
River towns. This proved a blessing during the embargo and war years when
British frigates again patrolled the Sound—under the overall command of
Admiral Nelson's second in command at Trafalgar, Captain Thomas Hardy, no less! By the mid 1830s the Rowayton packet trade had prospered to
the degree that tiny Five Mile River boasted two piers and four small warehouses.[4] Onions were grown abundantly, especially in New Canaan and in
Brookside, and were warehoused here with other produce awaiting shipment.

Strong competition relegated the coastal packet trade to the shallower harbors unavailable to larger vessels, and consequently to small cargoes. The
steamboat, invented in 1796 by John Fitch of Connecticut descent, rather
than Robert Fulton in 1809 as some contend,[5] improved and developed so
rapidly that by 1818 the *Mechanic* with three cabins, 42 berths, and proportionate cargo space, left Norwalk for Peck Slip, New York, on a regular

Watermen from the Start

The "Sarah R. Bell" c. 1939, the very last local schooner converted to powered propulsion. Edward R. Smith was owner and master.

schedule each Wednesday and Saturday, and returned Monday and Thursday. The competition between steamboat operators was so intense that as early as 1825 sixteen to twenty steamers were docking in Norwalk daily![6]

With the advent of the railroad along the Connecticut shore line to New Haven in 1848 and later to Stonington and Providence, the steamboat monopoly was to be shared with the iron horse. Surprisingly the small packets hung on tenaciously. The ship *Chief*, depicted by artist, Alfred Avison, in the Rowayton Library mural, was so engaged until the late 1890s, one of the last survivors of the packet trade.

Small coastal schooners, only slightly larger than the packets, became their successors and lasted for another half century. They, too, frequented the Five Mile River. During the early days of the twentieth century Rowayton was home port to the ketch *Clarence*, Captain William H. Lockwood; and the schooner *Mary E. Cuff*, Captain Charles W. Conklin. Later, during the years between the two World Wars, the *T.W. Anderson, Joseph R. Murray*, and *Sarah Bell* were owned and operated by Captain Theodore Smith and sons Howard, Edward, and Lester, all Captains in their own right. Originally two-masted vessels, the schooners were later powered with auxiliary engines, the main mast removed entirely and the foremast often shortened. The engine soon became the principal source of power, the sail became the auxiliary. After World War II the days of working sail on Long Island Sound were as dead as a salt mackerel.

Rowayton on the half shell

Of Schools And Churches

*E*DUCATION WAS a major concern of the earliest settlers, to their ever-lasting credit. They made provision for the first school at their November 1699 town meeting, to be a one room affair on lower East Avenue. Essential supplies, such as writing paper, were scarce. Until 1690 when the first paper mill opened in Philadelphia, all writing and wrapping material had to be imported from England. As settlement spread, lack of transportation spawned separate schools in each settled area of the town. An unconnected district school system evolved. Each loosely defined district was responsible only to itself for administration, curriculum, and operation. As the town grew, so did the school districts. By 1840 there were twelve of them in Norwalk! The system, if it may be so called, became so chaotic "school societies" were abolished by the state in 1856.

PLEASE PRESERVE THIS BILL.

Rowayton, Ct., *June 19* 1878

M *Mary B Raymond*

To SOUTH FIVE MILE RIVER SCHOOL DISTRICT, Dr.

To amount of Tax laid on List of 1878 $ 4-20

Received Payment, *Aug 22* 1878

E F Rile _____ Collector.

Three per cent. will be abated on this bill if paid on or before July 3d, '78.

E. F. RILE, Collector,
OFFICE AT HIS RESIDENCE,
OPEN EVERY EVENING TILL 9 O'CLOCK.

South Five Mile River School District tax receipt dated June 19, 1878.

Two-room district school at Rowayton Avenue and Cudlipp Street was in service from 1848 to 1894.

Rowayton's first schoolhouse of record was built by such a school "society" soon to be designated the "South Five Mile River School District." School districts often crossed town boundaries. Ours was comprised of residents of both sides of the river, as did the Middle and Northern Five Mile River School districts (Brookside and West Norwalk). The Southern District was organized in 1820 and promptly set about providing a schoolhouse, one room, measuring maybe 12 x15 feet. It was located across the road from the property of Andrew Bell who probably donated the site, now 11 Hunt Street. The teacher is reported to have received sixteen dollars a month (a bit excessive for that day, if true) and boarded in the neighborhood.[1]

The second Rowayton school was built in 1848 on the river bank at the intersection of Cudlipp Street and Rowayton Avenue. Although larger and more comfortable than the first school, a second room had to be added some twenty years later. A reporter for the *Norwalk Gazette* visiting the village in 1869 "noticed the foundations going up for a considerable addition to the schoolhouse in 'Grantville,' more than doubling its present capacity. 'More room for scholars' seemed to be the cry all over the town - thanks to the benevolent law."[2] The school was a long narrow building facing the street on what is now 1–3 Cudlipp Street. The school was divided into two rooms, one called the "big" room and the second, of course, the "little" room, al-

Rowayton on the half shell

The four-room district school at Rowayton Avenue and Witch Lane operated from 1895 to 1940.

though according to pupils of the time, the rooms were about the same size. The addition was a square section added to the rear of the building, making it "L" shaped.

The teacher in the "big" room also served as principal. Both the "big" and "little" room teachers came to school by train from South Norwalk, and walked down "Main Street" from the station. One was very conscious of the daily temperature and invariably read the outdoor thermometer each morning. The students were well aware of his habit. On cold mornings the big boys would put the thermometer in a bucket of ice where it was left until the teachers approached to within sight. Then the thermometer was hastily re-hung on its nail by the door. When the principal looked at the doctored instrument, he decided it was too cold to hold classes. School was cancelled for the day!

When the building was replaced in 1895, it was sold to a former associate editor of the *South Norwalk Sentinel*, Emma Walker. Miss Walker had the older part of the school detached and moved across and up Cudlipp Street, where it still stands as a residence overlooking the White Bridge. Part of the rear section also survives, having been incorporated into the residence at 3 Cudlipp Street.[3]

In the early 1890s the local school district acquired property at the corner of Witch Lane and Rowayton Avenue from Captain Edward Smith, a natu-

Of Schools and Churches

The first Rowayton Baptist Church at 15 Cudlipp Street;
1858–1905.

ral growth oysterman. A two-story, four-room school, complete with full attic, basement, bell-tower and separate outdoor privies opened in 1894. A soaring flagpole stood on the front lawn and a steep hill, ideal for sliding and romping, was close behind the building that was to serve as the Rowayton School for nearly fifty years.

Rowayton children going beyond elementary levels commuted to and from classes in South Norwalk by train and later by trolley. Two school districts in South Norwalk combined to form the Union School District. Two rooms were set aside in their Concord Street School as a high school open to all. The first class graduated in 1901, and contained a few Rowayton students.

After much wrestling, Norwalk, South Norwalk, and the East Norwalk Fire District consolidated into one governmental administrative unit—The City of Norwalk—in 1913. With consolidation came a single city-wide school system. The Rowayton school was deeded to the city Board of Education. The South Five Mile River School District ceased to exist; the building they had built in 1894 was to be used, however, until 1940.

Soon after the Civil War a number of good quality private preparatory and girls' finishing schools prospered in Norwalk, accommodating both boarding and day students. Soon after World War I such a school opened

Rowayton on the half shell

The Rowayton Methodist Episcopal Church at Rowayton Avenue and Pennoyer Street, c. 1868. It was erected on land donated by Elias Pennoyer.

in Rowayton. The Thomas School was founded by Mabel Thomas at the head of Wilson Cove in October 1922. Enrollment totalled eight pupils.[4] A small beginning, but a healthy start. Within six years the staff numbered twenty-five teachers, three of whom had masters' degrees. The Thomas School flourished here for forty-five years, providing instruction from kindergarten to college entrance. Enrollment eventually reached 375 students.[5]

The coming of the railroad in 1848 did little to alleviate the problem of getting back and forth to church services for the residents of Rowayton. It would be twenty years before a station would be built here. By then the two prominent local religious denominations had built their own houses of worship. In 1859 the Baptist Ecclesiastical Society of Five Mile River acquired land on the east bank of the river just east of the White Bridge. A small church was soon erected. It was the first house of worship to be built here. Heretofore the Baptist group, made up of residents from both sides of the river, had met in members' homes - an unsatisfactory arrangement at best. The Baptist creed called for baptism by total immersion. It must have been a source of satisfaction and comfort to have the church situated on the water's edge,

Of Schools and Churches

The same church after renovation and Anglicization with the aid and guidance of Mr. and Mrs. John Sherman Hoyt, c. 1908.

especially during the warmer months. Timing of baptism, of course, had to coincide with the time of high tide behind the church.

The church building was extensively remodeled and converted into a residence many years later. It remains to this day at number 11 Cudlipp Street. A second Baptist church was built in 1905. It stood between the present United Church and the Raymond cemetery. Its dominant feature was a turret-like bell tower. There was a large Sunday school room, baptismal, choir stall and sanctuary. It was to serve until 1966.

Those residents of the Methodist persuasion organized formally in 1868, as the Third Methodist Episcopal Church Society (the First and Second being in Norwalk and South Norwalk). They erected a one-room church at the corner of Rowayton Avenue and Maple Street, later renamed Pennoyer Street in honor of Elias Pennoyer, donator of the land for the church and parsonage.

The original church was a wooden colonial unornamented type building, painted shining white, with the entrance on Rowayton Avenue. Among the Methodist parishioners were Mr. and Mrs. John Sherman Hoyt of Tokeneke. While travelling in England the Hoyts had been smitten by the charm and

Rowayton Baptist Church at 210 Rowayton Avenue; 1906–1966.

The United Church of Rowayton at 210 Rowayton Avenue was built in 1966.

Of Schools and Churches

grace of a small country church. Upon returning home, Mrs. Hoyt became instrumental in designing and financing extensive renovations to the original building patterned after the English model. The attractive church and Sunday school rooms we know today are the result of her commitment.

In the post World War II years church attendance fell off sharply. Neither Rowayton church was prospering and costs were steadily rising. At the instigation of the Methodist minister, Donald Emig, the daring idea of combining the two churches was broached. It did not meet with universal approval, of course, but after many meetings and much heart rending, the concept gained acceptance and was adopted in 1951 by both congregations. Rivals for generations, the two were now to be one—almost.

The plan to combine was not to be wholly successful. It soon developed that ownership of the Methodist property was in the name of the District Methodist Conference rather than in the local congregation. The conference denied the congregation permission to transfer the property and unite with the former Baptists. The Methodists were split. Those favoring union joined the new church, those opposed remained Methodists.

The Baptist property at 212 Rowayton Avenue was offered and the church used initially for services of the United Church of Rowayton. Mr. Emig resigned from the Methodist faith and was retained by the new church, soon after affiliated with the Congregational denomination. A meetinghouse was first built, to be followed by the present house of worship, finished in 1966. The edifice of 1905 was then razed after being a fixture of life in Rowayton for some fifty-six years.

After many lean years religion generally experienced a resurgence. Both the old and the new Rowayton churches have been invigorated and are effectively meeting the challenges of modern times.

Rowayton on the half shell

The Railroad Cometh

*T*HE EFFECT OF the arrival of the Iron Horse in this area is immeasurable. The population of Norwalk, according to the 1830 census, was 3702. Rowayton and vicinity lacked enough people to warrant consideration for a railway station. When the railroad came through eighteen years later, it is doubtful there were more than thirty homes on both sides of the river. Norwalk, sad to say, systematically resisted the railroad during the 1830s and 1840s.[1] This may have been a contributing factor to the twenty-year wait after the first train chugged its smokey way from New Haven to New York in December 1848, before a station was authorized to be built here in Rowayton, when the necessary land on both sides of the track was granted by generous local owners.

With the railroad came the idea that cramped New York City dwellers might seek the peace and quiet elbow room of the Connecticut shore, at least during the summer months. One of the first steps to accommodate the sun-worshipers was the erection of the Rowayton Hotel. During the eventful year 1848, Charles L. Raymond proved the courage of his convictions by having a four story summer hotel (sans heat and water) built on the southeast corner of Main and North Streets.* It was the start of a Rowayton tradition that was to flourish for a hundred years.

After an initial flurry of catering to the "Summer Visitors," it was not so very many years before most of the shoreline, especially Hickory Bluff, Bell Island, and Pine Point, was covered with summer cottages (also sans heat and

---

*Now Rowayton and Wilson avenues. The building still stands. After a varied career, including a period as an elegant private dwelling, circa World War I. It is currently called the "Winthrop House."

George Palmer Putnam residence at 130 Rowayton Avenue after renovation by Robert S. Barclay in the 1890s.

Vincent Colyer residence, Contentment Island, Tokeneke, c. 1870.

Rowayton on the half shell

water). Of course, many year-round "native" residents with an extra room or two "took in" boarders, many of whom later returned to rent, build, or buy houses of their own. The summer trade became a mainstay of the local economy.

The Civil War was scarcely over when the desirability of having a railroad station here at "Five Mile River Crossing" took root. After all, the spur line to New Canaan was about to open and the trains to New York and to New Haven didn't even slow up for Five Mile River "Crossing," as we were known by the railroad at that time. George Palmer Putnam, founder of the New York publishing house, had moved to Rowayton in 1861, the year the war began. He purchased a large home on the river edge at the present site of 131–135 Rowayton Avenue. For the remainder of his life, Putnam took an exceptional interest in the affairs of Rowayton. A near neighbor, Vincent Colyer, of Contentment Island, Tokeneke, was prominent in Washington circles, having served as national chairman of the Christian Commission during the recent war. The commission provided medical and religious materials to sick and wounded Union soldiers.[2] President U.S. Grant was soon to appoint Colyer Superintendent of Indian Affairs, an office only a step below cabinet rank. Both Putnam and Colyer were anxious to obtain a railroad station.

A petition favoring a station was circulated and presented to the railroad company by the distinguished committee consisting of both Putnam and Colyer in early 1867. To sweeten the request, two unusually generous citizens came forth and offered, free of cost, land on both sides of the tracks for station platforms and buildings. Lester St. John, who later built the large residence high on a knoll at 344 Rowayton Avenue, offered a sizable tract on the north, or west bound, side. Jacob Grant, a former private in the 8th Connecticut Volunteer Infantry Regiment, donated a large piece of his property on the south, or east bound, side. Railroad directors of fledgling lines were not too proud to accept free land grants in those days, the New York and New Haven men being no exception. Permission was granted, and the Five Mile River Depot opened February 24, 1868.

There were other valid reasons to build a railroad station: the slow but steady growth of permanent and seasonal residents, and the fact that Rowayton had a product to ship in quantity—oysters! In addition, coal was coming into broad use for home heating which would soon lead to large quantities being stored in dealers' yards along the route. Demand for lumber grew also with at first one, and later two dealers on the local scene.

One important factor leading to the erection of a railroad station was that during the previous year the postal department had authorized establishment

The Railroad Cometh

Rowayton railroad station, stuccoed and tiled after renovation and elevation of the track bed in 1894.

of a post office here.* Post offices and railway stations went hand-in-hand during the years of great railway expansion. The mail was carried by rail, and what better place for government to rent post office space than in the convenient railway stations?

There was, however, a bitter local conflict. The post office had been designated "Rowayton" in 1867 by the Post Office Department. The railway station had been designated "Five Mile River" by the railroad company. The area had always been called one or the other, or some variation of both—Rhoaton, Roton, Rocatan, etc., as well as Five Mile River Landing, Five Mile River Crossing, and now Five Mile River Depot! Strong sentiment prevailed that the generosity of Jacob Grant at least be recognized—the railroad station and post office should be called "Grantville!" It is to be remembered that the hero of the recent war and newly elected president also bore the name Grant.

A series of village meetings was held during 1868 to select the preferred name.³ As the supporters of one group would prevail, a subsequent meeting would soon be called, revoking the action of the previous one, and declaring the choice of the present majority. The advocates of "Five Mile River

*Also at the urging of George Putnam, who brought the mail from his New York office to help meet the volume required to meet postal department minimums.

Rowayton on the half shell

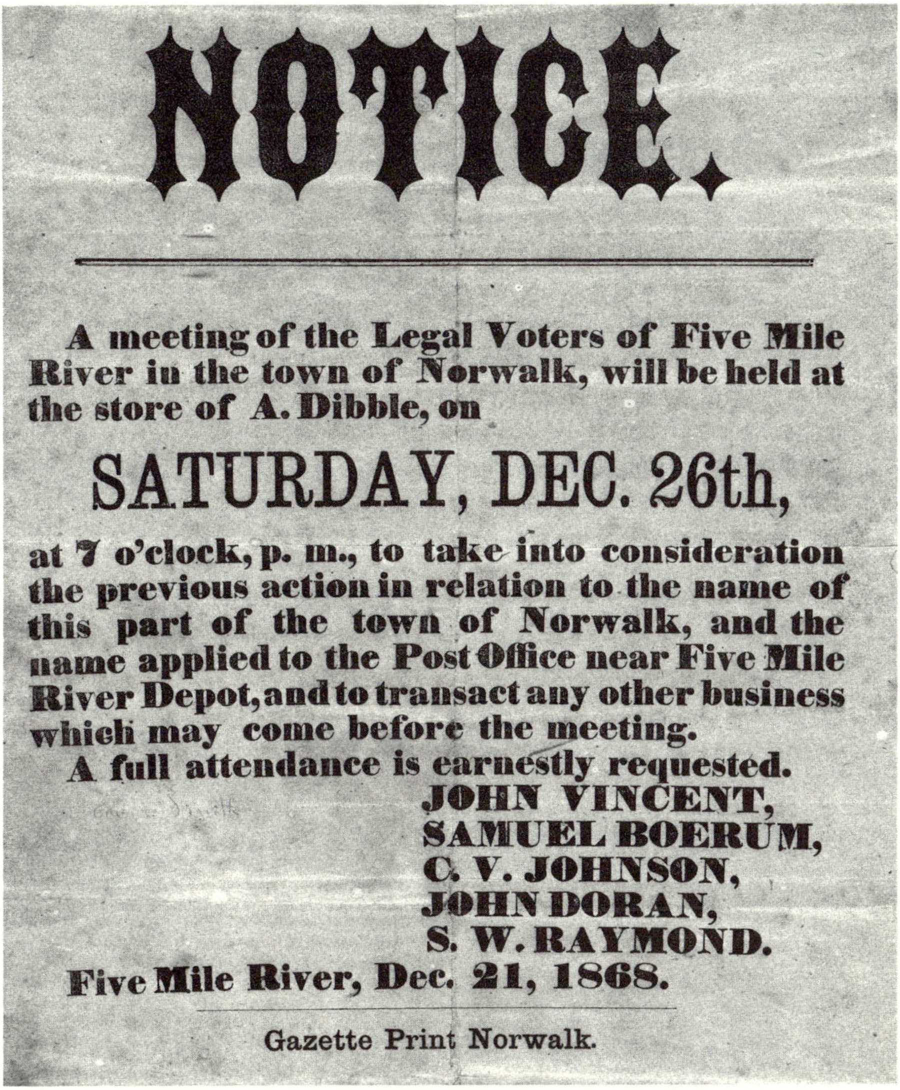

NOTICE.

A meeting of the Legal Voters of Five Mile River in the town of Norwalk, will be held at the store of A. Dibble, on

SATURDAY, DEC. 26th,

at 7 o'clock, p. m., to take into consideration the previous action in relation to the name of this part of the town of Norwalk, and the name applied to the Post Office near Five Mile River Depot, and to transact any other business which may come before the meeting.

A full attendance is earnestly requested.

JOHN VINCENT,
SAMUEL BOERUM,
C. V. JOHNSON,
JOHN DORAN,
S. W. RAYMOND.

Five Mile River, Dec. 21, 1868.

Gazette Print Norwalk.

Notice of special town meeting in 1868 to consider renaming of Five Mile River.

The Railroad Cometh

East bound train crossing culvert at Five Mile River in the 1880s. The falls at Chasmer's pond dam are visible in the background.

Steam engine scooping water from trough near Rowayton station while going 50 miles per hour.

Rowayton on the half shell

Landing" carried one meeting only to be shot down by the postal authorities—there were simply too many digits to fit a cancellation cachet!

Subsequent meetings were held. At one on June 15, 1868, "Five Mile River" was chosen, only to be voted down one month later. On July 15, "Rowayton" seemed to have been the favorite and won the day. "Grantville" was still in the running, however. After some months another meeting was called to assemble on the day after Christmas.

In the January 1, 1869, issue of the *Norwalk Gazette* it was reported the name of "Grantville" had been approved at a recent meeting by a vote of 67 to 2, listing the names of those who voted "yes" and "nay." Presumably the article referred to the December 26th meeting. Subsequent issues of the *Gazette* referred to "their friends and neighbors to the southwest" as residents of "Grantville." Whether the railroad or the Post Office Department ever adopted the name is a matter of conjecture. Apparently it was some twenty-five years later before the railroad gave in and changed their sign, but they chose the name used by the post office rather than respect the wishes of the town meeting held so many years before. "Rowayton" emerged victorious!

George Putnam died suddenly in 1873. In honor of his memory the packet sloop which carried on the water-borne commerce with New York City was rechristened *George Palmer Putnam*. It was the highest honor the village could bestow upon a distinguished citizen.[4] One wonders how many town meetings were necessary to arrive at a consensus.

The Railroad Cometh

The Civil War Strikes Home

*I*N 1861 BEGAN the nation's most dreadful tragedy—the Civil War.* It was to be fought on a scale so vast as to be felt in every town and hamlet North and South. The war was to inflict more fatalities during the next four years than were killed in all the nation's wars combined until Vietnam. Approximately 622,000 men died, and an additional 1,700,000 – 2,000,000 were seriously wounded.[1]

Norwalk boasted some 7582 souls in the 1860 census, and sent 655 to save the Union, only a half dozen of whom can be definitely traced to the forty-odd homes in the Five Mile River area. It is very difficult to determine exactly how many Rowayton men enrolled. They enlisted in a number of different towns, and to further complicate matters used South Norwalk, Norwalk, or Darien as their place of residence. We do know George O. Tuttle, Private in "A" Company of the 17th Connecticut Volunteer Infantry Regiment was from Rowayton. Private Tuttle was killed May 2, 1863, at Chancellorsville, Virginia. It was the day Confederate General Thomas J. (Stonewall) Jackson executed his daring encircling march around the Union right, struck the Fairfield County regiment, routed the Eleventh Corps, leading to the defeat of the Union Army. That evening Jackson was accidently shot by one of his own men while making a reconnaissance and died a week later.

On the day Jackson was shot, Tuttle's Company A had been bivouacked on the farm of the Talley family near Chancellorsville. After the war a local veteran, William H. Lockwood, of Company B, 28th Connecticut, returned

---

*By far the best treatment yet written of Civil War Norwalk is found in *Norwalk – Being an Historical Account of that Connecticut Town*, by Doctors Deborah W. Ray and Gloria P. Stewart, 1979, Chapter 10, pages 118–129.

In the Rowayton Union Cemetery on Rowayton Avenue twin stones mark the graves of the Ferris brothers; Stephen, age 21, and William H., Jr., age 28, who gave their lives during the Civil War, "that this nation might live."

to the Talley farm and married the young Miss Talley he had met on the day of the battle. The Lockwoods lived the rest of their lives in the Roton Avenue home on the present site of Pond Ridge Road. The ex-sergeant engaged in oystering and coastal freighting with his ketch, *Clarence*. Their son, Henry, was a life-long employee of Roton Point Park.

The Rowayton family of William Henry Mills★ suffered severely during the Civil War. William's brother, Edward, after being released from the notorious Confederate prison camp at Andersonville, Georgia, died of typhoid fever. William's son, William Henry, Junior, was killed in action. William Senior, aged forty-three, was killed in the attack upon Port Hudson, Mississippi, in July 1863.

A stone mason, William Sr. built the wall which defines Wilson Point along Wilson Avenue (Route 136), for either Lewis Wilson or the Belden family. The wall was built with large flat top-stones, many of which remain to this day.

A veteran who moved here after the war served as minister of the Methodist church. Henry Wing wrote a book concerning an experience during

---

★William Henry Mills was a great-grandfather of Mrs. Lola Baxter Seiffert, teacher at the Rowayton School for many years.

The Civil War Strikes Home

68

GEN. GRANT!

The Funeral Services over the remains of GENERAL U. S. GRANT, will be held in New York city on

Saturday, August 8th.

On that day the commodious Steamer,

"City of Albany,"

will leave So. Norwalk and Wilson Point at the usual hour. Returning will leave New York, Pier 23, E R., foot of Beekman St., 4:45, foot 23d St., at 5 o'clock, p. m., thus giving ample time to all who wish to attend the funeral of the dead soldier.

A Special Train will be in waiting at Wilson Point upon the arrival of the Steamer for the convenience of those living on the line of the D. & N. R. R.

☞ Trip Tickets from all Stations on Danbury & Norwalk Railroad at the following rates:

Danbury,	$1.50	Branchville,	$1.20	South Wilton,	$ .90
Bethel,	1.45	Ridgefield,	1.45	Winnipauk,	.85
Redding,	1.40	Georgetown,	1.15	Norwalk,	.70
Sanfords,	1.30	Cannons,	1.05	South Norwalk,	.60
		Wilton,	1.00		

GAZETTE PRINT, NORWALK.
1885

Rowayton on the half shell

Steamboat "City of Albany" (formerly "Adelphi") shown here between Bell Island and Sheffield Island. In 1878 the "Adelphi" suffered heavy damage from a boiler explosion in Norwalk Harbor with loss of life. When rebuilt, she was also renamed.

the Wilderness campaign in the spring of 1864, titled *When the President Kissed Me*, published by Eaton & Mains, New York, 1913. At the end of the first day of battle, May 5, 1864, ex-Private Wing, then a correspondent, was sent by General Grant to Washington with a dispatch for the president. Shot at and chased by the Confederates, Wing managed to jump upon a moving train. Upon his arrival at the White House, he interrupted a meeting of the cabinet. Finally cleared and admitted, he handed the message to Abraham Lincoln which read: "Tell the President there will be no turning back." Wing wrote, "tears streaked down the cheeks of the tall man as he leaned over and kissed my forehead."[2] It was the type of message Lincoln had waited three long years to receive.

The nation's worst tragedy, made up of hundreds of thousands of horrible individual experiences, dragged on for four years before the final curtain. By then sixty-eight Norwalkers, over 10 percent of the total enlistment from the town, lay dead on the many battlefields. In addition to saving the Union (no serious thought has been given to seceding since) and freeing the slaves, the war stimulated the industrialization of the North. During the years after Appomattox out-livers in this area were able to travel to Norwalk and Stamford and seek gainful employment in mills and shops that had benefited by war demands. It was another period of growth for the village of Rowayton, economically and physically.

The Civil War Strikes Home

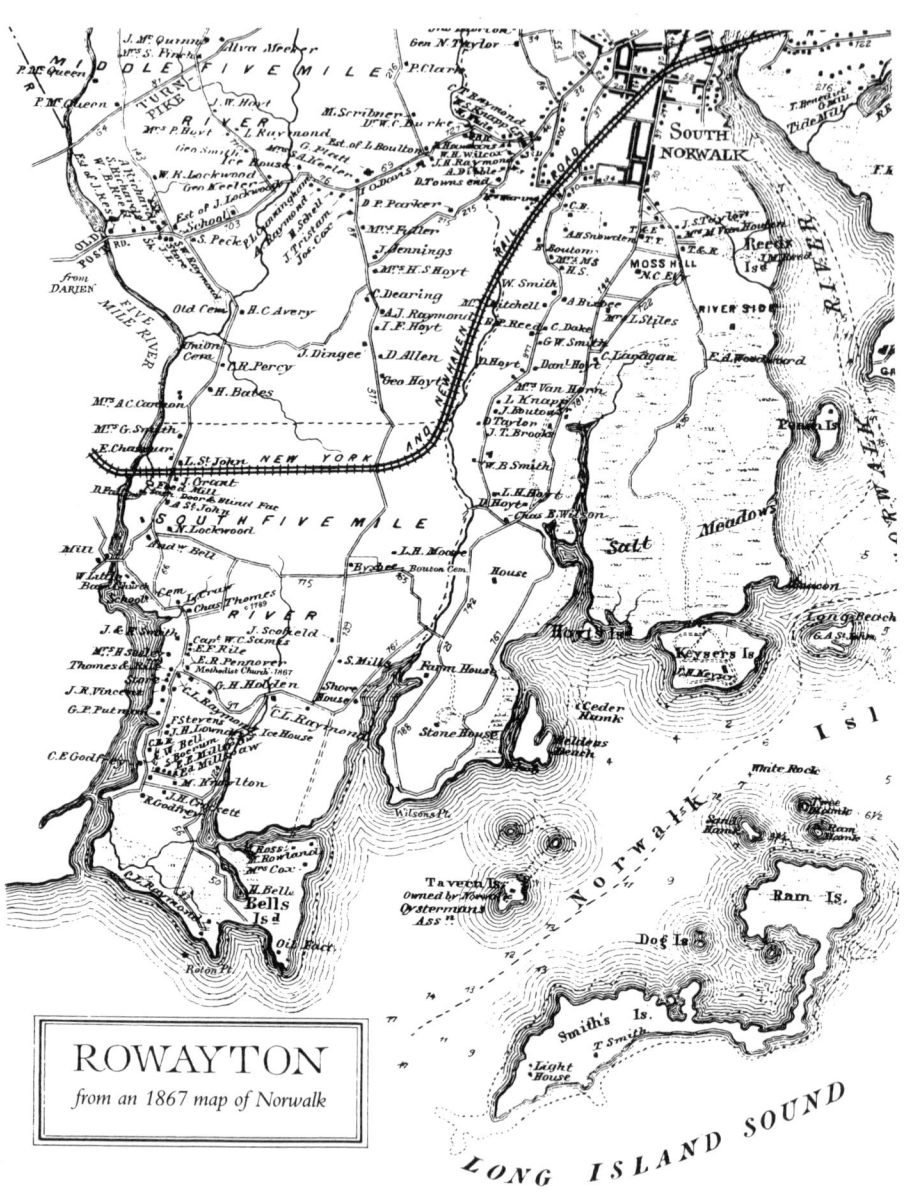

ROWAYTON
from an 1867 map of Norwalk

Rowayton on the half shell

A house-to-house survey map was prepared by a Philadelphia firm in 1867.[3] It shows quite a bit of new development: near the south end of Main Street (Rowayton Avenue), two small streets, both dead-end, Bay Street (Pond Street) and Logan Place. The latter was named for Major General John A. Logan of Ohio, first commander of the Grand Army of the Republic, the Union veterans' association. (Logan was a political-general who proved to be an effective troop commander.) Farther down Main Street a new through street to Roton Point Road is pencilled-in on the map, named for a family of one of Rowayton's veterans, William Gardiner Crockett.[4] Since 1850 the only house south of McKinley Street had been that of William H. Godfrey, which still stands at present 64 Rowayton Avenue.

The influx of new residents to the village was made up of a high percentage of veterans. The principal burial ground in the area had been established in 1849 by a group of civic-minded citizens with admirable forethought, and appropriately named Rowayton Union Cemetery. It became the final resting place of numerous Union veterans of 1861–1865, and still serves the community to this day. Veterans' organizations became powerful social and political influences throughout the post-war period. Indeed, if you had not served in the armed forces during the great conflict, it was useless to stand for public office. Norwalk, always divided, had two posts of the Grand Army of the Republic, Buckingham Post in uptown Norwalk named after the wartime governor, and The Douglas Fowler Post in South Norwalk, named for the lieutenant colonel from there who was killed at Gettysburg, Pennsylvania, July 1, 1863, while commanding the 17th Connecticut Regiment. He is buried on the field in an unmarked grave, his body never identified.

Some thirty-five years after the war the Douglas Fowler Post was in a financial position to purchase and place a monument in memory of those who fought that "this nation might long endure." A cannon the post had planned to use became surplus and was offered to the veterans in Rowayton. The local boys accepted the offer and set about raising money to erect a monument of their own. Many small contributions were received by public solicitation, plus an offer by Elias Pennoyer to use his front lawn as site for the monument. This gift made it possible for them, and us, to have the fine war memorial we proudly share today.*

*The cannon, dedicated in 1901, total cost $150, was cast in Cold Spring, New York, in 1864. It was mounted on the Union gunboat *Tallapoosa*, but, alas, was never to be shot in anger. The Civil War Secretary of the Navy was Gideon Welles, a Hartford newspaper editor and publisher, who held the office throughout the presidency of Andrew Johnson. In 1869 when he retired back to his home in Connecticut, his family and his furnishings were safely transported from Washington to Hartford on the *Tallapoosa*. (See Niven, John, *Gideon Welles, Lincoln's Secretary of the Navy*. Oxford University Press, New York, 1973, pages 567–568.)

The Civil War Strikes Home

Oysters packed for shipment. Wooden barrels with burlap tops were used to allow the oysters to breathe.

Rowayton on the half shell

The Succulent Bi-Valve

*A*T THE SAME time the railroad was being built, a discovery was made in Rowayton waters that was to revolutionize the growing of oysters from a back-yard operation to a full fledged multi-million dollar industry. The oyster had been a staple of the American diet since long before first settlement. Oysters were abundant along the entire Atlantic coast, and especially so in shallow estuaries of fresh water rivers and streams. Connecticut with more than its share of such waterways was a foremost producer of the succulent bivalves.

Natural oyster beds, where all the natural essentials to growth prevailed, were until then the only source of oysters. Most of the vast bottom acreage of the Sound was barren. Left to grow unmolested, oysters at all stages of development gather in a rough mix on the bottom. When harvested, only one oyster in five would be marketable. Some unknown imaginative natural growther got the idea to transplant the immature, unmarketable oysters to barren ground to mature, thus opening new acreage to cultivation. Transplanting made it possible to sort, categorize, and replant by age grouping.

Connecticut was the first state to enact legislation to enhance this practical idea. The new law provided that anyone interested was eligible to two free acres of barren oyster ground, which meant all natural growth oystermen almost without exception. To certify the titles to the ground, warranty deeds were issued by the coastal towns.

In 1851 a Bell Island oysterman, not surprisingly named Captain Henry Bell, busied himself conducting experiments on the oyster grounds in Wilson Cove, or perhaps around the point behind Tavern and Hoyt islands. He observed that oysters during their earliest stages of reproduction tended to

Rowayton-built oyster sloop "Harp" at Stevens dock departing with youngsters for a picnic c. 1912. The burned oyster house was replaced by this one of more modest proportions.

attach themselves to clean smooth surfaces and remain there until fully developed. As has been the case with countless other discoveries and inventions, other people in other places were independently arriving at the same conclusions at relatively the same time. Observant oystermen working the waters off City Island and Staten Island, New York, had hit upon the same idea. Although the City Islanders were a year or so earlier than Captain Bell, he reached his conclusions independently.[1]

The discovery led to the idea of saving opened oyster shells which were available in large quantities and spreading them back over recently harvested beds. If timed properly this method would provide a suitable surface for that season's embryonic oyster spat, or "set," to attach itself and thrive. Scientifically conducted experiments later explained the phenomenon Captain Bell had deduced in 1851. It was as of that date that oystering was transformed from a mom-and-pop operation to a full-fledged industry by first, cultivating heretofore barren ground, and, second, preparing a clean bed for the infant oyster to lie in.

Scientists have since shown that oysters live best in certain shallow bays, sounds, creeks, and estuaries where salinity, temperature, food supply, bottom condition, and other factors, provide favorable combinations for reproduction or growth. Flow of current, wave action, water quality, depth

Rowayton on the half shell

of water, and the amount and quality of food available are of vital importance. Oysters feed on a variety of microscopic sea life called phytoplankton, a portion of which comes from rivers and streams—by filtering it through their gills, with as much as twenty to thirty quarts of water an hour. An especially important influence is the location and nature of the bottom or bed upon which the oyster lives. As Captain Bell discovered, young oysters prefer clean beds. Deep mud will smother them and they die when overgrown with other animals. After setting, they live a completely sedentary life, resting on a bottom firm enough for them to open and close freely while filter-feeding the minute marine life in the water. All these delicate features must be in balance in order to maintain life.[2]

In Long Island Sound both male and female oysters spawn several times during late June, July, August, and early September. Each female oyster releases 23 to 85 million ova, and the male oyster an almost infinte number of sperm cells. When the sperm meets the ova, purely by chance in the vastness of the water, fertilization occurs. Only a small percentage, of course, of the cells are fertilized. The fertilized eggs soon become free-swimming larvae called "spawn." For a few days they have some locomotion, but are mostly carried by the tides and currents.

The fragile, microscopic larvae have no adequate defenses and are thus drastically reduced in numbers by prolonged drops in temperature, storms, lack of food, and predators, such as jellyfish, sea anemones, and fin fish. At the end of the free-swimming stage, which may last up to two weeks, the larvae, now about 1/75 of an inch long, attach to firm clean surfaces—shells, which they seem to prefer, bottles, twigs, even old boots or shoes, piles, or floats. They cement themselves to the surfaces by their left valves, and the young oysters, now metamorphosed, and called "spat" or "set," commence their sedentary life. Where no such materials are available, they eventually die.[3] Cultivation—cleaning and preparation of the bottom with a suitable surface—supplanted mere oyster planting. Oystering became the mainstay of the Rowayton economical base for the next fifty or more years.

By the 1860s oyster cultivation was mastered.[4] Certainly no other single influence on the long term sociological and physical development of Rowayton matched that of the oyster industry. Once the concept of oyster cultivation became accepted practice and had time to develop widely, the abundance of oysters in the waters nearby, and their superior quality, enabled Rowayton residents to enjoy a relatively high degree of prosperity for generations. The homes on the east side of Rowayton Avenue today, along the bank of the river from Witch Lane south to the Rowayton Beach gates, attest to their standard of living made possible by the oyster. Almost without exception,

The Succulent Bi-Valve

94 Rowayton Avenue, Captain Charles H. Bell, 1888

86 Rowayton Avenue, Captain John Monsell, c. 1890

82 Rowayton Avenue, Captain Stanley Lowndes, c. 1880

Rowayton on the half shell

78 Rowayton Avenue, Captain John H. Lowndes, c. 1870

11 Craw Avenue, Josephine Craw, c. 1875

The Succulent Bi-Valve

Small natural growth oyster sloop with meager catch of three bushels on a flat day, c. 1890. Homes along Five Mile River Road in the background.

the homes were built by oystermen, and Main Street became "Oysterman's Row." Some of the homes are larger than others, none are extravagant nor ostentatious, but all radiate a solid, comfortable lifestyle. Many homes on the expanding side streets also were owned or occupied by those whose livelihood depended on the oyster.

The entire Rowayton water front opposite Oysterman's Row was devoted to the oyster and satellite businesses, plus a number on the west side of the river as well.* Opening and shipping shed-type buildings, large and small, sprung up cheek by jowl along the east bank.

Oyster cultivation before 1865 was confined to the rivers and harbors of the state and to the shallow area inside the Norwalk Islands. In that year, however, offshore cultivation in twenty to twenty-five feet of water began off Norwalk. By the early 1870s all of the available inshore property was designated, and the spacious floor of Long Island Sound, always considered com-

*As a result, when zoning came to Rowayton in 1929, the entire waterfront was designated as "Commercial" classification.

Rowayton on the half shell

pletely unfit for any kind of oystering, remained the only underwater land left in Connecticut.[5] By 1875 the Rowayton oyster production exceeded all expectations. A single New York City dealer reported purchasing 32,000 bushels of Rowayton oysters that year. In 1879, which was considered a poor year, Rowayton produced something near 50,000 bushels.[6] During the three years previous to 1880, Rowayton supplied a large proportion of the oysters shipped to Europe, partly by direct shipment. At that time oysters here were sold wholly in the shell, and almost always by the barrel or bushel.

The census taken in 1880 by the United States Department of the Interior found about thirty-five oyster planters or firms, and nearly as many families were so supported here. "The little creek-mouth is perfectly filled with oyster-boats and other conveniences of the pursuit. There are some twenty-eight sloops and sail boats which belong here, some of them very large and well built." (In addition, of course, there were many lesser craft, skiffs, sharpies and rowboats used for tonging.) Tongs had basket-like claws operated by scissor type handles often eighteen feet long, very heavy to lift from the bottom and over the sides of the boat when filled with shell fish, stones and plain muck. The value of the "sail" and other floating and shore property at Rowayton directly concerned with the oyster trade of the port was estimated to be not far from $30,000.[7]

This was still the days of sail for the oyster fleet. Virtually all shipments were made by rail, some to dealers across the country from Rowayton, but mainly to the New York market. Steam came late to the oyster fleet. The first experimentation in the use of steam powered oyster boats was conducted just around the corner in Norwalk Harbor. In the year 1874, nearly three-quarters of a century after John Fitch, Captain Peter Decker installed a small steam engine in his sloop *Early Bird*. He is quoted as follows:

In 1869, I invented a drum with gearing attached to make easy the hauling of oyster dredges. One of these drums was placed aboard the sloop Peri *owned by my brother, Captain Abram Decker. In 1870, the burning of a factory in South Norwalk left a small engine without use, and it was bought and placed on board the* Peri *to wind the drum and thus haul the dredges.*

The following year I put a like hoisting apparatus on my own sloop, the Early Bird, *a vessel of eight and one-half tons old measurement. Both sloops still used sail to propel them. The next year a propeller was added, but sails were still used to supplement the power of the boat. It was thought that propulsion by steam would prove impractical in oyster dredging. Men wondered how I would steer the boat, and claimed the dredges would render the boat unmanageable. This was the case with a powerful steamer built at City Island in 1876. The steamer was built with a very broad stern and attempted to tow*

The Succulent Bi-Valve

Large natural growth sloop on the oyster beds off the mouth of Five Mile River.

Rowayton on the half shell

*The blacksmith shop of Charles H. Guider at 3 McKinley Street made dredges and hardware
for the oyster industry. The single story portion of the building still stands.*

six dredges all fastened to the stern. She proved a failure.

*But about the year 1874, I put in a large wheel, boiler and engine, discarded sails,
retained the same hoisting gear, put out a single dredge well forward on each side, and
the problem of oyster dredging was solved.*

In 1877 Albert A. Geib and William Lockwood of Norwalk had the steamer *Enterprise* built. In 1878 Captain Henry Lockwood of Greenwich built the
W. H. Lockwood described as the most efficient and convenient oyster steamer in the country and perhaps in the world, 63 feet long, 16 feet beam, 5.5
feet draft.[8]

Rowayton was not far behind. In 1880 Captain William Isaac, (*Ike*)
Stevens,★ had the first steam-powered oysterboat designed and built for the
purpose, constructed in the sideyard of his home at 124 Rowayton Avenue.
The master builder, another Rowaytonite, was his brother-in-law, Moses
B. Hart. The vessel, named for a daughter, *Mabel L. Stevens*, was 60.6 feet
long, 16.3 feet beam, and 4.8 feet draft. The *Mabel* was the first of three steamers to be built for Captain Ike who had started as a natural growther in his
sloop "Dora Dean" in the early 1860s. Thirty years later with four boats,
and a large opening and packing house at 65 Rowayton Avenue employing

★A great-grandfather of the author.

The Succulent Bi-Valve

Oyster sloops dredging on the natural growth beds off Bridgeport. Most Rowayton oystermen worked the state-owned beds off Bridgeport which were forbidden to power boats.

up to twenty-five during the peak season, his business, the Stevens Oyster Company, was Rowayton's largest. For a time, with oyster grounds and opening houses also in New Haven and Greenport, and with a total work force exceeding ninety, it was the second largest oystering operation in the state.[9] Politically, Captain Ike was an ardent Democrat. At election time he religiously decorated his home with a huge American flag, yard upon yard of red, white, and blue bunting, portraits of the Democratic candidates, slogans, etc. He was especially partial to Grover Cleveland, even to the extent of naming his youngest daughter Kathryn Cleveland Stevens! Such devotion to the cause did not go unrewarded by the local Democratic sachems. One year they nominated the captain for state senator. Knowing he owned oyster grounds in Norwalk Harbor off Goose Island, the Republicans promptly dubbed him the "Goose Island Senator." That did it. He never stood for public office again. He did, however, continue to decorate the old homestead every time election rolled around.

There were other large-scale oyster operators in Rowayton: the Lowndes Oyster Company, Oliver Cook, Craw and L'Hommedieu, John H. Monsell, Charles W. Bell, John DeWaters, the Cole Brothers—Hickson and Dexter. Dexter Cole was a designer and builder of oyster boats as well. By 1885 there were eight steam oyster boats in Norwalk, the second largest steam powered fleet in the state, New Haven having fourteen.[10] Steam did not take over completely, however. As late as 1910 the Connecticut Shell Fish Commission listed forty sloops working out of the Five Mile River.* Astonishing as it may seem, the 1896 list of merchants vessels in the United States

*For a list of owners and boat names, see appendix.

Rowayton on the half shell

Oyster shell pile at Standard Oyster Company, Water Street, South Norwalk, c. 1908.

devoted more than twice as many pages to sailing vessels, 209, than to steam vessels, 102.[11]

The introduction of steam power to the oyster business made the natural growther feel his life work threatened. He worked from skiffs and sloops with tongs and hand dredges, and on grounds limited to two acres. Natural growthers throughout the state immediately recognized the superior working capabilities of the steamers, but they most feared complete depletion of their beds in time. Furthermore, power placed the sail owners at a decided disadvantage which would inevitably drive them out of work. Their complaints reached the state legislature, which in 1879 restricted employment of power boats on the natural beds to only one week per year. Continued objections led to the complete ban of steam boats on the public beds the following year. This law, similar to those on the Chesapeake and Delaware bays, kept commercial sail alive.[12]

For years, the Connecticut legislature had been continually bombarded with bills regulating the taking of oysters, with the result that in 1881 the Connecticut Shell Fish Commission was created to administer the numerous regulations. A number of state-owned natural beds had been established over the years which were, of course, open to all—except powered vessels, as we have seen. The waters directly off Rowayton, from a range line running from the southern tip of Bell Island to the western tip of Sheffield Island on the east, to the Fish Islands on the west, and comprising some 307

The Succulent Bi-Valve

Opening and packing house of Stevens Oyster Company at 65 Rowayton Avenue, c. 1905. It burned to ground in December 1909. The flat-bottomed ketch-rigged oysterboat in the foreground is known as a "New Haven Sharpie."

acres was designated a natural bed (hence the term "natural growthers"*). It was one of only four such beds the commission felt important enough to stake out at their expense. The Bridgeport-Stratford beds which the Rowayton men also worked were by far Connecticut's largest natural beds measuring 3398 acres.[13] As many as 450 sail have been sighted there at one time and even then the huge beds were not crowded!

The Roton Point—Fish Island grounds are state owned to this day, but the ban on powered vessels has been rescinded, and the beds partially leased. To the many natural growthers of yesteryear the nearby beds were a great boon. Bountiful during their heyday, until about 1905 or so, they had been diligently harvested for more than fifty years. All of the bottom land of the outer Norwalk harbor to the state line south of the Norwalk Islands was plotted and assigned by the state through sale or lease to both natural growthers or commercial cultivators—those who cleaned and coated the beds, planted or grew seed oysters, and when mature, gathered and sold them. The labors of Long Island Sound oystermen had carried oyster culture to the highest point of perfection in the country.[14] The abundance and quality of the local oyster, and the proficiency and diligence of local oystermen, placed South Norwalk first in the amount of oysters shipped in the mid 1880s. It was tru-

*Self-employed oystermen who harvested oysters produced without benefit of cultivation.

Rowayton on the half shell

The oyster steamer "Kate C. Stevens," pride of the Rowayton based Stevens Oyster Company in South Norwalk, c. 1890.

ly the Oyster Capital of the World.

In 1889 Norwalk had more oyster boats on her grounds, public and private, than any other city in the state. She could boast a total of 208, steam, sail and row boats, New Haven being second with 111. That same year Norwalk stood second in the state with number of acres included in natural beds, there being 1650 acres under town control and 160 under state control. Norwalk stood first in the number of seed oysters taken from private grounds, 140,790 bushels valued at $81,978. She also stood first in the number of native oysters taken in the shell from her private grounds, 127,442 bushels, worth $127,746. Where public grounds were concerned, Norwalk stood second with 12,500 bushels valued at $5,750. The total amount of oysters taken from all Norwalk grounds, not including shells, in 1889 was 275,841 bushels worth $215,117.[15] Statewide, in 1898, Connecticut exceeded New York State in oyster production for the first and only time.[16]

But, alas, the Connecticut oyster industry after a very few more years went into a disastrous decline. The last really plentiful set was in 1904, and by 1928 Connecticut production hit a new low. By then only a hardy, tenacious few oystermen clung to the tongs and dredges. The most successful of these has been the Bloom brothers, Hillard and Norman, owners of Tallmadge Bros. Oyster Company, South Norwalk. By virtue of a great deal of pluck, hard work, judicious acquisitions, and sagacity they have become the largest oyster operators in the nation.

The Succulent Bi-Valve

The oyster sloop "Ruby" - Judson Williamson, Five Mile River Road, owner and master - lying in wet storage during the lean years of oystering in the 1930s.

By the time of World War II there were only a handful of oystermen left in Norwalk and none in Rowayton. What had happened to kill the golden goose? The most often cited reason is pollution, but that is an over-simplification. Granted, it doubtless had ill effects. However, when the decline was precipitous the full length of the Sound as early as 1905, it seemed doubtful the volume of human and industrial waste at that time would have been the principal reason. The myriad factors necessary for the delicate reproduction process mitigate against that concept. The industry diminished due to set failures, storms, pollution, and the oysters most dangerous predator—man. Over-fishing was certainly a contributing factor, possibly the main factor. The complete answer is so complex that all the advances of modern marine science have yet to solve it after forty-plus years of study.

It would be a mistake to imagine the standard of living of all oystermen was luxurious. True, the large oyster operators, the planters, dealers, and cultivators generally did pretty well. But for the small oysterman, the natural growther (and there were many more of them), it was a hard, meager living at best. The oyster business was seasonal, and like farming, vulnerable to the vagaries of nature. Ideal conditions were necessary for a bumper crop, and it is a rule of life that things are seldom ideal. Oystering was far from a secure living. Captain Ike Stevens was highly regarded by Rowayton oyster-

Rowayton on the half shell

Smith (or Sheffield) Island Lighthouse erected in 1868 served to mark Green's Ledge at the western entrance to Norwalk Harbor and as a range for oyster ground identification.

men as he provided a stable price of fifty cents per bushel for all the oysters they could catch regardless of market price. As few as eight bushels could represent hours of tonging or pulling in a dredge hand-over-hand in order to make four dollars a day during the short season. The daily average catch ran between eight and fifteen bushels.[17]

The season was set by state and local law and through the years varied considerably. Usually it extended from fall through spring. Hard, honest work, in sun, rain, and snow marked the life of a typical natural growth oysterman. From fall to spring he pulled heavy dredges, tended sails, managed his boat, and delivered his cargo—always outdoors, exposed to the wind and wave. The oysterman's work was always tough, but physically and emotionally rewarding, and his good health and vigor often carried him through to a rewarding old age. He was justly proud, for as a free lance oysterman he was completely independent, accountable to no one but himself.

He usually owned his own boat, hired a crew of one to six men, harvested oysters on the public ground, and sold them to oyster companies. Ordinarily he did not own oyster ground and did not cultivate oysters as the companies did. He was comparable in a sense to the man who might earn a living by scouring the countryside for wild strawberries. But he was a crack sailor and expert oysterman who frequently had learned his trade as a boy

The Succulent Bi-Valve

on the deck of his father's sloop. Fathers and sons, uncles, and even grand-fathers worked together on the same boats year after year. When the father retired, the son continued to work the old sloop. In this way, and with lov-ing care, boats sometimes lasted two and three generations. At the end of the season he outfitted the battered sloop again for the summer's work of freight-ing farm produce between Long Island and Connecticut, and taking out fish-ing and sailing parties. Many also worked as clam diggers, farmers, and some "took in boarders."[18] Fishing commercially in Long Island Sound was not a financially rewarding alternative.

The oyster industry affected Rowayton in a variety of ways. The architec-tural style of the village homes, the eventual zoning of the eastern bank of the river, and also the design of the Five Mile River harbor were shaped by the oyster. As recently as 1894, when the tide went out, there was but a small drainage ditch narrow enough to step across left in the middle of the river basin. In that year the governmental agencies in Washington were persuad-ed to dredge a channel to accommodate the sizable oyster fleet. Increasingly larger vessles were using the harbor regularly. The *Kate C. Stevens* measured 85 feet overall, 25.5 feet beam, and 6.8 feet draft—a very large oyster boat indeed. There were half-a-dozen other steamers owned in Rowayton, some thirty-odd sloops, plus numerous sharpies, skiffs, and floats.

Because the Rowayton oyster business was almost wholly concentrated on the eastern shore, the channel, 100 feet wide and 8 feet deep, was dug close to that shore rather than down the center of the estuary. By then the Wil-liamson brothers, Frank and Judson, who docked their sloop *Ruby* on the west side of the river near the foot of Five Mile River Road, and the Oberlander family who operated a small boatyard at Ivy Point near the head of naviga-tion, were the last vestiges of commercialism along the far shore. After they ceased to exist, and zoning had come to Darien, the entire west bank was restricted to residential use. Land use for marine-oriented businesses was limited to the Rowayton shore.

Rowayton on the half shell

The Prettiest Park On Long Island Sound

*T*HE NATURAL advantages of that section of the Long Island Sound shoreline which was to become known as Roton Point Park—easy access, fine sandy beaches, cool shady groves of tall oaks—were readily apparent to all. As early as 1868 the property was being used for outings and bathing.[1] Accessible only to local residents at first, with the rapid improvements in public transportation, the popularity of "The Point" for recreation grew immensely. (Conversely, it was the lack of transportation caused by World War II shortages that ended its life as an amusement park.)

By 1892 the park was well known. During the intervening years under various family ownership, but principally of the heirs of Charles L. Raymond, actual operation was leased to concessionaires for the summer seasons.[2] Among those, for one or more seasons at least, were the Jacobs brothers, Mike and Joe, later famous boxing promoters and editors and publishers of *Ring* magazine. It is difficult to establish when the first excursion steamers arrived carrying many hundreds of people from New York City on their decks; but certainly prior to 1891.

In that year James S. Kelley, together with Catherine and Julius Finkelstein, became interested and within two years acquired title to all Roton Point as well as high land to the east, known as Pine Point—seventeen acres of Pine Point for $1,000, Roton Point for $3,000 ($1,000 cash and $2,000 mortgage). In 1892 Kelley and the Finkelsteins formed a New Jersey corporation, called "The Roton Point Improvement Company." The company started to develop the Roton Point section of their holdings, a consortium of Norwalkers having undertaken development of the Pine Point section, and had Ro-

The dance pavilion and small boat pier of Roton Point Park when it was operated by the Ackert family, c. 1880.

ton Point mapped. This map is on file in the Norwalk Town Clerk's office as Map No. 91, dated 1892. The map shows the hotel (still standing today) with horse sheds behind, a merry-go-round, dancing pavilion, and bath houses all across the north edge of east beach, and the pier and wharf. The company signed a bond–mortgage for $50,000 in 1892 and another in 1895. Extensive renovation was at hand.[3]

One of the greatest advancements in public transportation during the 1800s was wrought by the trolley car. Horse-drawn trolley lines had been established between Norwalk and South Norwalk via West Avenue, the Red Line (the color of the upholstery), by LeGrand Lockwood of Lockwood Mansion, and others. Soon after another group opened a line along East Avenue known as the "White Line." By 1890 both had been electrified and were pushing out into the suburbs. In 1894 the Red Line extended north to the Winnepauk and Cranbury areas, and the White Line to Westport, Broad River, and south to Roton Point Park.[4]

The Roton Point Improvement Company had entered into an agreement to operate the park with the Connecticut Company which had absorbed the local tramway companies. The Connecticut Company promptly built a trolley route from South Norwalk along the west side of Wilson Avenue from the foot of Meadow Street to the western end of modern-day Martin Luther King, Jr., Boulevard, thence through dense woods (Trolley Way and Cove-

Rowayton on the half shell

People flocked to Roton Point Park on trolley cars similar to this for a five-cent fare.

wood Drive) to Wilson Avenue near Highland Avenue then south along the west side of Highland Avenue to Farm Creek, crossing on a long trestle or bridge over the creek, and on into the park. It was ready just in time for the 1894 summer season. During peak season there was a car to or from South Norwalk every twenty minutes. The fare was all of five cents.

In winter the "cars" ran only to the Sammis Street intersection before returning to the Norwalks. Bell Island and "down street" Rowayton residents walked up to the stop at the corner of Highland Avenue and Wilson Avenue (Jake Raymond's corner). As an accommodation to the lower Rowayton folk, a spur of track was laid across open fields from Highland Avenue to Guider's corner on Rowayton Avenue where it terminated. As the paths beside the tracks transformed into a road, the road was named Lincoln Avenue, later to be renamed McKinley Street for the more recently assassinated president. The trolley spur was opened September 24, 1894, amid appropriate ceremony and speechifying—long after Roton Point Park was closed for winter.[5] The next year track was extended north up Rowayton Avenue and Cudlipp Street to the White Bridge. There another special trestle was erected to cross the Five Mile River just south of the highway bridge. The track then ran over the hill and through the woods to Darien. This made the time opportune to shorten and straighten the road from Rowayton to Darien. Tokeneke Road was built concurrently and adjacent to the trolley tracks, replacing the Five Mile River Road–Old Farm Road–Hog's Hill route.

The Prettiest Park on Long Island Sound

Long skirts, straw hats, and sun bonnets were the vogue in the 1880s before the bandstand was built on the rocks in the background.

When the trolley tracks linked the Stamford-Darien tracks, it was possible to travel, and ship parcels, straight through between Bridgeport and Stamford. Rowayton had a second connection by rail with the outside world!

The tracks into Roton Point made a large loop where the club tennis courts are today, turning the car for the return trip, and providing side trackage in the center where extra cars could lay-by awaiting the high-volume return rush hours. The large open cars used throughout fair weather had capacity for over two-hundred persons, a crucial factor in the success of the park.

Improvements to the park included a new building for the merry-go-round built in the northwest corner of the grove. The old building was then used as a vaudeville theatre for a time, later as a roller skating rink. The bath houses originally extended from the southeast corner of the grove across the full length of the beach to the wharf road. They were split into two sections, turned to right angles with the beach, and attached to either side of the ex-merry-go-round shed. It was customary in those days for swimmers to don bathing suits upon arrival at the beach, and re-dress after swimming. At "The Point" there were more than four hundred bath houses ready to accommodate them for a small fee. Men's and women's bathing suits, each solid black with "RPP" smartly stencilled in white, bathing slippers, towels, beach chairs, and life saving "wings" were available at moderate rates—all clean and tidy as can be.

Indeed, throughout its existence Roton Point Park enjoyed a reputation

Rowayton on the half shell

for always being clean and tidy. The sale of beer and liquor was discontinued many years before prohibition; gambling and rowdyism were not tolerated. It was an especially pleasant place to take the family. In the earliest days the police and security force consisted of but one man, a local constable, which led to tragedy. One day, screened by the crowd, a prankster picked the constable's pistol from its holster. When word spread, the unsuspecting officer became the butt of jibes and torment which troubled him deeply. Soon after the incident a cartoon with a derisive caption appeared in a New York newspaper depicting Roton Point Park with a seedy law-man peering from behind a tree as a hooligan pilfers a gun from his pocket. Public ridicule proved too much for the poor man to bear. He took his own life.

As a family park Roton Point attracted church and fraternal organizations, Sunday school picnics, lodge outings, conventions, marching and chowder societies, band concerts, and a week-long "Society Circus" sponsored by the Reliance Hook and Ladder Company boys of Rowayton. It soon became a full-fledged amusement park with a wide variety of attractions and an already wide public acceptance. Starting as a bathing beach and picnicing grove, a small dancing platform was placed in the center of the grove with music provided by William (Billy) Offen and son of Pound Ridge, New York, twenty-five miles from Roton Point. Undaunted the Offens walked both ways carrying their instruments, a fiddle and a base violin, with them.[6]

A two-story building was located where the hotel still stands, with a central hall, dining room, bar, and bowling alleys. The manager, A. K. Ackert, resided in Rowayton's "Montgomery House" (now Winthrop). Roasted fresh clams were sold from a shack located on a large rock where the bandstand is now located. A toll gate was placed at the western park entrance at the foot of Roton Avenue to collect ten cents from each person or carriage.[7] A shooting gallery was added. Games of skill abounded in booths throughout the park, "Ring the Canes," and later "Kill the Kaiser," (by hitting his cut-out wooden profile with squashy baseballs). Another popular attraction required the contestant to guess the winner of a race of billiard balls around a gravity course to win a stuffed doll or a box of undigestible salt water taffy.

One of the most popular early attractions was a glass blower's booth. As dainty beautiful glass pieces were shaped before their eyes, fascinated people would crowd in front of the skilled craftsman. Many objects of his handiwork were, and may be still treasured by local residents. Two sons of the glass blower, Frank and Charles Pfahl, were to spend their entire careers with Roton Point Park.[8]

On the glorious Fourth of July not only would there be a fireworks displays in the old days, but balloon ascensions as well. A fire was built near

The Prettiest Park on Long Island Sound

Looking east from Price's Rocks along Wee Burn and Bayley Beaches with roller coaster, merry-go-round, and dance pavilion.

the eastern entrance of the park, the gases generated used to fill the balloon. As the balloon filled, a dare-devil with parachute would take position in the basket attached. When adequate height was attained the parachutist would hang out over the edge, perform a few acrobatic stunts, and drop with open parachute to the ground, hopefully. Occasionally, however, he would land in Long Island Sound, or worse, on the mud flats - as one did, well remembered as gloriously attired in red satin tights![9]

Soon after the turn of the century a salesman for a merry-go-round manufacturing firm, named Neville Bayley, became interested in the park. He negotiated a lease with the Connecticut Company to manage the park on a long-term basis. This later led to his purchase of the property from the Connecticut Railway and Lighting Company, successors to the Connecticut Company, on March 15, 1928. The trolley company retained the rights to the trackage through October 19, 1941, when they released it.[10] Motor buses had replaced the trolley car on the Norwalk-Stamford run in 1933.

Neville Bayley was to rise to become an astute and successful entrepreneur. A shrewd manager, he surrounded himself with other capable businessmen, notably Charles Phafl, son of the glass blower, and Henry VonDwingelo, Sr., all officers of the new corporation. More rides, chance booths, and a variety of attractions were added. A long roller coaster stretching along the entire west beach to Price's Rocks (Bayley and Wee Burn beaches) had been previously built, to be razed in the early 1930s when a shorter, precipitous

Rowayton on the half shell

Prize booths, airplane swing, and the "Big Dipper" roller coaster along the Great White Way at Roton Point Park in the 1920s.

breath-taker replaced it. The starting and finishing platform now serves as bath house and pavilion at Rowayton's Bayley Beach. Dancing contests, beauty pageants, and band concerts were held.

People simply flocked to Roton Point Park.

Excursion boats from the metropolis brought them by the thousands. Carrying from one to three thousand passengers, the steam boats made regular runs daily, with added vessels on weekends and holidays. Often there were as many as three or five steamers nestled abreast at the pier. A record was set in the 1920s when nine excursion boats arrived in one day.[11] Only four could be berthed while five had to lie-to between Greens Ledge lighthouse and Sheffield Island.

Excursion boats were large vessels, usually between one hundred and three hundred feet long, with three, sometimes four, wide open decks. There were no accommodations to speak of. A refreshment stand or two, a first aid room of closet proportions, a room on each deck marked "Men" and another "Ladies," and that was about it. A place for the band to sit was near a small, highly polished area for dancing. Benches ringed the decks, and chairs, of course, but never enough.

There were seldom enough life preservers to go around either until after the *General Slocum* burned and sank in the East River en route to an amusement park on Eaton's Neck directly across from Roton Point. One life preserver for each passenger was required thereafter, which placed the

The Prettiest Park on Long Island Sound

Watching the bathers from the grove at Roton Point Park, c. 1929.

management in a quandry for space to stow them.

The sail from the lower end of Manhattan, through the East River and up the Sound, nevertheless, was grand. There was approximately two hours of smooth water, beautiful scenery, bands playing, flags flapping, dancing, and refreshment. Arriving about one o'clock and departing between four and five, depending upon their order of arrival, passengers enjoyed the park all afternoon. A belfry stood near the steamer dock. Tolling of the bell bemoaned the passing day and warned of departure time. The passage home was probably more quiet and less gay.

Excursion lines proliferated around New York City during the 1800s with trips up the Hudson, to Coney Island, the Rockaways, Asbury Park, Keansburg on the Jersey shore, up the Sound to Rye Beach, also beyond Roton Point to Pleasure Beach in Bridgeport and Savin Rock amusement park in West Haven. Where there was an amusement park, there was an excursion line serving it - McAllister, Mesick, Sutton, Wilson Line, and others. One of the larger lines was the Iron Steamboat Company with a fleet of ten or more vessels, easily distinguishable—large side-wheelers with huge walk-

Rowayton on the half shell

Excursion steamer "Rosedale": c. 1875, one of the earliest to run to Roton Point Park from New York City. It was operated by the Iron Steamboat Company.

ing beams rocking up and down high above the upper deck. Their *Grand Republic* was one of the largest to come to Roton Point regularly, 282 feet long, 13 feet draft, built in 1878. One fine moonlight night the tide at Roton Point Dock dropped below the thirteen foot mark, delaying the departure of the *Grand Republic* many hours. Passengers were estimated to be two thousand. To soothe the restless crowd, a lady residing on Bell Island, a concert singer and soloist in a large Brooklyn church, volunteered to entertain. "An audience was never quieter nor more appreciative. There was enthusiastic applause throughout the evening."[12]

There were other grounding incidents. One summer day Rowayton residents were fascinated watching the crew of the *Crescent* ram her hard aground on Ballast Reef, right off the park at the start of their return trip. Earlier that day en route to the park the captain and crew had sampled confiscated booze stashed in the pilot house by a police officer. It was only with difficulty that the crew had managed to dock the steamer upon arrival. They were in considerably worse shape when the *Crescent* left the wharf for New York. Rowaytonites talked about it for weeks. Fortunately, there were no casualties.[13]

Around 1900 the Starin Steamboat Company of New York leased the

The Prettiest Park on Long Island Sound

The "Grand Republic" at 282 feet was probably the largest steamer to run regularly to Roton Point. She extended well beyond the Roton Point dock as this shot plainly shows.

beach west of Price's Rocks (Rowayton Beach) and extended a pier a great distance out to deep water to accommodate excursion traffic to the park, but little came of the venture.[14]

In 1925 the park management had their own excursion steamer designed and built for their exclusive use to run daily to Roton Point. The *Belle Island* was 200.5 feet long, of 842 gross tons measurement. Many thought her to be the prettiest of all steamers to serve the park. She remained in service until the park closed permanently. Commandeered by the government in 1942, she spent her last days on the Amazon River.

The park continued to change, to grow, to expand. Dining facilities were enlarged to seat hundreds on the vast hotel porch, the west side of the grove was filled with picnic tables and benches to accommodate five hundred at a sitting. A fortune teller's booth was nearby, also a weight guesser's scale, "Within five pounds of your weight or you win a prize (a walking stick or candy)." For the children, but not necessarily, a fish pond, penny arcade, ice cream stand, hot dogs, taffy, popcorn. At one game of chance, a spinning wheel, smoked Virginia hams were prizes. Operator of the stand, Sam Ireland, soon became "Sam, the man what 'am.'"

Fireworks and the dance hall were always major attractions. So many people came to see the weekly fireworks display, and especially on holidays, that

Rowayton on the half shell

Box lunches on tables in the picnic grove awaiting hundreds of Sunday school youngsters on a sunny day in the 1930s.

it became necessary to change the display location from the bathing beach to the parking lot. On holidays the pyrotechnical grand finale was invariably a full color rendition of the national flag. Soon after the finale, departing traffic choked and clogged the narrow roadways of Bell Island and Rowayton until far into the night.

Dances and dancing competitions were held from the earliest days of the pavilion, and always were popular. During the great depression, endurance contests, a short-lived fad with generous cash prizes as a come-on, were held. Literally a physical endurance test, the hardy partners danced continually for days until they dropped one by one exhausted to the floor. At long last, one couple would remain standing, sometimes holding each other up, often unaware they had won the dubious honor. It was a barbaric experience for participants and spectators alike, reminiscent of ancient Rome.

During the last twenty years of the park operation nationally known big name bands were scheduled for Sunday nights. Radio in every home had made the bands and their personnel household words. Personal appearances in dance halls and amusement parks were immensely popular. Thousands turned out to see and hear them in person. Few of the famous bands missed coming to Roton Point, thanks to Roton Point's enterprising booking agent, Leo Miller. Glen Miller, the Dorsey brothers, Eddie Duchin, Bunny Berrigan, Guy Lom-

The Prettiest Park on Long Island Sound

The "Belle Island" was built by the Roton Point Corporation in 1925. She made daily runs during the season until the park ceased to operate in 1941.

bardo, Wayne King, Fred Waring, Cab Calloway, Duke Ellington, as well as other big name bands all came. The largest attendance was probably when Rudy Vallee, with the movie star, Alice Faye as his thrush, overfilled the pavilion with some 1800 people, while ten thousand more jammed the entire park outside.

Bathing Beauty contests were annual events. For many years "Miss Connecticut" was selected and crowned at Roton Point before advancing upon Atlantic City, New Jersey, seeking national honors. In the nationwide contests in 1933, Marion Bergeron of West Haven won the Miss Connecticut title here at Roton Point Park, and went on to be triumphantly crowned Miss America in Atlantic City. She was the first Connecticut girl to be so honored.

A dozen or so Rowayton area men were employed by the park at all levels, management, operational, and maintenance. Local merchants, services, and suppliers benefited economically by the presence of the park, but it was a noisy, messy nuisance to the neighbors.[15] It was not unusual for residents of lower Rowayton, Pine Point and Bell Island to look out their windows and find park visitors gaily picnicking on their lawns, invariably leaving wrappings and other debris about for the property owners to pick up. After the demise of the trolley car, street traffic increased alarmingly. On peak days as many as sixty large buses from New York and elsewhere could be counted parked in long rows in the parking lots. At times the lines of buses await-

Rowayton on the half shell

The noise generated at the park was not easy to live with. The giant organ in the merry-go-round rotunda banged away incessantly and could be heard at Cannon Square. Roller coaster riders screeched without restraint as the coaster dipped and plunged. They, too, were heard far and wide.

Consequently the park had a strong influence on the development of Rowayton. People of means, who were able to choose, chose to live a sizable distance from the park—in Tokeneke or Wilson Point where things were apt to be more serene. With few exceptions, those less well-off tended to comprise the majority of Rowayton area residents, making for a more homogenous community, and therefore more friendly and less socially stratified than those of their neighbors.[16]

As all things must, Roton Point Park came to an end. Fuel rationing had crippled the 1941 season. After the declaration of war in December, the park management decided not to reopen in the spring. Mr. Bayley was of retirement age, and after selling off some of the rides piecemeal, wanted to sell everything else outright. Fortunately for Rowayton he was a public minded man. He offered the village first refusal.

Under the aegis of the Rowayton Civic Association, a committee was organized, chaired by the then current president, Frank P. Dunn. The property was offered at $75,000 with an acceptance date provision. The committee promptly canvassed the area for support and financial pledges. Rowayton was not as affluent then as later. It clearly became apparent the sum was far in excess of that readily available to make a commitment. A group of real estate investors from New Canaan, led by George N. McKendry, a summer resident here, came forth with the suggestion the property be divided: approximately 10 acres to Rowayton for $30,000 and 13 acres to the Town of New Canaan for $45,000.[17] Mr. Bayley was agreeable. That suggestion was to save the day for Rowayton residents, enabling them to acquire approximately one-third of the property for public use in perpetuity.

As agreed, the investors offered the remainder of the park to the Town of New Canaan at their cost. A series of town meetings was held during 1942. Finally, on March 3, 1943, the town voted against the purchase by a vote of 356 to 103.[18] The investors held on to the eastern two-thirds of the site and organized the Roton Point Beach Club. The Sixth Taxing District purchased the west beach and the property immediately behind it, the New Canaan group the east beach, pier, grove, and most of the buildings. It was quite possibly the best Rowayton real estate transaction ever. To his credit, Mr. Bayley was most cooperative and helpful, granting options to the two groups and allowing them time to arrange the details of subdividing, etc. He very

Neville Bayley, owner of Roton Point Park, speaking on the occasion of the transfer of the park to the Sixth Taxing District and a group of private investors. To the right are: Congressman Leroy D. Downs; Frank P. Dunn, Chairman of the Rowayton Civic Association; Clarence E. Crofut, Chairman of the Commissioners of the Sixth Taxing District; and George F. McKendry, Chairman of the investors.

much preferred to have the property used for public, rather than private use.★[19]

However, he did require a deposit of $10,000 from the Rowayton group as evidence of good faith. It had been decided to finance the purchase by a bond issue based on the full faith and credit of the Sixth Taxing District (Rowayton). Legislative approval was necessary for a bond issue, and the legislature would not meet until January 1943. A public subscription was taken to raise the necessary deposit, to be returned without interest to the subscribers after sale of the bonds. The Bayley Beach Fund, Inc. was organized to handle money matters. The $10,000 was collected from those residents

★The total sale price was much less than the actual value for development purposes, or as an amusement park. One appraisal made at the time was over $200,000 if the land use continued as an amusement park.

Rowayton on the half shell

in favor of the purchase in amounts varying from ten to less than a thousand dollars each. Later the bonds sold readily.

With a public beach, and later tennis courts, ball field, and picnic grove restricted to residents, Rowayton became even more attractive as a place to live. Property values started to rise immediately. Much credit is due Neville Bayley for his patience and consideration throughout the long drawn-out negotiations. When the suggestion was made, there was no opposition to having the Rowayton portion of Roton Point Park named in his honor.

FOR ROTON POINT.

1885—SEASON OF—1885.

Steamer "Pinto"

Will run regularly between South Norwalk, Wilson Point, Bell Island, and Roton Point on the following Time-Table:

								Lv. Ar.							
7.00	—	—	3.20	1.30	10.05	—	7.05	South Norwalk	—	10.00	12.05	3.15	—	6.80	10.35
xx	—	xx	xx	xx	xx	8.20	7.45	Bell Island	8.10	9.25	xx	xx	xx	xx	—
—	6.00	5.10	—	—	—	8.25	7.55	Wilson Point	8.05	9.20	—	—	l. 5.10 a. 4.30	5.50	—
7.35	—	5.25	4.00	2.05	10.85	—	—	Roton Point Ar. Lv.	—	—	11.30	2.40	4.05	5.40	10.00

xx   Bell Island Flag Station—Boat Stops when Signalled.
—   Signifies Boat does not stop.

SUNDAY TIME-TABLE.

On and after SUNDAY, JUNE 14th, the boat will run as follows:—LEAVE SOUTH NORWALK FOR ROTON POINT at 2 and 6.80 p. m. Returning will LEAVE ROTON POINT FOR SOUTH NORWALK at 4 and 7.30 p. m.

The Prettiest Park on Long Island Sound

The Urge To Read

DESPITE THE TIME and effort George Putnam devoted to pressing for civic improvement projects, creation of a railway station, and approval for a post office during 1867, he still had enough energy to also advocate establishment of a public lending library. Then a partner of Wiley and Putnam, publishers, New York, it was his desire to elevate the social and educational standards of the villagers and thus to broaden and promote their well being in a variety of ways. He was sometimes misunderstood and some of his efforts proved abortive.[1] In characteristic fashion he did more than advocate a public library, he acted.

On Saturday evening, October 8, 1866, a meeting of Rowayton and vicinity residents was held, pursuant to public notice, in the basement of the store of Alphonso Dibble (now Rowayton Market). On motion of Mr. G. P. Putnam, so read the minutes, Edward T. Rile was appointed chairman, and Henry Taylor secretary. Mr. Putnam stated the object of the meeting. Those present were invited to organize a library association by signing a general agreement. Fifty-six names were affixed including several ladies. Mr. Putnam moved a committee of two be appointed to nominate officers and prepare a set of by-laws and a constitution for the association. He and the Reverend Arthur Day were appointed outright.

The committee submitted a detailed set of by-laws and a constitution at a meeting held May 18, 1867. The group was to be called "The Lyceum Library Association." Elias R. Pennoyer, president, Reverend Day and Charles Thomes, vice presidents, George Cudlipp, treasurer, and Henry Chasmer, secretary. Messrs. Putnam, Vincent Colyer, Dibble, Grant, Wamsley, Crockett, Craw, and Murdock were named to the executive board. A motion was

The meat and grocery store of Alphonse Dibble at 155 Rowayton Avenue. The first public library in Rowayton, the "Lyceum," was opened in the basement of this building in 1867, only to be short lived.

made to give Mr. Putnam a vote of thanks for so kindly fitting out the room (in Dibble's basement) and doing so much to establish this institution. The motion was seconded and carried by the association with a most hardy voice! It was signed by H. H. Taylor.[2] Books were collected, sorted, and catalogued, a librarian chosen and a schedule of fines posted.

Alas, the Lyceum proved one of those efforts of Putnam's doomed to failure. After a short life span of but two years, in face of declining circulation and disappearing funds, the Lyceum Library Association disbanded, a victim to having been born before its time. Not too many years later another group got together for the same high purpose and proved much more hardy, to be known as "The Association of the Free Library and Reading-Room of Rowayton, Incorporated." In spite of its cumbersome title, the library took root and is flourishing to this day.

The present library association was organized December 18, 1903, at Doctor Charles E. Hackley's home, corner of Logan Place and Rowayton Avenue. Mrs. Hackley was appointed chairman of the meeting and her daugh-

The Urge to Read

Organized in 1903, the present library association soon outgrew its first location at 91 Rowayton Avenue (now Capt'n Henry's Luncheonette) and soon moved to 101 Rowayton Avenue (now also a luncheonette) shown here, remaining until 1926.

Interior view of "The Free Library and Reading Room of Rowayton"
at 101 Rowayton Avenue, c. 1925.

Rowayton on the half shell

ter, Mary, secretary pro-tem.* A rough draft of a constitution as presented provided for a board of "five ladies." Duly elected were Mrs. Josephine Craw, Mrs. Charles H. Guider, Mrs. John Slater, Mrs. Edgar Lane, and Miss Hackley - the doctor barely making it as "fourth man" on the Advisory Committee! The board subsequently elected Mrs. Craw, president; Mrs. Guider, first vice president; Mrs. Slater, second vice president; and Miss Hackley, secretary-treasurer.

With a loan of one hundred books from the state for three months, plus twenty-five books to be exchanged monthly from the Bodley Club Library Service, together with $154.80 in cash, they were away and running. President Craw made a room in her building at 101 Rowayton Avenue available "at very low rent." Low rent or no, it was obvious the cash position was shaky. A fund drive was authorized following which a motion was made to express the appreciation of the board to Edward Ladrigan, local livery stable owner, for "driving the young ladies around the village at no charge during the canvass." The library fostered dues paying book clubs which used their funds to purchase books for the library, the donation being made only after the books were circulated among the group. The Monday Book Club, for instance, passed their books to the next member on the list promptly on the first day of each week.

Soon after selling his steel mills to the United States Steel Corporation in 1901, Andrew Carnegie started to dispose of some of the profits by making generous grants for public libraries across the nation. The Rowayton Library, as it was to become conveniently known, applied for a grant from Carnegie, but was turned down as the area the library served was too small to qualify. Mrs. Craw's "Room" was to serve as the home of the library for twenty-three years.[3]

In 1926 the association purchased the former fire house of the defunct Reliance Hook and Ladder Company, at 145 Rowayton Avenue, from Francis Machette, and moved in soon after. The fire doors were replaced by a large window, modern lighting was installed, and the meeting room on the second floor was made available for public purposes. A considerable mortgage was assumed,** eventually paid by dues, fines, and income from an annual "Silver Tea," which in itself became a notable social event in the village. When the Sixth Taxing District was created, a clause was included in its charter,

*Dr. Hackley was a retired surgeon who had served as Chief Surgeon, Third Calvary Division, Army of the Potomac, during the Civil War. He later had a private practice in New York City. His daughter, a Vassar graduate, retained her interest in the library into the late 1920s.

**Courtesy of Mrs. Robert S. Barclay.

The Urge to Read

In 1926 the library association purchased the former Reliance Hook and Ladder Company building at 145 Rowayton Avenue, currently the Rowayton Arts Center.

over some opposition, let it be noted, requiring the taxpayers to support the library by appropriating a sum of not less then one hundred dollars annually. In our wisdom of today, nearly all the monies necessary for operation of the library are raised by taxation.

As Rowayton grew, the library outgrew first the ground floor and soon, indeed, the building itself, the second floor having been utilized as the children's library. In its quest for a new location, the Building Site Committee of the Library Board of Directors in 1966 realized the potential of the barns and stable buildings of the former James A. Farrell estate at the corner of Highland Avenue and McKinley Street, then owned by the Remington-Rand Corporation. The committee broached the idea to the Commissioners of the Sixth Taxing District of acquiring all or part of the property for library use. An option was readily obtained. After a series of open-house visitations and district meetings, overwhelming approval was granted. The present library and community center property was acquired for $142,500 in early 1966.

An exceptional community asset, even by Fairfield County standards, the property comprises six landscaped acres. To many, the library and commu-

Rowayton on the half shell

In 1966 the Sixth Taxing District purchased the farm buildings and gardens of the former James A. Farrell estate. The Rowayton Library now occupies the former garage and stables at 33 Highland Avenue.

nity center buildings are reminiscent of an English country estate, which is exactly the effect the architect sought. Built in 1912, the complex consisted of barn, stables, garage, ice house, tool and wagon shed, blacksmith shop, greenhouse, potting shed, and root cellar. The first floor walls of the main building were of hand-cut fieldstone, with the second story half-timbered stucco and oak, capped by heavy slate roofing. The walls of the ice house, also fieldstone, four feet wide at the base, repelled the heat of summer. The stone-walled courtyard dominated by the tall clock tower and weather vane exudes old world charm. Inside the meeting room the immense fireplace of selected stone predominates. In 1966 a master stonemason was heard to remark that the fireplace was the finest example of stonemasonry he had ever seen. A high compliment, indeed. The centerpiece of the entire complex is the library itself.

Today, book inventory exceeds 25,000 volumes. Circulation amounts to 24,000 volumes. It is a fine tribute to the founders and to the many men and women who have so ably succeeded the original "five old ladies."

The Urge to Read

Of Roses And Orchids

URING THE thirty years that followed the Civil War there were very few opportunities to earn a living in Rowayton other than the employment afforded by the oyster and associated businesses. The "DIRECTORY" for 1885/86 reported fifty-two farmers in Rowayton, which, like the premature statement of Mark Twain's death, "would appear to be greatly exaggerated," even allowing for an average of three farmers per farm.[1] There were scarcely that many houses here. Most homes during that period had fruit and vegetable gardens of varying sizes, but hardly large enough to qualify as farms requiring outside laborers.

Rowayton could boast of but one factory during the postwar period, the Boylston Carriage Works, at 295 Rowayton Avenue abutting the railroad tracks. Manufacturers of baby and doll carriages, invalid chairs and velocipedes, they were first with the idea of using steel springs for mounting the carriage bodies to the wheels. The bodies were of woven reed, like baskets. Boylston products were of high quality and sold through a company-owned outlet in Brooklyn. Probably at no time did employment exceed twenty-five or thirty persons at the local factory.

The plant superintendent was George W. Bryan, who moved to Rowayton with the Boylston company. He later became postmaster and promptly moved the post office from near the railroad station into a small one-story building on his front lawn at the corner of Thomes Street - nearer the postmaster. The assistant superintendent at Boylston's was Harvey Ackert, who, upon succeeding his boss as postmaster, lost no time moving the post office, building and all appurtenances across the street and attaching it to the side of his house, surpassing his predecessor for proximity.

During the second half of the nineteenth century the only manufacturer in Rowayton was the Boylston Carriage Works at 293–299 Rowayton Avenue, makers of baby and doll carriages and invalid chairs, c. 1880.

Boylston carriages were sold direct from the company store in Brooklyn, New York.

Of Roses and Orchids

The railroad enabled Rowayton men and women to be employed away from home, many in the needle trade in South Norwalk. The R. & G. Corset factory on Ann Street produced 7,500 garments daily.

About the time of World War I, the Boylston operation ceased. The factory buildings were thereafter occupied by a variety of small operations employing fewer workers. During the early 1930s one such was a dye works long remembered for discharging excess dyes directly into the Five Mile River. The river water was discolored and could be seen sparkling in a variety of brilliant hues downstream as far as the White Bridge. The Boylston buildings, one of three stories with mansard roof, were totally destroyed by fire one frigid evening in February 1944.

During the 1890s a few Rowayton men, and practically no women, commuted to work by train. A handful of boys and girls took the train to South Norwalk to attend advanced school classes, a privilege only the more well-to-do could afford. A number of quite good "finishing" schools were established in the Norwalk area during the Victorian era with both day and boarding students. It was not until the 1890s, however, with the advent of the trolley car that Rowayton girls had access to public education beyond the elementary school level.

Indeed, before the coming of the trolley, women's lives were strictly confined to domestic and household duties. Their entry into the local wage-earning force in appreciable numbers took place only after the easing of travel. Lacking job opportunities, ladies devoted much of their time to church activities, church societies, clubs, lodges, etc., frequently with a charitable connotation—The King's Daughters, for instance, the Ever Ready Circle,

Rowayton on the half shell

Good Will, Epworth League, Daughters of the Eastern Star, Christian Endeavor, The Deft Finger Circle, etc. Baptist ladies attended strawberry festivals held by the Methodists, and the Methodists sat in on lecture series put on by the Baptists.[2] With little access to the outside world Rowayton remained a tight little peninsula.

The mobility of the trolley immeasurably enabled Rowayton men, but especially women, to commute to work in the many nearby shops and mills. Most of the larger local employers were involved in the clothing industries— hats, shirts, shoes, corsets, lace, woven labels, etc., affording employment in large numbers to women, young and old. Women worked long hours for low wages in sordid conditions. Nevertheless, their horizons had been lifted at long last. A few years before World War I, the Nash Engineering Company built a large plant on Wilson Avenue in close proximity to Rowayton. It was to provide steady employment for many local area men and women from that day to this.

At about the turn of the century another sizable business was established here.[3] Frank H. Traendly started as a runner for a wholesale florist. He later became a partner of the New York wholesale florist firm of Traendly and Schenk when he started to acquire property in Brookside, notably from Jacob M. Layton, the William Lockwood heirs, and others. Eventually Traendly held large tracts along both sides of Rowayton Avenue together with other chunks of neighboring properties extending down the east side of Raymond Street as far south as the railroad. The Traendly family moved into the Layton home and started to grow their own flowers under the name of Mr. Traendly's father, George Traendly, and later as "Rowayton Greenhouses." Initially 10 "small" greenhouses, measuring 125 feet, were erected south of Rowayton Avenue, later to be augmented by 10 more along Raymond Street measuring 500 feet each, together with a huge boiler plant to heat the many acres of flowers growing under glass. The Rowayton Greenhouses became the largest growers of roses in the United States. Their reputation was based on the quality of their flowers, consistently winning prize after prize at flower shows far and near, especially in New York City. In addition to roses, they cultivated carnations, peonies and later orchids, all flowers much in demand.

Both the "small" and "big" greenhouse clusters required heating systems of their own, and the boilers had voracious appetites for fuel—bituminous (soft) coal. The warm months were spent storing the coal in huge piles exceeding twenty feet in height, each containing many tons of coal. Four teams of Clydesdale type horses drew the dump wagons piled high with coal from the Rowayton railroad station in a steady stream. There were no conveyor belts at either end of the haul. Coal shovelers worked ten hours a day, six

Of Roses and Orchids

Close after the railroad came the United States Post Office. The one-room post office on the right at Rowayton Avenue and Thomes Street was in the postmaster's front yard, c. 1890.

Later the same office was moved across Rowayton Avenue conveniently attached to the home of the succeeding postmaster, c. 1913.

Rowayton on the half shell

A view along the row of the Rowayton Greenhouses, the world's largest growers of roses, on Raymond Street, Brookside.

days a week. At the greenhouse site the soft coal was packed and graded on an incline. The horses were rested and then hard-driven to run up the incline and stop to dump the load at the top, then slowly descend the opposite slippery slope. Seems impossible, but that's how it was done. All winter long coal was hand shoveled into the boilers.

At the peak of operations the Rowayton Greenhouses employed more than thirty men. Many were first or second generation immigrants of Italian or Hungarian extraction, both laborers and gardeners. Almost all lived in the Springwood ("Whistleville"★) or Soundview Avenue section of South Norwalk. It was not unusual for some of the more recent immigrants to take up temporary residence in sheds and barns on the premises. Housing for few long-time employees was provided by a scant half-dozen frame houses scattered about the properties. Working hours were ten a day, six days a week. Everyone walked to and from work.

The Rowayton Greenhouses attained a high degree of self sufficiency. Water for flowers, animals and humans was pumped from a pond to a large capacity, elevated storage tank. Acres of corn were grown and ground for silage—the tall silo filled by hand. Ice was cut by hand and dragged by horses to be stored in an ice house nearby. The dairy herd numbered some forty head. Milk, in forty-quart steel cans, was hauled by team down the Boston

★East bound trains blew their whistle as they rounded the sharp curve west of the South Norwalk station.

Of Roses and Orchids

Houses like this on Flax Hill Road were rented by
the Rowayton Greenhouses to their employees at the
level of foremen and higher.

Post Road to Stamford to be sold wholesale. The manure from both horses and cows was used to fertilize the flowers. Many fields were held in hay requiring huge barns for storage. Two apple orchards of about a hundred trees were trimmed and picked. Some of the apples were shipped to the company store in New York to be given to customers as a dividend, one to each. Peonies were grown by the acre in open fields, to be gathered, packed, and shipped in time to meet the Decoration Day demand.

In the mid 1920s motor trucks replaced the horses. A garage was built to house them, plus the family cars. There was not only ample parking, but a spacious packing and shipping room, next to a large refrigerated area. Ice, along with the horse, was passe. The new delivery truck to the New York market proudly bore the title "Miss Rowayton" emblazoned across the front above the cab. The bulk of the record keeping was done at the New York office requiring but one office secretary-manager here. Half a dozen girls were hired for grading roses (by length of stem), work previously performed by men, but the Traendly work force remained over-whelmingly male, some to the third generation.

Frank Traendly died in the early 1940s. After his death the business was divided and operated by his sons, John (orchids) and Charles (roses), for a few years. But the value of the real estate, eighty-three acres in Norwalk and fifty-two in Darien, far outstripped the value of the business. Where prize

Rowayton on the half shell

The Danbury and Norwalk Railroad extended trackage to the tip of Wilson Point in 1882.

roses, carnations, orchids, and peonies had bloomed to fruition, comfortable, commodious, private residences now stand on half-acre plots, some with flowers.

The Spanish-American War of 1898–99, one of the shortest of modern wars, had little lasting impact on New England in general, or upon Rowayton in particular. Only a few Rowayton men enlisted, George Cudlipp, son of a prominent local family, being one of them. Some time after the war, Commander Provost Babbin, USN (Retired) acquired Revolutionary War Sergeant Paul Raymond's home at 26 Wilson Avenue, in which to live out his life in retirement. It soon became part of Rowayton folklore that Commander Babbin had stood at the side of Admiral George Dewey on the bridge of the flagship USS *Olympia* in Manila Bay when the Admiral uttered his deathless phrase, "You may fire when ready, Gridley," and proceeded to pound the Spanish Grand Fleet into submission, with the loss of but one man. The *Olympia* is today preserved in Philadelphia as a national shrine. Among the memorabilia is the duty roster of the officers and crew of that historic day. Commander Babbin's name does not appear among them. This should not be construed to mean, however, that he was not present on the bridge at that time in some other official capacity. As a matter of fact, it is quite possible he was.

It was not long after Colonel Theodore Roosevelt of Spanish-American War fame became President of the United States that he sent the better part of the United States Navy on a trip around the world as a show of strength. All the ships were painted starchy white and were universally called "The Great White Fleet." Upon their triumphant return the president scheduled

Of Roses and Orchids

For a short time in 1890 the New York and New England Railroad operated the ferry boat "D. M. Martin" between the Wilson Point dock shown here and Oyster Bay, Long Island, for passengers en route to New York City.

a grand review off his home at Oyster Bay, New York—diagonally across Long Island Sound from Rowayton. On the day of the review harbors on the Connecticut side of the Sound were denuded of boats. Crafts of all kinds were carrying sight-seers to the grand event, including the three steamers of the Stevens Oyster Company, decks covered with Rowaytonites. The Great White Fleet was an unforgettable spectacle. Indeed, Long Island Sound has not witnessed such a day, before or since.

As in the case of all other major wars, a rash of building followed the Spanish-American War in Rowayton. Many of the residences along upper Rowayton Avenue, Highland Avenue, Roton Avenue, and Bell Island were built during the short period between the Spanish-American and World War I.

World War I took a long time to get to America. Commencing in Europe in August 1914, it was April 1917 before the United States was sufficiently provoked to fight.* Recruiting offices sprouted throughout the land. When peace came on November 11, 1918, fifty-one Rowayton men had enlisted in the Army, Navy, and Marines, more than 10 percent of whom were to become officers in the Naval Reserve. Years later, Fred Oakes recalled sitting with his friend, Harvey Jarvis, on a bench at the Guider's Corner trolley stop a few weeks after the declaration of war. The Stamford bound trol-

*In May 1915 a German submarine sank the British passenger liner, *Lusitania.* Aboard were the Rowayton playwright Charles Klein and Mrs. Klein, his producer Charles Frohman and Mrs. Frohman. The sinking stiffened American sentiment to enter the war.

Rowayton on the half shell

A Lilliputian War Shop
That is helping one little town do its bit

By MARY FRANCES HACKLEY

During World War I Miss Hackley operated a small shop at 135 Rowayton Avenue, the proceeds of which went to the war effort.

ley stopped and discharged a lady passenger. As she crossed the street she noticed the two young men lounging comfortably and said, "Why aren't you two loafers in the army?" and stomped past. They looked at each other and took the next trolley to South Norwalk and enlisted. Jarvis was caught in a German gas attack in France the following year and was to suffer ill effects for the rest of his life.★ Oakes lived until his ninety-eighth year.

As did many Rowayton men, Jarvis and Oakes served with the 26th Division, known as the "Yankee Division," made up principally of Connecticut and Vermont troops. Of the fifty-one Rowayton enlistees, fifty were to return home to hearth and home. There was but one fatality, Rowayton-born G. Lester G. James, who died of disease in a training camp in the Carolinas.

The war made a strong impact upon domestic life in and around Rowayton. For some years before the war wireless telephone experiments were conducted by the government from the tip of Wilson Point. When war came, knowing of the location, the government leased the southwestern end of the point for its merchant marine wartime agency, the United States Shipping Board. The property was encircled with barbed wire, and guards with riot

★One of the lesser remembered aspects of WW I was the effort made throughout the United States to have school children save and collect peach pits which were used in making filters for gas masks.

Of Roses and Orchids

The Rowayton Fife and Drum Corps, organized in 1914, poses on the steps of the Benjamin Franklin school on Chestnut Street in South Norwalk, c. 1920.

During World War I small cargo ships were built in coastal shipyards and sent to outfitting and finishing yards before commissioning. Shown here is a fleet of eight awaiting completion at the facility established at Wilson Point, c. 1918.

Rowayton on the half shell

A welcome home parade for Rowayton veterans was held in the spring of 1919. Here the leaders step off smartly on Rowayton Avenue to fifes and the beat of drums with Winthrop House in the left rear.

guns were stationed to protect the entrances.★[4]

Acutely short of ocean tonnage at the outbreak of war, the United States hurriedly instituted a crash program of shipbuilding. The program eventually produced quite a number of small freighters. Some of these were called "Hog Islanders" after their building site. Immediately upon launching, these ships were towed to finishing yards and depots for final equipping and commissioning. Wilson Point became such a location, employing as many as eight hundred men, enhancing the local economy. Marine equipment of all kinds was stockpiled, but only a few of the partly completed hulls were actually finished here. The armistice came too soon. Building and outfitting ships is a complicated and time-consuming business. By the time the program was entering its production stage, the war was over. Tons of surplus material were auctioned at Wilson Point in May 1922, including a number of steel lifeboats.

★Extensive docks and warehouses, including a roundhouse to reverse direction of the railroad engines, had been built at the point by the New York and New England Railroad, a threatening competitor of the New Haven Railroad (Morgan) and Harlem Railroad (Vanderbilt) interests. Docks and buildings had been built as a terminus for a railroad-ferry. Barred from entry onto Manhattan Island by the monopoly of the Harlem Railroad, the New York and New England devised a route from Boston to New York circumventing the Bronx. It came down the Housatonic Branch of the NY & NE, to Wilson's Point, was ferried across the Sound to Oyster Bay, New York, thence to New York City on the tracks of the Long Island and Eastern States Line (aka Long Interval and Empty Seats Line). Morgan and Vanderbilt need not have worried. The competition lasted less than a year, but the docks remained.

Of Roses and Orchids

They were approximately twenty-five feet long, could be bought for approximately twenty-five dollars, and could be seen rusting away along local shores for approximately twenty-five years later.

The Wilson Point docks were soon to be used by the Standard Oil Company of New York (SOCONY) to supply their tank farm at the corner of Wilson and Ely Avenues. Pipe lines were extended from the water-borne tankers and barges to huge land-bound storage tanks.

The year 1918 marked the end of the Great War, but it was also to be remembered as the year of the influenza epidemic which took more lives locally than the war had, and for one of the severest winters on record. The cold was so intense and protracted that western Long Island Sound froze over, making it possible for pedestrian and vehicular traffic to cross safely. Not until 1934 was there such a deep freeze with thick ice extending beyond Green's Reef Lighthouse, but not to the Long Island shore as in "eighteen."

Rowayton on the half shell

A Taxing District Is Spawned

$\mathcal{T}$HE IMPACT OF the motor car during the post World War I period was the most significant influence on suburban living ever. The mobility provided by the automobile changed the lifestyle of the outlivers beyond recognition. Roadside businesses bloomed. Rowayton broke out in a rash of gasoline staions. Diagonally across from Hartog's Rowayton Garage at 105 Rowayton Avenue, the Sinclair Oil Company installed a two pump prefab station on the southwest corner of McKinley Street. Harry S. Street, with an eye on the luxurious cars housed in posh Tokeneke garages, decided to open a gas station on a corner of his land at Tokeneke Road and Five Mile River Road. As Harry told the author: "I went into the Darien Town Hall and said, 'Clarence, I want a permit to use a piece of roadside for a gas station.' 'How many feet?' he asked. 'One hundred and fifty,' I said. 'Why not make it three hundred?' he asked, so I did. He wrote out a permit right then and there. As I was about to leave, I said 'Oh, by the way, Adolph Brown wants a permit to build two stores, with apartments over, across the street from my place.' 'O.K.' said Clarence, 'wait a minute and you can take the permit with you and give it to him.'"[1] Things tended to be a little less formal in those days. Another gas station, this one offering refreshments, soon opened on an opposite corner to Street's, to be known as "The Gables," Abraham Modney, proprietor.

The increased demand for marine fuels had to be met. Earlier Andrew S. Mills had installed a two-thousand gallon tank for marine gasoline on the end of a long wooden pier opposite his home at 78 Rowayton Avenue. Others followed suit and facilities for fuel were available at the Rowayton Marine Works and still later at W. P. Jenkins Boatyard. As the demand for marine fuel expanded, the number of local outlets declined. Costs for attendants, tank installation, maintenance, and insurance, as well as a short season and low volume obliterated profit even as the number of power boats more than tripled. Today there is but one fuel dock in Five Mile River—open weekends only!

Gas stations ashore have fared little better. There is only one in the immediate vicinity—on the site of Modney's "Gables Inn," where many years before Harry Street's great grandfather operated a landing for his packet boat and a warehouse for local farm produce.

Back in 1913 Norwalk, South Norwalk, and East Norwalk took a major step towards reducing the sectionalism that fragmented the town. An intricate system of taxing districts dating back to pre-Civil War times had evolved in Norwalk. (In those early days there were eleven school districts alone levying separate taxes for the expenses and setting the curriculum of each school!) Geography and lack of communication were major developmental factors. South Norwalk was far enough distant from Norwalk and East Norwalk to be awkward. Both Norwalk and South Norwalk had long before received recognition from the State Legislature by being designated the Borough of Norwalk and the City of South Norwalk. Norwalk was later acclaimed a city, and East Norwalk named a separate fire district. The 1913 legislation designated these three entities numerically—Norwalk, 1st Taxing District; South Norwalk, 2nd Taxing District; and East Norwalk, 3rd Taxing District. Collectively they became the 4th T.D. for certain services provided the inner city such as fire, police, sanitation, etc. The entire town became the 5th T.D. to provide administration, education, highways, vital statistics, etc.

A city council of seven members was created, two each from the inner cities, and one each from East Norwalk, Rowayton, and the rest of the outer city. The first councilman from Rowayton was George W. Stevens of McKinley Street (and McKinley's party). It would be twenty-five years before a Democrat would gain the Rowayton council seat. John M. Gloetzner, Sr., of Bell Island, was elected in 1938.

After a series of deliberative meetings in Rowayton, a bill was introduced at the 1921 session of the Connecticut General Assembly that would make Rowayton a separate taxing district of the City of Norwalk, effective in 1923, if approved by local referendum. The issue that instigated the idea of a separate district was how to arrange for street lights throughout the village. Attempts had been made during the previous few years, but to little or no avail. There were two good reasons against: 1, street lights would cost money, and 2, they would not guarantee safe passage after dark anyway.

Rowayton on the half shell

Jacob B. Raymond was quoted as stating at one of the meetings that "since hand lanterns were good enough for my father, they're good enough for me!"[2] But Jake was on the short end of the vote. The referendum held in June 1921 voted in favor of becoming a taxing district to provide street lighting (and other specified services) at public expense. The district concept, from the local view, at least, proved to be a boon for Rowayton. One by one, other public services were assumed by the Sixth Taxing District (its numerical designation) that could not, or would not, have been provided by the inner districts—garbage collection, library support, fire protection, park land acquisition, etc. The district system was the ideal vehicle to facilitate acquisition of several parcels of real estate that so enhance the quality of village life.

One important piece of Rowayton real estate came into the public domain just at the time the Sixth Taxing District was being created. The welfare of Rowayton in general was of much unselfish interest to the John Sherman Hoyt family, near neighbors living in the Tokeneke section of Darien. They were most generous contributors in both time and money to charitable, church, and civic causes regardless of town boundaries. The Hoyts owned a piece of waterfront on lower Rowayton Avenue, between the former oystering operations of Craw & L'Hommedieu and the Stevens Oyster Company, which they used as a private landing for their yacht. The landing fell into disuse upon completion of a stone breakwater which enclosed a dock and slip in front of their Contentment Island home. In June 1923 they gave of their own free will eighty feet of waterfront opposite Cook Street to the City of Norwalk for public use. "Community Beach" proved to be a godsend.

In those long-gone days many Rowayton swimmers used the numerous Sound beaches, but predominately the beach at Rowayton Beach, then known as Columbus Grove, walking, rowing, or paddling to get there. When Rowayton Beach proper was developed, the beach itself was restricted to property owners and renters within the development. The no longer welcome town-folk turned to the newly available Community Beach. Hoyt had built a retaining wall and bulkhead. The Sixth Taxing District, of very few years of age, contracted with Captain Theodore Smith to bring over a few deck loads of Long Island sand on his schooner *T. W. Anderson* to be spread upon the shore. A swimming float complete with diving board was anchored off shore, Arthur Ladrigan was hired as lifeguard, and a swimming beach was in operation on the small parcel. It served throughout the 1930s to an ever-increasing horde of swimmers until replaced by Bayley Beach in 1942. Community Beach graphically showed that it is astonishing how many hot and humid people can crowd into the water at a tiny bathing area if they have to.

A Taxing District is Spawned

The channel of the Five Mile River hugs the Rowayton shoreline and pleasure craft utilize it fully.

Rowayton on the half shell

The largesse of the John Sherman Hoyt family continues to be appreciated to this day. Community Beach provides the only publicly owned access to the Five Mile River—on either side—for those interested in boating. During the post World War II years, with the advent of mass-produced fiberglass boats of all sizes, and the resulting tremendous expansion of pleasure boating, the Five Mile River estuary has become a highly congested yacht harbor. Virtually landlocked, it is a desirable, safe boating facility during all weather conditions, truly a "hurricane hole," but very limited in area. The only navigable water at times of low tide is the federally dredged channel, last dredged in 1968. Originally dug to a width of one hundred feet, bank and shore erosion, silting and land run-off have reduced the channel width to less than eighty feet. A major limitation to the full utilization of the harbor is that public access is available on the Rowayton side only, resulting in severe traffic congestion and inadequate parking on narrow busy streets during the peak season. Realizing the acuteness of the problem, the legislature in 1971 created the Five Mile River Commission to deal with the situation.

In a stroke of rare good fortune, the finest parcel of land on the Five Mile River became the property of the people of the Sixth Taxing District in 1966. The Seeley-Dibble-Pinkney house, built circa 1820, on four acres of tidewater near the village center was offered to the district by the widow of William Pinkney, Jr., whose family had lived there for one hundred and fifty years. Realizing the historical significance of the property to the community, Mrs. Pinkney contacted the Sixth District Commissioners, offering the district first refusal on a direct sale basis, the price to be $200,000.[3] Approval by the district electors was readily granted. Temporary financing was arranged through a Norwalk bank until a bond issue could be authorized by the legislature. It was only three years since a similar bond issue had been sought for the purchase of the Community Center. This time, however, it was not necessary to solicit the public for the down payment as in 1942.

The original part of the Seeley-Dibble-Pinkney house, the front, was leased to the Rowayton Historical Society for its headquarters. The rear part, added circa 1850, was made into an apartment for the caretaker family. The spacious grounds have proved ideal for community affairs, picnics, church fairs, and open air services in summer. The site is a community asset of inestimable value.

Not all proposals to purchase property for public use made since the district's founding have met with success. When Community Beach was found to be inadequate to the demand for swimming space in the mid 1930s, a proposal was made to purchase the Charles H. Wells property, now Cavanaugh

A Taxing District is Spawned

Marina, at 82–86 Rowayton Avenue, for a waterfront park. In 1975 it was suggested the district acquire property owned by the Second Taxing District used for a high, standing water storage tank east of Highland Avenue for $350,000. It was proposed in 1986 that the district buy the former Hickory Bluff Store with bathing beach and bath houses, for use as a yacht club for $1,000,000. All three proposals fell short of approval by the electorate.[4]

In the earliest days police protection was in the form of an elected constable, described at the time "as the arm of the law and the embodiment of His Majesty." As the town population increased, and police problems with them, so too, did the number of constables. With the establishment of the Borough of Norwalk in 1836, the City of South Norwalk in 1871, and then the City of Norwalk in 1893, both centers established police departments for their separate areas. The rest of the town had to rely upon only a handful of constables for their safety.

After the consolidation of 1913, the three taxing districts comprising the Fourth Taxing District provided uniform police service for the inner city only. It has been said the automobile necessitated the establishment of the Department of State Police. In Norwalk the State Police proved to be a God-send to the constables trying to maintain order in the outer areas. The levy of an equal town-wide tax to extend police protection throughout the town had been proposed for a number of years by Independent-Socialist Mayor Irving C. Freese. During the 1951 legislature session the local contingent, Republicans, agreed with him, and a law to that effect was passed. Many out-livers felt their cost would be disproportionately high since so large a percentage of police work is concentrated within the inner city. The volume of outer city calls, however, is a constant reminder of the necessity of full-time, city-wide police protection.

Sanitary sewers were another vital service enjoyed by the inner city, but denied the out-livers since the 1930s. By then the ubiquitous outhouse had long been unfashionable, of course. The last such facility still in active service was at 10 McKinley Street as late as 1948! Sanitary systems with either cesspools or septic tanks with leaching fields, some adequate, some not, had long been in use throughout the outer city. The cost of extending sewers to the entire town seemed prohibitive. But the concept, modified to include only the more densely populated outer areas, took root. By 1975 the necessary pipes were buried throughout most of the Rowayton area, together with three pumping stations at Bell Island, Sammis Street, Wilson Avenue at Martin Luther King Highway. More and more streets, both inside and outside the

Rowayton on the half shell

Since the 1900s a drug store has occupied virtually the same site at 159 Rowayton Avenue. In this 1940 photo druggist George Soybel is shown on the front sidewalk.

Sixth Taxing District, have since been tied into the system. To underwrite the cost equitably, that area within the sixth receiving sewer service became the Seventh Taxing District. It was another triumph for Mayor Freese, who abhorred the district system, but found it to be a useful instrument of government.

Rowayton has boasted a drug store almost continuously since 1900 when Charles Bartlett opened a small store next to Dibble's meat and grocery at 159 Rowayton Avenue. Patent medicines were so abundant the phrase "a drug on the market" was coined. Many, or most, were out-and-out fakes. Often they were called "Elixirs" or "Extracts" or "Bitters." Advertising claims were extravagant: "Never failing ague cure, for the blood, liver, skin and heart," "Expectorant for coughs, colds, croup, asthma, bronchitis, and all lung diseases - it surely expels worms!" "Vegetable Pills - Cure Dyspepsia, Colic, Sick Headache, Constipation, Diarrhea, Worms, Fever and Ague, Indigestion." Liquid "medicines" usually were high in alcoholic content, some tested the same as corn whiskey. One of the very popular brands was Indian "Kickapoo Juice" made here in staid Connecticut, of all places! There were cure-alls for every ache or pain known to man or beast. It was said they claimed much, but cured little. Samuel Hopkins Adams wrote in 1905, "Gullible America will spend this year some seventy-five millions of dollars in order to swallow huge quantities of alcohol, narcotics, dangerous heart depressants and insidious liver stimulants."[2] But not for long.

A Taxing District is Spawned

In 1926 the post office was moved to the center of the village at 153 Rowayton Avenue next to the Rowayton Market.

Although bills had been introduced in Congress four years before, it was not until the last days of the session of 1906, spurred on by President Theodore Roosevelt, that the Pure Food and Drug Act was passed. It was to be the death knell for the "Pink Pills for Pale People," "Wahoo Bitters," and "Indian Doctor" wonder drugs. The act also made a severe dent in the pockets of druggists nationwide, including poor Mr. Bartlett, not to mention the ingenious advertising industry.

About twenty-five years later Dibble built a new store adjacent to the market for the express purpose of opening a drug store complete with a marble ice cream soda fountain. By then ice cream sodas had become synonymous with drug store. The new store was promptly occupied by Frank Ritter, not a professional pharmacist, but a confectioner. In 1927 the store was bought by Sedgwick M. Allen, who hired a full-fledged pharmacist. "The Rowayton Drug Store" was legitimatized. Allen later sold to Chester Andrus, a salesman who employed a pharmacist. In 1939 a New Haven druggist, George Soybel, purchased and revitalized the store. Nine years later, in 1948, Soybel acquired vacant land adjacent to the north, which even then was still part of the Winthrop House property, where he built the block of stores we know today.[3] The centerpiece of the new block was a spacious new drug store, also with an ice cream soda fountain, alas, now gone. George Soybel is to be remembered as the first to realize the retail potential of the center of the village.

Others were quick to follow Soybel's example. The east side of Rowayton Avenue, with the exceptions of the corner at Wilson Avenue and at

Rowayton on the half shell

Captain Frank R. Stevens of the oyster family was
appointed postmaster in the early 1930s.

McKinley Street, was entirely residential. The property directly opposite the stores, post office, fire house, etc., was owned by Mrs. Charles Ambler of Wilton. (Mrs. Ambler's mother-in-law, Hannah Raymond, was an heir to the Raymond estate.) One day while shopping in New Canaan, Mrs. Ambler was smitten by the quaintness of a block of stores there, and thought how nice it would be if Rowayton had a similar complex. She contacted an architect and decided to build in 1949. The post office block is the result, anchored by a restaurant on one end and a hardware store on the other. The Post Office Department leased the keystone building. Unfortunately, it was not finished in time for the post office to move in before their current lease expired. Temporary quarters were located in the rear of the old Guider's store with an entrance from McKinley Street, for a number of months. The new building, completed at last, was dedicated in the summer of 1949.

The property adjacent to the north of the post office tract, once a large fenced lawn of the Winthrop House, was developed commercially. A small block of stores was erected. Both business blocks provided for head-in parking on their front aprons, resulting in cars having to back out into the state highway, which is now illegal. Illegal or no, the parking problem in Rowayton center goes on. Businesses on the river side of the avenue provide no off-street parking; those on the east side inadequate off-street parking. Not an

A Taxing District is Spawned

The present post office building was dedicated June 30, 1949.

easy problem to solve, nor a healthy one to allow to continue to fester. Ironically, before these three business developments were started, two other locations that would have provided adequate parking space, the Ambler property behind the post office, and the then-open land between McKinley Street and Sammis Streets, and Highland Avenue and Farm Creek, had been discussed and considered at meetings of the Civic Association, but to no avail. Rowayton was not ready for a shopping mall.

It had long been the hope of local civic leaders that someday a branch of one of the nearby banks would be located in Rowayton. A number of Rowayton residents had served as officers and/or directors of Norwalk banks: Lawrence Paul, Lewis Wardell, Frederick Stabell, and others. Their interest in a branch bank in Rowayton led to the taking of feasibility surveys periodically during the 1940s, '50s and '60s, all with negative results. Historically bankers had emphasized the rate of interest paid as the prime inducement to attract new business. They slowly came to realize their depositors were more concerned about convenience of location rather than a fraction of a percentage point of interest.

In 1974, perhaps in celebration of the one hundredth anniversary of its founding, the Fairfield County Savings Bank of Norwalk purchased the Shell gas station on the Rowayton Avenue - McKinley Street corner.[4] After extensive alterations to the building, Rowayton's first bank opened its doors in October that same year. The time was ripe. Deposits far exceeded expec-

Rowayton on the half shell

tations during the first six months of operation, and continued to grow for many years. The strong market for local real estate swelled the demand for mortgages, a traditional investment field for savings banks. Convenience banking seems here to stay. And Rowayton's bank physically continues to resemble a Shell gas station.

A Taxing District is Spawned

But One Life To Give

*A*T THE END of the summer season in 1929 no one in Rowayton anticipated the financial disaster that was but one month away. During the boom years of the 1920s, more and more local families had enough extra money to own a pleasure boat of their own. The Five Mile River and the coves to the east and west were soon serving as home ports to more and larger yachts. The full effect of the fall of the stock market prices was not felt by the wealthy immediately. It was three or four years before the local yachtsmen retrenched or curtailed their enthusiasm for boating drastically. Three large high-speed yachts left from this area each day with owners and a few breakfast guests for the yacht club landings in the East River at 59th and 23rd streets, New York City. The run took approximately two hours. Some of the yachts would lie at the landings until the end of the day to return His Highness in style. The boats themselves were called "Commuters."

Two from here were sister ships, seventy-two feet in length, built by the Luders Marine Construction Company in Stamford: *Eepee*, Edward E. Plaut, New Canaan, and *You'll Do*, Walter Sachs, Darien. A third "commuter" from here was *Catamount*, eighty-five feet long, of similar design, also built by Luders, and owned by Bradford Ellsworth of Butler's Island, Darien. Ellsworth owned and operated two other noticeable yachts (all three named for cats), a forty-two foot express cruiser *Bob Cat* (presumably for shorter commuting), and a ninety-six foot schooner, *Lynx*. Since she drew nineteen feet of water, *Lynx* was necessarily moored out near Green's Ledge Lighthouse. A number of lesser craft were to be seen in and around the river. The *Sunswyck*, Edward H. Delafield, seventy-two feet; *Mendota*, sixty-five feet, and *Satel-*

The Pennoyer residence at 168 Rowayton Avenue. The wing at the left dates to the 1790s; the 2½-story portion at the right is c. 1845.

lite with her tenders, *Parasite* and *Flea*. With the boats came the boatyards to service them.

Ferdinand Hartog changed the focus of his waterside business from automobile sales and service to marine sales and service. It was a good move to make. True, by 1934, the very depth of the depression, most larger yachts were shelved. Pleasure boating was confined to considerably smaller craft. But fortunately there was enough work for small boatyards to hold on until better days. The ex-Rowayton Garage, now Rowayton Marine Works, became a dealer for Mathews yachts as well as Marblehead Cruisers, a popular thirty-four foot single-screw boat, and distributor for Gray Maine Engines. In due time the business would prosper.

One segment of the economy most seriously affected during the Great Depression was the construction industry. Then, as now, it was a principal employer of younger men. A good many Rowayton men were employed in the residential and commerical building trades and suddenly found themselves without work. As more were laid off or let go, the number of men hanging around the firehouse grew. Few could turn to the land. A few did turn to the water—to dig clams, oysters, mussels, scallops, often from borrowed rowboats. It was not unusual to row as far afield as Westport or to

But One Life To Give

Erected in 1901 in memory of veterans of the Civil War, Cannon Monument also honors veterans of both World Wars. The land donated by Elias Pennoyer was formerly his front yard.

Stamford beaches, as well as throughout the Norwalk Islands. A bushel of clams brought $1.65, oysters $.75; a day's pay occasionally $5.[1] A job that paid eighteen to twenty-five dollars a week was much sought after.

To stimulate employment during the depression, the federal government established, among other agencies, the Works Progress Administration. One project fostered by the WPA aided artists by underwriting their works in public buildings and places. Many of the remaining works of this program are in the form of murals in public buildings across the country. One fine example is the large oil painting in the Rowayton Library by a local artist, George Avison. It depicts market day in Rowayton as the packet boat *Julia* lies loading at the wharf—Rowayton as it might have looked in the 1830s, a full century before.

By the end of the decade of the 1930s war had exploded in Europe for the second time in twenty-five years. The American economy at last began to show signs of survival, there were fewer idlers hanging about the firehouse and the village center. In much less time than it took during World War I, the United States joined the European war effort in only twenty-six months, thanks to the Japanese attack on Pearl Harbor. Air raid wardens appeared instantly on the local scene to prevent any artificial light from filtering out from behind drawn shades and thus contribute to silhouetting coastal shipping off Long Island, making it easy prey for German U-boats farther off shore. Just how lights shining on this side of the Sound would aid in il-

Rowayton on the half shell

A huge welcome home celebration was held at Roton Point in the spring of 1946 for the men and women who served in World War II. The refreshment committee shown here were all members of the fire department.

luminating the south shore of Long Island was never satisfactorily explained, but the lights here were effectively doused anyway.

Local draft boards, ration boards, price control boards, etc., spawned prolifically. Perhaps the first is to be longest remembered. All males aged eighteen to forty-five were required to register during October 1940, fourteen months before Pearl Harbor. Some local boys, Albert ("Ubbie") Lawrence, among them, had already joined the armed forces. Draft selections were drawn by a blindfold celebrity from a tumbling barrel. One of the first numbers to be selected in Norwalk's initial drawing was that of a Rowayton lad, Joseph R. Morrison. Many more were to follow. When the war was over and it came time to place a tablet on the base of the cannon monument, space for one hundred and seventy-eight names was necessary to list those men and women from Rowayton who served in World War II.

Amazingly, there were no more fatalities than during World War I. Again, only one Rowayton man lost his life, Albert Lawrence, who had volunteered more than a year before Pearl Harbor, December 7, 1941 ("A day that shall live in infamy!"), died during the infamous Japanese Death March on the Ba-

But One Life To Give

taan Peninsula. A vivacious, natural athlete, "Ubbie" excelled in all fields, especially friendship.

Rowayton men and women served in all services and branches of the armed forces and in all theaters of war. They were united, consoled, and informed of each other's activities, and the state of siege at home by a monthly mimeographed newsletter, appropriately named "The Clamdigger." It was prepared, published, and posted by a group of dedicated local young ladies, some of them temporary "war widows," who really cared and who showed it in a most welcome manner: Dorothy C. Johnson, Grace Kiggins, Florence P. Pettus, Esther B. Raymond, Jane P. Russell, Emily Stevens, Myra Soybel, Doris Gale Mason, and Mrs. Elizabeth Moseley Merrill.

The major effect of World War II in Rowayton was psychological. A predominantly residential community, no factories, no assembly plants, no ship finishing facilities (as Wilson Point in World War I) were located here.★ Nevertheless every resident was personally involved on a daily basis throughout the entire war.

With over a 170 men and women enlisted from so small a community, there was deep emotional concern upon each and every resident. The nation's war effort was conducted on an all-inclusive scale. Everyone in Rowayton had at least one relative, friend, or acquaintance actually in the armed services or employed in war production. When the war was suddenly over in August 1945 the relaxation of tension and anxiety was universal. In Rowayton there was real thankfulness for so few local casualties.

The close of the war was the dawn of a new era here. The main physical effect of the war on Rowayton—the demise of Roton Point as an amusement park—was to have far-reaching results. Never would newcomers experience the vicissitudes of having a noisy amusement park as a near neighbor.

★A few wooden lifeboat type craft were built here at the Wm. P. Jenkins Boatyard.

Rowayton on the half shell

Developer's Delight

DURING THE later part of the 1800s dealing in real estate as a developer or commission agent became a bona fide livelihood. From the earliest days real property was bartered and swapped as a medium of exchange by landholders, as well as mortgaged or sold outright as a means of providing immediate liquidity. From the 1870s until World War I the Rowayton area enjoyed a period of steady development. Materials and labor were both cheap and plentiful, resulting in the building of numerous roomy, comfortable, middle class homes we now loosely categorize by that all inclusive term, "Victorian." (The good queen reigned from 1839–1901, but the architectural styles we encompass by the term cover an amazingly flexible time frame.)

By the 1890s the Foster brothers of Danbury had acquired and were developing much of Bell Island, building on speculation and renting or selling outright as the situation dictated. Dudley E. Hoyt was operating on a similar basis and scale at Pine Point. Theophileus Euphrat was one of the first to realize the potential of Rowayton real estate development. He seemed to specialize in the rather larger tracts. He sold to the Traendlys, and over the years built a large home on the northeast corner of Rowayton Avenue and Hunt Street, as well as other homes, the Ed White–Charles Klein estate at 33 Wilson Avenue, the Hart Castle at 34 Sammis Street, etc. It is said that while showing the 261 Rowayton Avenue property to a lady prospect from New York City, she expressed concern about the possibility of mosquitoes breeding in the close-by riverbed. "Mosquitoes?" the incredulous Euphrat replied, "What is those?" Another Euphrat story popular at the time, and perhaps apocryphal, is that when presenting a Brookside residence for sale which

The oldest house south of McKinley Street is at 64 Rowayton Avenue. Built in 1850 for William R. Godfrey, subsequent owners have been Charles Scofield, Frank P. Dunn, and Charles Dunn.

relied on a backyard well for water supply, he had had two holes drilled into the wall above the kitchen sink into which he inserted a pair of faucets! The real estate profession has played a continuous role in the Rowayton story to this day. There are presently four or more real estate offices, and at least twenty-five men and women employed as full time Rowayton real estate specialists.

Two of Rowayton's grandest estates of all time were created near the turn of the century. At Pine Point, B.F. DeKlyn, a bakery owner, candy and ice cream manufacturer (also from Danbury), developed a sizable estate with a huge summer house and guest houses on the tip of land that juts out into the Sound. The main house was located at the northern extremity of the property, requiring Roton Road, as both Crescent and South Beach roads were then known, to make two ninety degree turns before reaching Roton Point Park.

The mansion with observation tower and copious porches on three sides contained over thirty rooms, including two kitchens. A long pier stretched southeast from the front lawn diagonally across much of Pine Point Beach in order to accommodate the large DeKlyn steam yacht. Stables and carriage house were located on West Avenue (now Westmere Avenue), Bell Island. Here was kept the family coach, drawn by four white well-groomed horses. They were often followed by the classic Dalmatian coach dog nipping at their heels, half a step ahead of the left front wheel, all driven by a liveried coach-

Rowayton on the half shell

The huge residence of B.F. DeKlyn dominated Pine Point from 1890 to 1927.

man and footman! When the house was dismantled in the late 1920s it was separated into three residences. Two were moved to numbers 73 and 75 Roton Avenue, and the third to Ensign Road.

Bell Island and the Hickory Bluff area attracted members of the James A. Farrell family in the 1890s, where they rented cottages for the summer season. At the time Mr. Farrell was manager of one of the many steel mills owned by Andrew Carnegie. In 1901 J. P. Morgan acquired the controlling interest in the Carnegie mills, which together with the American Steel & Wire Corp., American Bridge Corp., Tennessee Iron and Coal Corp., among others, he consolidated to form the world's largest industrial enterprise, the United States Steel Corporation. For president of the corporation Morgan chose his lawyer, Elbert H. Gary. A few years later Morgan selected Farrell to become president of the vast operation. It was a position Mr. Farrell was to hold for over thirty years.

Around 1910 Mr. Farrell chose Rowayton as his permanent residence. He purchased two large tracts on both sides of Highland Avenue between Wilson Avenue and McKinley Street from the heirs of Charles L. Raymond, and proceeded to build an elegant country estate modelled upon the English Elizabethan style. A spacious half-timbered, "pseudo Tudor" mansion and gatehouse were erected on the east side of the avenue, gardens with farm and out-buildings on the west side. The mansion was to be short-lived. In the spring of 1913 during a wedding reception for a Farrell daughter the house caught fire and could not be saved. A new house was soon designed and built

Developer's Delight

The original James A. Farrell home "Rock Ledge" at 40 Highland Avenue from Bluff Avenue. Finished in 1912, it burned to the ground during the wedding reception of a Farrell daughter in June 1913.

of granite which was to be lived in and cherished by Mr. and Mrs. Farrell until their deaths in the early 1940s. Their lifestyle had been such as to require eight full-time employees to cater to their comfort.

In the late 1940s James Rand of Darien, chairman of the board of the Remington Rand Corporation, became enamored by the attractiveness of the James A. Farrell estate, and acquired the property for corporate headquarters. Executive offices were housed in the mansion and research offices in the building across the street. The firm was a large manufacturer of office furniture, machines, and systems. It was one of the first to turn its attention to the computer field. Remington Rand developed one of the earliest working computers which was trade-named "Univac." Much of the research, design, and engineering of the Univac was done under very tight security in the present Rowayton Community Center building.

To enhance corporate prestige, engineering skill, and foreign markets, Chairman Rand recruited prominent WW II army leaders as corporate executives, among them General James (Jimmy) Doolittle; General Leslie R. Groves, former head of the Manhattan Project, developers of the atomic bomb; and even General Douglas MacArthur himself, Allied Supreme Commander, architect of victory in the Pacific theatre over the empire of Japan.

Rowayton on the half shell

A fire-proof "Rock Ledge" was built of fieldstone which housed the Farrell family until the 1940s. It has since been owned by the Thomas School, Sperry-Rand Corporation, Continental Can Corporation, and Hewitt Associates.

General MacArthur became chairman of the board of the Sperry-Rand Corporation. The new corporate name reflected consolidation with the Sperry Corporation. It is doubtful General MacArthur spent many arduous hours behind his desk in the former Farrell mansion, but he often attended board meetings there and was frequently seen in the area. It is reported he was not too pleased with the mansion, as he found it to be dark within and not adequately lighted for office purposes.

Mr. Rand, or possibly the corporation, owned and operated a series of large yachts while located in Rowayton. The largest was called the *Galaxy* which measured one hundred and twenty-five feet, and was docked at a pier at 75 Five Mile River Road. Considerable dredging was required in front of the property to provide a turning area for so large a vessel in the small harbor. The additional dredging, alas, was not always quite enough. On one notable occasion, when the three generals and Rand were aboard, the *Galaxy* became hopelessly stuck in the mud while turning prior to docking. It became necessary for the august personages to wait patiently for the tide to come to their rescue, just like anybody else.[5] The embarassed yacht captain must have been thankful not to have been on active army duty that day.

Developer's Delight

144

The Sperry-Rand Corporation yacht "Galaxy" on which such notables as Douglas MacArthur, Jimmy Doolittle, and Leslie R. Groves dallied.

Probably the most significant aspect of the Rowayton story following the two World Wars is the use, and abuse, of land. During the 1920s Rowayton experienced a postwar building boom on a far vaster scale than heretofore.★ On Bell Island William Crimmins replaced the Foster Brothers as the leading real estate entrepreneur. He brokered existing dwellings for rent or sale, and built a number of others, mostly along the South Beach waterfront. In Rowayton, Ralph Case, native son and grandson of oystermen, bought the swampy marshes which extended from the high ground at the foot of Craw's woods (now roughly defined by Richmond Road and Craw Avenue) to the Sound, spanning from Farm Creek to the Five Mile River. Most of 1923 and 1924 was spent dredging the river bed as landfill for the marshes. The muck was pumped through twenty-four inch diameter pipes onto the marshland, filling it to a grade above sea level. Another eighteen months were spent allowing the oozie, smelly stuff to drain and settle.

Heretofore the roller coaster of Roton Point Park skirted along the shore of the Sound westward to Price's rocks, partly over land now owned by Case. When the lease expired the roller coaster had to be dismantled. A new coaster was designed and built to fit the more limited space. A higher, faster, more thrilling, and noisier ride resulted.

The area Case developed was designated "Rowayton Beach." Rowayton

★Norwalk's population increased by 23% from 1920–1930. (U.S. Census)

Rowayton on the half shell

34 Sammis Street; Edward Hart owner - c. 1914

33 Wilson Avenue; Edward White, Charles Klein, and Dr. Anson Hurd, owners - 1900–1940

260 Rowayton Avenue; Major Lucky, Melville Moore, and other owners - photo c. 1930

Developer's Delight

Rowayton Beach was tidal marsh before development. This view is from Price's Rocks c. 1921 with Five Mile River at the far left.

Avenue was extended; new streets were laid out to be named Sunwich, Juniper, Meridian, etc. The Sound beach front from the mouth of the Five Mile River east to Price's rocks was reserved for members of the Rowayton Beach Association—owners and tenants of Rowayton Beach plots. The remaining Sound beach front from the rocks east to the Roton Point Park line was held by the Case management group for a private beach and tennis club. Courts, bath houses, and club house were provided. It was to be known as the Ballast Reef Club, with membership also open to other than Rowayton Beach residents.

Construction of homes started in 1925. One of the first promoters of Rowayton Beach properties was Charles Hayes. Hayes built some half dozen frame houses along both sides of Rowayton Avenue within the confines of the "Beach." The Beach attracted people in the upper-middle income brackets, the fields of entertainment, publishing, etc., among them, Don Herold, famous cartoonist, as well as radio announcer Don Wilson and tenor Frank Parker, both of the Jack Benny show. From the start there was a certain tension between the newcomers in the beach development and the old timers of longer residence in Rowayton proper. The tension increased when the Rowayton Beach Association, Charles Hayes, president, declared beach roads private and that trespassers would be prosecuted. Chains were strung between the entrance gates, guards were deputized and placed to intercept intruders. It was the practice of some Rowaytonites to take an eve-

Rowayton on the half shell

ning walk occasionally along the off-limits roads. Alexander Robertson, treasurer of the Bowery Savings Bank in New York City and a summer resident of nearby Crockett Street, an epitome of virtue, was a regular evening walker. One evening while quietly strolling below the demarcation chain, Robertson was arrested, at the instigation of distraught beach residents, for trespassing on private property. A trial was held. The court maintained the roads were in the public domain. The accused was exonerated.

Before prohibition ended in 1932, at least one resident of the Beach, owner of a good sized fast run-about type motorboat, then known as a "speed boat," was suspected of participating in the illicit trade of "bootlegging" alcoholic beverages. Again, as in the days of the Revolution, the myriad inlets and coves along the Connecticut shore were ideally suitable for the nefarious night traffic so essential to successful bootlegging. Also adding credence to waterfront gossip, one of the houses across the river, near the end of the Five Mile River Road, had a set of port and starboard electric marine running lights mounted on the river-side porch uprights, quite visible from Long Island Sound. What other purpose could they possible serve than as a signal to rumrunners offshore if the coast was clear to off-load a case of hooch or two? At least three successful raids by prohibition enforcement officers, government men commonly called "G-Men" or "Revenooers," were effected near here with the aid of local police forces; one in Norwalk, one in Scott's Cove, and one on Bell Island. But none took place on Rowayton Beach.

Two of the earliest homes still standing within the Beach compound are 48 Rowayton Avenue and 24 Meridian Road. Many of the original houses have been remodeled, rebuilt, expanded, or razed. There are presently some eighty homes at Rowayton Beach, and virtually no unused building lots. Possibly the only exception is one lot on Roton Avenue long held by the heirs of Ralph Case. Property values peaked, temporarily at least, in 1987 when the owner of a river front home was reported to have offered a million dollars for an adjoining empty lot and was refused!

The trolley car rattling and clanking through Rowayton's streets gave way to the motor bus in 1934. Buses travel on roadways, not tracks, which liberated land on both sides of abandoned tracks through wooded areas, like present day Covewood Drive. Frederick P. Stabell, a civil engineer and surveyor, spearheaded the construction of quality homes along the tracks at the head of Wilson Cove. He also developed Flicker Lane. At about this time Bittersweet Trail and Indian Spring Road were being laid out and development started by Alvah Kellogg, a local builder with foresight to appreciate the advantages of this locality. Close by, across Wilson Cove, similar plans for Wil-

Developer's Delight

The swimming area at Rowayton Beach c. 1921 with Price's Rocks in the center foreground.

son Point were also afoot. Reed Haviland, a real estate agent with offices in South Norwalk, together with two other men from New York City, purchased 154 acres from the heirs of Boardman Burchard in 1920. Rather than subdivide into one-quarter acre plots, as in Bell Island, it was felt that larger plots, as in Tokeneke, would be more desirable. Eventually sixty-four plots were agreed upon. During the first ten years more than half had been sold or built upon.[1]

Two large tracts of land behind the old Rowayton school site on Rowayton Avenue were opened to development in the mid-1920s. Crest Road was widened and extended, Ridgewood Road and Milton Place laid out, subdividing the former pastures and gardens of the Dibble family. Bryan Road was built, separating the former White-Klein farmland owned by Harry S. Bryan, son of the early postmaster. Both tracts were slow to develop because the properties were sold piecemeal as vacant building lots. The day of the speculator-developer building and selling completed homes was yet to come.

Years later much of the Bryan property was sold to John P. Oakley. He put in a cul-de-sac, with swimming pool in the center of a circular turnaround, around which he erected a series of homes. One day he happened to be travelling in upstate New York at the time the famous social landmark, the Unit-

Rowayton on the half shell

The Knob Club at Wilson Point in the 1880s. A number of its founding members were associated with the corrupt Tweed ring in New York City during the post Civil War era.

ed States Hotel, in Saratoga Springs was being demolished. Much of the flooring of the ground floor of the hotel had been white marble. Noticing the marble slabs stacked here and there, he inquired as to their disposition and was told they were to be broken up and dumped as fill. Oakley seized the opportunity and arranged to have the heavy slabs hauled away the next day at no cost to the contractor! Consequently some of the homes surrounding Oakley Court today boast elegant floors of beautiful white marble.[2]

With the steady influx of people many areas of Rowayton gleamed in the eyes of residential developers. The land between Highland and Rowayton avenues north of Witch Lane to Devil's Garden Road was virtually vacant, holding barely half a dozen homes. Gilbert and eastern Thomes streets were laid out in the late twenties, but left undeveloped, as were Vanderbilt, Timberline, Possum and Briar roads in the vicinity of ancient Mount Misery. During the late 1930s and early '40s George Philcox, together with sons, Harold and Stanley, became a prime mover in the development of the Crooked Trail, Range, and Ledge roads areas. Little Brook Road was developed by John Coates, Clement Albrecht, and Theodore Chadeayne.

The property south of McKinley Street at Highland Avenue had been pur-

Developer's Delight

Wilson Cove looking west. The steam yacht "Kestral" at left was owned by James Trowbridge, and was one of the oldest listed in "Lloyd's Register of American Yachts," c. 1940.

chased from the Charles L. Raymond Estate by a local fuel dealer, Alfred Brown, in the early 1930s. He built a home on the northeast corner lot and laid out a subdivision. The plot called for two roads, Farm Creek Road, running parallel to the creek, and Topsail Road in the form of a horseshoe looping from and back to Farm Creek Road. The entire property was promptly dubbed "The Loop." Brown's plans were sidetracked by the depression. Few, if any, lots were sold. Twenty years were to pass before active development commenced. In the meantime Brown had died. The tract was acquired by William Kulse of Rowayton Beach for ten thousand dollars. In 1954 Harold Galzer, a Norwalk home builder, took title and erected some thirty-nine dwellings. In so doing he altered the layout for Topsail Road, eliminating the loop configuration. "The Loop" disappeared from the local lexicon.

Attendance at the old wooden schoolhouse on the Rowayton Avenue - Witch Lane corner had long since surpassed the capacity of the four rooms to house kindergarten, plus grades one through six, by 1939. The City of Norwalk, through its Board of Education, also acquired a tract of the Raymond estate north of McKinley Street east of Roton Avenue. The tract measured approximately ten acres and contained a large pond. The sale price was $10,000.[4] The following year the present Rowayton school building opened. The acreage was filled and landscaped, playgrounds for the young and old installed—jungle gyms, softball fields, tennis and basketball courts—all resulting in a fine outdoor facility.

Rowayton on the half shell

Present-day Rowayton School at Wilson and Roton avenues.

Two large additions to the school were added between 1950 and 1970 to meet what seemed to be an ever-increasing demand. Population of the school of late, however, has been declining to a point where closing the school has been seriously considered. The area high cost of living here is beyond the reach of many middle-income younger families with children of elementary school age. If the school is closed, it would be a misfortune to the entire community.

The Old Field Road, Old Trolley Way area, Pond Ridge, etc., have been developed comparatively lately. The former Thomas school tract on Bluff Avenue is the site of current construction, incorporating condominium type multi-housing units—the first of that type in Rowayton proper for sale to the public. Twelve condominium units built by the federal Department of Health and Urban Development on land donated by the United Church of Rowayton, at 212 Rowayton Avenue, as housing for seniors, were completed and occupied in 1982.

Two major steps had been taken over the years to preserve much of Farm Creek in its natural state. The marshland adjoining the creek between McKinley and Sammis streets was donated to the National Conservancy by the owner, William Kulse, upon his retirement to Florida around 1970. Some years later the City of Norwalk purchased the marsh tract south of Sammis Street from the Edward Hart family for preservation purposes.

Sperry-Rand moved their offices from Rowayton in 1963, and the man-

Developer's Delight

"And the band played on." Students parade in front of Rowayton School in 1957.

sion was sold to their near neighbor, the Thomas School. Soon thereafter the need for classroom space exceeded the capacity of the building. Kindergarten and first grade classes met in the basement of the Community Center until that building was purchased by the Sixth Taxing District in 1966. The Thomas School was absorbed by the Low-Heywood School of Stamford, and the mansion sold to Continental Can Corporation in 1975 for executive offices for their World Trade Group. Denied a permit to expand by the strength of spirited community opposition, Continental sold the property two years later. The purchaser was Chicago based Hewitt Associates, one of the nation's largest actuarial firms, for their eastern divisional headquarters. Hewitt soon applied for permission to expand also. Community opposition was not as widely spread as against Continental Can, and the permits were issued. A large addition to the mansion of contemporary design, together with a parking area extending over much of the former lawn, was completed in 1988.

The 1960s, '70s, and '80s witnessed an epidemic of office building along the Rowayton waterfront unprecedented in history. Brooks and Pack, a local building firm, acquired the former John Vincent residence, more recently the up-river branch of the Wm. P. Jenkins Boatyard, at 137 Rowayton Avenue in 1966, and built a four-story office-apartment building. Not only was it the tallest building in the village, but aesthetically one of the plainest. Many residents considered it a monstrosity and out of place, and urged the Planning and Zoning Commission to restrict further development of the

Rowayton on the half shell

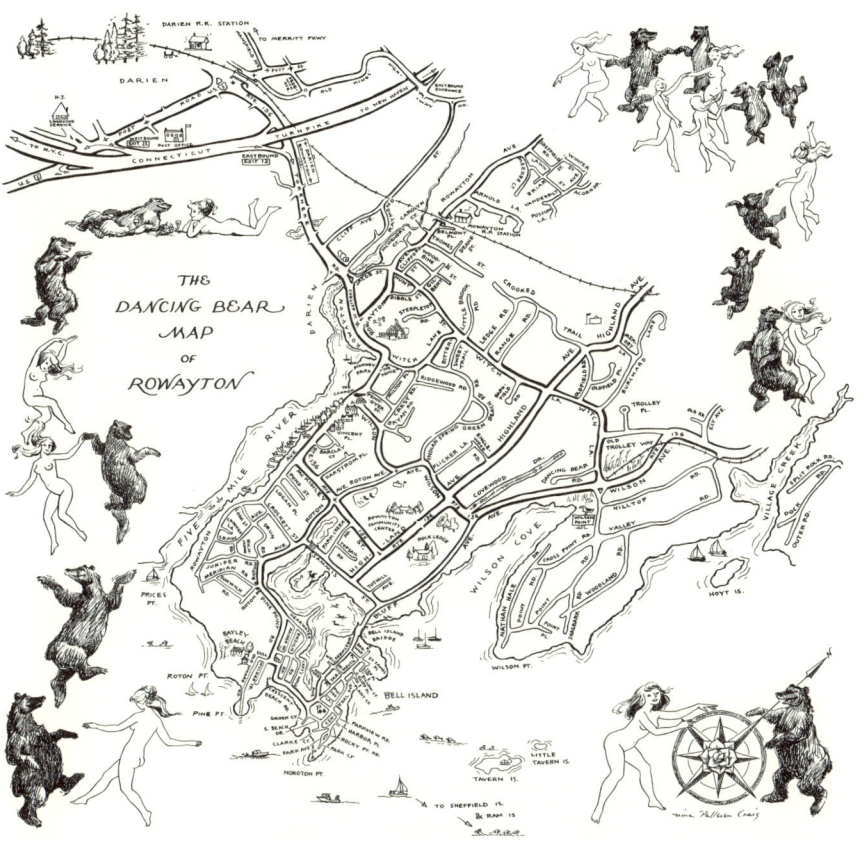

THE
DANCING BEAR
MAP
OF
ROWAYTON

waterfront. The commission responded by upgrading the regulations in a series of steps, first from Commercial zone to Business #1, requiring a side-yard setback of twelve feet; then to Business #3, increasing minimum open space to 40 percent of the land area. In 1977 most of the former Putnam-Barclay property at 123–135 Rowayton Avenue was covered by an office building of the Cold Water Fish Corporation. The following year future waterfront buildings were limited to two stories and a maximum height of thirty feet. Since then the maximum building size has been modified still again, allowing two and one-half stories and a height of thirty-five feet.

Zoning restrictions failed to hamper construction in Rowayton. Guider's store on the McKinley Street-Rowayton Avenue corner was expanded, renovated, and converted into offices. Roy M. Boe of Darien, owner of professional basketball and hockey teams in New York, built office buildings at

Developer's Delight

154 119 Rowayton Avenue, and at the White Bridge on Tokeneke Road. Lee F. Hartog, owner of the Rowayton Marine Works, remodeled the Aaron Stevens homestead at 107 Rowayton Avenue into offices. R. G. Ely built new office-apartment buildings at 65 and 75 Rowayton Avenue.

In the 1980s two-story office structures were erected at 121 Rowayton Avenue, and at number 105, site of the former Rowayton Garage-cum-Marine Works, completed in 1988. During that same year the storage and spray painting shed and the spar and repair shed at the Boatworks, Inc. (successors to Wm. P. Jenkins Boatyard at 95 Rowayton Avenue) were converted to office use. The rush to provide office accommodations in picturesque Rowayton was influenced, of course, by nearby Stamford as it became the fastest growing city in the nation. Tiny Rowayton was not in the same league, but was swept along like the tail of Stamford's kite.

By the early 1980s the appetite for Rowayton real estate bordered on the ravenous and seemed equally insatiable. Cost was no object. Prices soared. A one-quarter acre lot in B zone, which sold for $2,500 twenty-five years before, was worth $150,000. Today virtually every building lot has been built upon. New construction is nearly nonexistent. Builders are temporarily turning to repairs and renovations to keep busy.

Rowayton on the half shell

For Whom The Bell Tolls

*I*N 1875 THE City of Norwalk (then known as the Second Taxing District) established a water company, piping water from a reservoir in Wilton to serve South Norwalk. The City of Norwalk ("uptown" Norwalk, the present First Taxing District) had its own water company to serve that section of the city. Twenty-six years were to pass before water mains were to be extended down into the Rowayton area. The prime mover for water extension was Dudley E. Hoyt, descendent of earliest settlers, Highland Avenue resident, and local building contractor. Hoyt had built a number of cottages at Pine Point, as well as a large mansion for B.F. DeKlyn on the point itself (hence NYLKED Terrace—DeKlyn spelled backwards). In 1894 Hoyt had built the first Norwalk Yacht Club building at 59 Bluff Avenue. More recently he had acquired a number of building lots along Pine Point Road adjacent to Roton Point Park.

Hoyt proposed to the water company that these various properties be serviced. In November 1901 he was awarded a contract to install a water main from Flax Hill Road down Highland Avenue, across the railroad bridge, onto the trolley trestle across Farm Creek to Pine Point.[1] The contract was for $11,000! Soon after, the water main was extended into Rowayton proper with a sprinkling of hydrants here and there.

With the installation of hydrants came a whole new concept in fire protection. Until then the principal conveyance of water to fight fires in rural areas without city water was the trusty "Bucket Brigade." Men and boys, and sometimes ladies, would form a line stretching from the scene of fire to the nearest water source. Filled buckets would be rapidly (and carelessly) passed to be emptied upon the flames, and fro to be refilled. Not only ineffi-

155

The general store of Charles H. Thomes was situated in the center of the village between 145 and 151 Rowayton Avenue. Totally destroyed by fire during the winter of 1901–02, it instigated organization of the Rowayton Hose Company, No. 1. Miraculously, Vincent's saloon adjacent to the store survived unscathed.

cient, but usually ineffective!

During the decade preceding the coming of hydrants, local residents had been terrified by a series of serious fires in and around the immediate neighborhood. In 1894 the large residence of Captain John H. Lowndes, corner of Crockett Street and Rowayton Avenue, had burned unhindered. Soon thereafter a virtual conflagration eliminated eight or ten "cottages" from the Bell Island hilltop during a nor-westerly gale. Only the previous year one of the larger stores in the center of the village, Charles H. Thomes' General Store at 149 Rowayton Avenue, was destroyed by huge flames that threatened the entire center. Rowayton firemen telephoned the nearest fire department, South Norwalk, to come to their aid. And come they did, with the buckets and pike poles, by the fastest transportation possible—trolley car!

The hour was late. Trolley service had ended for the day. The trolley barns were more than a mile away in the center of Norwalk. It was necessary to hire a special car. To make matters worse, the trolley tracks terminated at the corner of McKinley Street and Rowayton Avenue, a good running distance from the blaze. Not surprisingly, when the South Norwalk lads finally got there, only embers remained. (Surprisingly enough, however, the saloon of John Vincent, which stood next door, was inexplicably spared.)

Rowayton on the half shell

These fires, one after the other, stimulated the birth of not one, but two fire companies in Rowayton. Some time in the 1890s—it is difficult to establish exactly when as the records are nonexistent today, as are the participants—Rowayton's first fire company was organized to be known as the Reliance Hook and Ladder Company.* The membership of the "Hooks" represented a goodly cross section of the males of the village, but the dominate ones were those middle-aged and over, better heeled, less apt to be receptive to innovation, including the additional expense for city water, for instance. After all, who wanted to be beholden to that far-away place, South Norwalk? But the water mains came. They were to cause a crisis.

A schism developed among the Reliance members. It was brought about, as so often happens, by the younger members frustrated by the staid policies of their elders. The leader of the movement was Edwin Lee Stevens, son of Civil War veteran, James Stevens. A home painter and decorator, he later built the residence at 132 Rowayton Avenue. Now that hydrants were here, Stevens and friends advocated more Hose and less Hooks. They sought advice of their friendly fireman in South Norwalk, David Harford, secretary of the State Firemen's Association. Harford worked full time as a bridge tender, and part time as a volunteer fireman. He later became chief of Norwalk's fire department.

Harford advised the young turks to resign from the Reliance Hook and Ladder Company and form a second company, a Hose company. On November 8, 1902, the following stalwarts did just that and established the Rowayton Hose Company: Herbert M. Arnold, Harry S. Bryan, William O. Clark, E. Howard Evory, Frank J. Lockwood, Elbert J. Marsh, Royal A. Mills, George Moore, William Moore, Jr., John Plander, Joseph S. Pennell, Moses H. Rackett, Edwin L. Stevens, George W. Stevens, Earl F. Thomas, and Charles W. Wells.[2] So started a heated rivalry between Rowayton firemen that was to last for twenty years.

"Eddie" Stevens, the founding father, became the first chief (foreman). Dudley Hoyt, who was primarily responsible for the installation of fire hydrants, was elected to lifelong honorary membership. Soon after organizing, the Hose Company attained statewide recognition by admission to the

*It has been a common misconception these many years that the reverse was true - that the Hose Company was founded earlier than the Reliance. This was the opinion of the author, until researching for this book. However, two factors mitigate against this theory: 1. Mrs. Emily Stevens Merriman, of Canaan, Connecticut, daughter of an early fireman, Earle P. Stevens, clearly recalled her father stating the Hose Company splintered from the Reliance when they formed in 1902. He was there. 2. A contemporary picture of some members of the Reliance exists. None of those shown were ever enrolled as members of the Hose Company, which would have been very probable had the Hose Company been older.

For Whom the Bell Tolls

Firefighting equipment in 1903 was rather modest by today's standards.

Connecticut State Firemen's Association, aided and abetted by their sponsor, the Association Secretary, David Harford.

The barn of William Cushman at the head of Logan Place was to serve as the first headquarters of the Hose Company. The next to serve was the barn of Charles Thomes which stood at number one Witch Lane. In 1902 the Hose Company moved to the water's edge into the boathouse of Charles Klein at 169 Rowayton Avenue. The rolling equipment consisted of a two wheel hand-drawn jumper and a converted grocery wagon bedecked with lanterns, helmets, and buckets. A "Grand Fair" was held in the building December 4th and 5th, 1903, to initiate a fund drive for a proper firehouse. The drive culminated in 1905 with the construction of a two-story structure, appropriately adjoining the Thomes store fire site at 151 Rowayton Avenue. The new building was complete with full basement, equipment room (including pool table), meeting room, with a second-floor porch across the front and back which overlooked the river, all capped by a jaunty bell tower. Inside the tower hung the same bell that for years had signalled the arrival and departure of excursion steamers at Roton Point Park. A massive casting, the bell is now mounted on the roof of the present fire station, no longer used to pierce the stillness of a fiery night.

Rowayton on the half shell

QUARTERS OF THE RELIANCE HOOK & LADDER CO., ROWAYTON, CT.

Built on the site of Thomes' store by the Reliance Hook and Ladder Company in 1905, the building still serves the community as the Rowayton Arts Center.

The men of the Reliance Hook and Ladder were not to be outdone. That same year, 1905, they built a very similar firehouse for themselves. It was also of two stories with porches overlooking the river, also measuring 25x50 feet, with full basement, meeting rooms, a dumb waiter, and of course the essential pool table. It, too, was adjoining the site of the Thomes store fire, at 145 Rowayton Avenue. The building now serves as the Rowayton Arts Center. The two firehouses stood less than a hundred feet apart, making for spirited competition and undoubtedly enhanced the quality of fire protection generally. The Reliance men purchased a long heavy iron truck laden with extra long, extra wide, extra heavy wooden extension ladders. Loaded with axes, pikes, and other gear, the truck required a good strong team of horses to get it to the scene of a fire. John Brundage, a farmer who lived directly across the street, was surely their most important member. John had just such a team right handy which was hired to pull the truck. On the way to a fire, John would swing up and ride one of the horses bareback off to glory, his long white beard flowing in the wind.

A thick iron ring some five feet in diameter, from a railroad engine drive wheel, hung in the alley way between the firehouse and John Vincent's saloon. It was used in lieu of a bell to summon Reliance members. The ring was struck with a sledge hammer kept nearby—a constant source of merri-

For Whom the Bell Tolls

ment for the youth of the village whether there happened to be a fire or not.

It would be the height of understatement to say the splitting into two of the firefighting forces was not without rancor. The wounds were deep and were slow to heal. Evidence of sharp and not always friendly rivalry was apparent at the sounding of each alarm. Perhaps it peaked in ugliness in 1915 when the chief of the "Hooks," a great uncle of the author, was playing a Hose Company hose from a neighboring porch onto the hot fire of the Albert Hartog home at 105 Rowayton Avenue. Suddenly the hose went dead, leaving the chief in a seriously exposed position. One of the chief's brothers at the scene of the fire traced the cause to the hydrant which he found had been shut off by a Hose Company member. Why? Simply because the hose belonged to the Hose Company and was in the hands of a bloody Hook![1] Grabbing a heavy iron spanner wrench the faithful brother reopened the hydrant, and brandishing the wrench high above his head, defied any Hose Company member to tamper with the hydrant further at the risk of sudden death.

Another long remembered event took place on one snowy winter's night. An alarm signalled a house on fire "up the street." The Hose Company boys, being spryer, were first to respond with their hand-drawn jumper and wagon. Driver John Brundage of the Reliance rapidly hitched up the heavy horse-drawn hook and ladder truck. The race was on. Up ahead the Hose boys had bogged down in the snow and ice at Bee-Hive curve, at the foot of United Church hill. As John and the Hooks approached at full gallop, the Hose men with that extra strength that only panic can supply, pulled and pushed their rigs into a snow bank. Just in the nick of time. Without missing a stride, the Hooks breezed merrily past without so much as a glance.

There was, of course, a warmer side to the rivalry that centered around the pool tables. Pool was a great pastime in the early part of the century. The Hose and the Hooks held tournaments annually, scores tallied on overhead wires weighted with tally markers, prizes awarded, all amid an atmosphere of good fun, fellowship, and respect.

The ancient rivalry came to an end when the Reliance Hook and Ladder Company disbanded in 1923, a victim of the mortality tables. The young bloods of the village had been attracted to the Hose Company in ever-increasing numbers over the years, while their friendly enemies withered. After disbanding, only a handful of Hooks continued their interest in firefighting by joining the Hose Company. The much outdated horse-drawn ladder truck of the Reliance was difficult to dispose of. It was pulled across the street into a vacant lot and left there to rust away. But instead, it became a portent of things to come. That vacant lot is the present site of the Rowayton Hose

Rowayton on the half shell

Mead Brothers' store at 167 Rowayton Avenue was built in the 1880s. Rowayton's first "department" store and site of the first telephone in the village, it was destroyed by fire December 18, 1934. Photo c. 1905.

Company! With admirable foresight the surviving fire company acquired the property in 1956 from William P. Jenkins for five thousand dollars, obtained a mortgage, and built a four-bay masonry building to accommodate their expanding inventory of modern equipment.

The establishment and development of the fire companies had a great impact upon the social life of the community over the years. As both companies were always in need of funds, benefits of many kinds—dinners, recitals, plays, parties, and dances—were regularly held. The meeting rooms were made available for wedding receptions, scout and civic meetings, political rallies, as well as for the polls each election day.

Early in the 1920s the Hose Company members hit upon an idea that was to become a major community event—the Oyster Supper. How appropriately Rowayton! All you can eat for a dollar! Oysters fried, oysters raw, oysters stewed, potato salad, cole slaw, baked beans, bread or rolls, apple, berry, pumpkin or custard pie, coffee, tea, or milk. How could you miss it? The supper became so popular that two were held each year, fall and spring. Eventually the price of tickets inched upwards, to $1.10, $1.25, and finally to a staggering $1.50! When opened oysters hit $15 per gallon wholesale, the Oyster Supper became a thing of fond memory. Although the Oyster Sup-

For Whom the Bell Tolls

Some present-day firefighters - upon whom so much depends.

pers provided a great deal of pleasure for many, as well as a great deal of hard work for others, they failed to become a great provider for the cause.

The best source of revenue for the cause was the Firemen's Ball. The ball was held annually in mid-August for over fifty years from the early thirties to the nineteen eighties. Originally the ball was held in the dancing pavilion at Roton Point Park thanks to the generosity of the park management. After the hurricane of 1938 weakened the pilings beneath the dancing pavilion, the ball was held on the vast porch of the Roton Point Hotel. The Firemen's Ball became THE social event of the summer, and, incidentally, a major financial crutch to the firemen. Dance tickets were sold house-to-house to residents throughout the Rowayton area from the fire trucks. Hearing the sound of a fire truck in his driveway, the householder was often found standing ready at the door with cash in hand when the deserving volunteer rang the bell.

Rowayton has not been without its share of spectacular conflagrations. Among them have been the Stevens Oyster House on the "lower dock," 65 Rowayton Avenue in 1909; the two Hartog homes at 105 and 107 Rowayton Avenue in 1915; the Farrell mansion, a huge half-timbered house less than four years old, on the occasion of a daughter's wedding reception in 1913; Sam Mead's store at 167 Rowayton Avenue, December 18, 1934, where the heat was so intense the hose ignited at the hydrant; and the Boylston carriage factory on a snowy night in February 1944.

Rowayton on the half shell

Although many injuries from fires have been suffered through the years, no lives had been lost in local fires until December 26, 1947. During that fatal day a record twenty-seven inches of snow had fallen. Early in the evening Mrs. Donald MacKenzie was trapped in her home at 44 Roton Avenue, and perished before firemen reached her. Ironically, exactly one month later to the day, Harvey Cooke of Pine Point dashed back into his burning home and burned to death in the inferno. Fortunately there have been no other fatalities. May there never be.

Because of the devotion, regardless of motivation, of the Rowayton Volunteer Firemen, this is the only area of Norwalk still providing its own fire protection. All Rowayton firemen serve strictly as volunteers. None, including officers, are compensated. Their efforts are responsible for a greatly reduced tax levy. Purchases are for equipment only. The tools are furnished by the taxpayer, but the volunteers do the job. The job is done well, at untold savings, thanks to this energetic group of civic minded men.

ANNUAL OYSTER SUPPER

GIVEN BY

Rowayton Hose Co. No. 1, Inc.

AT

ROWAYTON HOSE HOUSE

Friday Evening, December 4, 1942

5:30 TO 9 P.M.

ADMISSION $1.00　::　TAX .10　::　TOTAL $1.10

For Whom the Bell Tolls

EPILOGUE

WHAT IS TO be learned from the long litany of Rowayton's land development? One fact that stands out is, situated as we are in the shadows of New York City and Stamford, we are in constant danger of becoming unbearably over-crowded. As urban population continues to grow unfettered, so too will the demand for desirable suburban real estate. With open land no longer available for development here, persistent pressure will be focused upon increasing the density of land use and air space. One thing is certain. Avarice and greed of property owners and developers will not cease with our generation. Multi-story, multi-purpose buildings will be continuously advocated.

Where, then, lies our hope and our strength to preserve and protect the high quality of life we enjoy in Rowayton? They lie in the zoing laws—the bedrock of our lifestyle. Zoning did not come to Norwalk until 1929, and not a moment too soon. During the first sixty years zoning has not been fully effective, primarily because of the sad lack of enforcement. Not until just recently has Norwalk enjoyed the luxury of a full-time zoning enforcement officer per se!

With strong stiffening of enforcement, combined with appropriate punishment for all offenders, there is hope. Strength lies in the active participation of all citizens that effective enforcement requires. The neighbor who knows of a zoning violation, and who, for whatever reason—fear of retaliation, loss of friendship, timidity, or sheer cowardice—shies away from notifying the zoning enforcement officer, fails in his obligation to his community and to his own fellow man. The zoning regulations must be constantly strengthened and enforced without favor if future generations are to enjoy the ambience and quality of life Rowayton offers today.

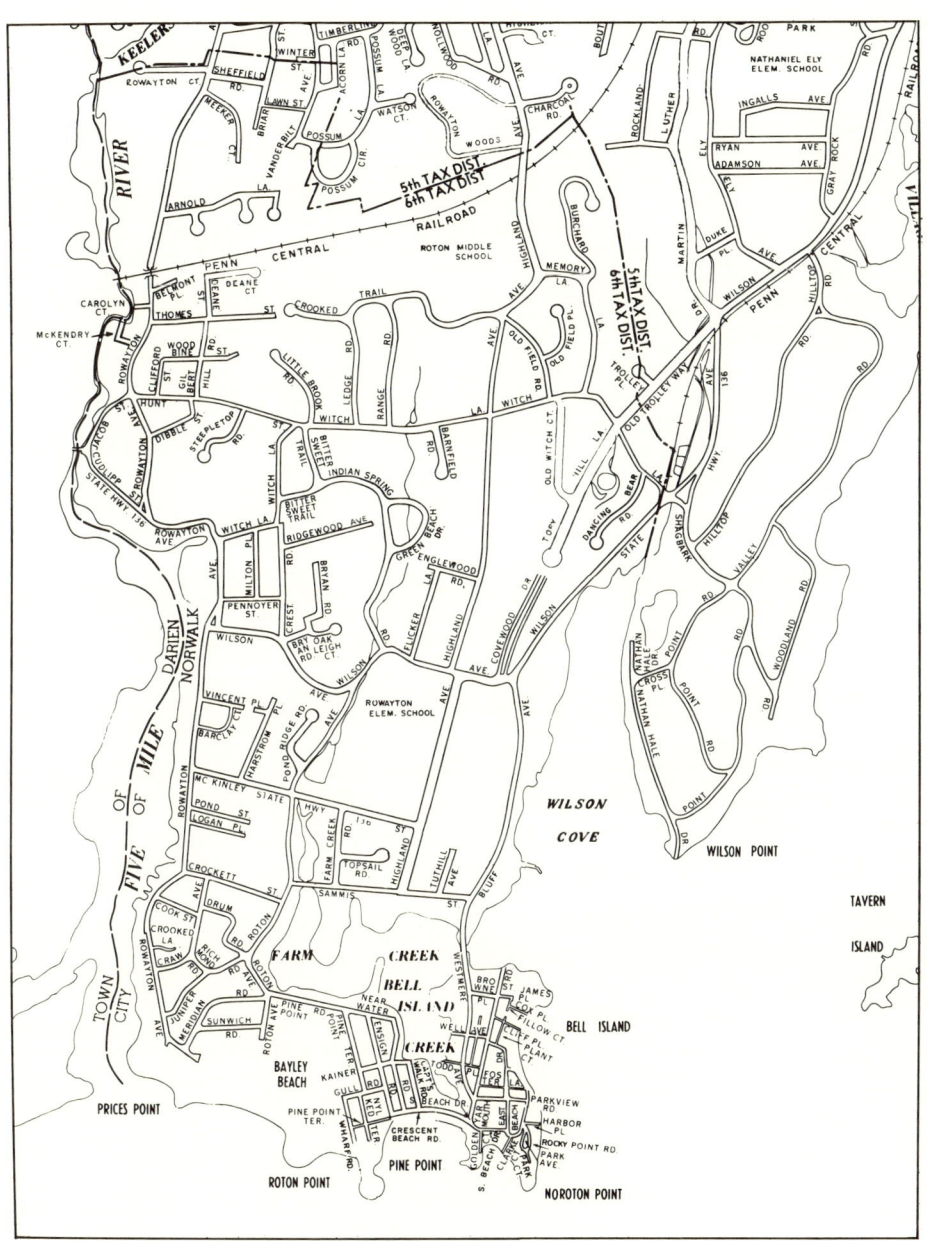

Map of Rowayton to-day

Epilogue

Today with some 1400 homes, around 4000 souls, its own churches, post office, railroad station, fire department, library, bank, parks, harbor, and beaches - a town in microcosm - with its own particular history, identity, and charm, Rowayton is in a word *unique*.

In the May 1952 issue of *Park Lane* magazine (New York), Paul Wallace probably synthesized Rowayton as well as anyone. In an article entitled "The Darien - Westport Axis" he wrote: "Jerry-built Victorian is Rowayton's major architectural style. It has no class whatever. In fact there is nothing much tangibly good about the village - it just happens to be one of the most engagingly cockeyed, delightful places in the Darien-Westport Axis, as is attested by its real estate values."

The power to control future growth and development lies in our hands. It is incumbent upon each of us, and upon those who follow, to exercise it wisely. A sage once said, "Eternal vigilance is the price of liberty." It is also the price of our way of life.

It is the civic, and moral duty of those who cherish Rowayton's lifestyle to perpetuate it.

Rowayton on the half shell

APPENDICES

Notes

Chapter 1

1. Ray, Deborah W., & Stewart, Gloria P., *Norwalk - Being a Historical Account of that Connecticut Town*, Norwalk Historical Society, 1979, p. 11 (Hereafter referred to as "Ray & Stewart").
2. Jones, Mary Jeanne Anderson, *The Fundamental Orders of Connecticut*, The United States Constitution Bicentennial Commission of Connecticut, Hartford, Conn.; 1988, pp. 19–20.
3. Dannenberg, Elsie P., *The Romance of Norwalk*, The States History Company, New York, 1929, pp. 58–60. (Hereafter referred to as "Dannenberg").
4. Wilson, Lynn W., *The History of Fairfield County, Connecticut*, J.C. Clark Publishing Company, Chicago, Ill., 1929, pp. 58–59 (Hereafter referred to as "Wilson").
5. Ray & Stewart, p. 13.
6. Hall, Edwin, *The Ancient Historical Records of Norwalk, Connecticut*, Norwalk, 1847, reprinted 1973 by Friends of Lockwood House, Inc., p. 48 (Hereafter referred to as "Hall").
7. Ray & Stewart, p. 13.
8. Dannenberg, p. 28.
9. Hayes, Nelson, *The Destiny of an Indian Village*, Norwalk, Conn., 1933, p. 8.
10. Lynch, William, arrowhead collection, Rowayton Historical Society.
11. Ray & Stewart, footnote, p. 11.
12. Ibid, p. 13.

Chapter 2

1. Hall, p. 16, Plan of the ancient settlement.
2. Selleck, Charles M., *Norwalk*, 1896, p. 55 (Hereafter "Selleck").
3. Hall, p. 57.
4. Ray & Stewart, p. 30.
5. Selleck, p. 31.
6. Street, Harry S., interview, December 1985.
7. Ray & Stewart, p. 30.
8. Ibid, pp. 22–23.
9. Hall, p. 84.
10. Hunt, Malcolm P., *Names and Places of Old Norwalk*, Friends of Lockwood House, 1976, pp. 22–221, Norwalk Land Records (1816).
11. Hall, p. 69.
12. McLean, Louise H., *Darien Historical Society Annual*, 1982, p. 6.
13. Hall, p. 52.

Chapter 3

1. Wilson, p. 41.
2. Ray & Stewart, p. 35, footnote. "Of the fourteen signatures, seven were Raymonds, probably all of the young male members of the family."

Chapter 4

1. McLean, L. H., *Darien Historical Society Annual*, 1982, p. 7, from Morse, Abner, "Genealogical Register of the Decendants of Several Ancient Puritans," Boston, Mass., 1861, Vol. 3.

Rowayton on the half shell

2. The Gershom Raymond family may have been typical. Just before the outbreak of the Revolution, February 6, 1775, the Norwalk town meeting appointed a committee of four to represent the town at the County Congress, of whom Gershom was one. The same meeting appointed his brother, Jesse, to a Committee of Inspection (for powder and arms) along with twenty others.

Gershom's son, Paul, however, enlisted in the American army subsequently becoming a sergeant. In 1781 Gershom and two dozen others were cited as "inimical and dangerous to the Liberties and Independence of the United States of America." They were ordered to appear before a committee of fellow townsmen "to show reason, if any they had, why their names should not be enrolled as aforesaid."

Names of other Rowayton property owners, then or soon after: Hazekiah Beden, John Beld(i)n, John Saunders, Jr. Their names were all duly enrolled on a list as "inimical and dangerous" filed with the town clerk.

3. Byrne, Leonard, "Nathan Hale - A Testament of Courage," *New England Galaxy*, September, 1975, c. Old Sturbridge Inc., 1975: used by permission. The text of the article follows:

"When in the summer of 1776 Nathan Hale volunteered to go behind the British lines on Long Island to obtain information sought by General Washington concerning their plans to attack the Colonials in New York City, many of his fellow officers pleaded with him to change his mind. His country had no right to demand such moral degradation of one so 'young, ardent, educated, accomplished, the pride of his commander.' A former friend at Yale, now Colonal William Hull, tried to dissuade him. Hale's reply was: 'I think I owe it to my country the accomplishment of an object so important, and so much desired by the Commander of her Armies - and I know of no other mode of obtaining the information than by assuming a disguise, and passing into the enemy's camp. I am fully sensible of the consequences of discovery and capture in such a situation. But for a year I have been attached to the army, and have not rendered any material service, while receiving compensation for which I make no return. Yet I am not influenced by the expectation of promotion or a pecuniary reward; I wish to be useful, and every kind of service, necessary for the public good, becomes honourable by being necessary. If the exigencies of my country demand a particular service, its claims to perform that services are imperious!'

"Along with Sergeant Stephen Hemstead, a close friend, Hale left the camp at Harlem Heights in September with instructions from Washington and a general order to all American sloops that they were to take him to Long Island. There were many British vessels in the Sound and on the East River. Hostile scouting parties roamed the shores. Hale travelled to Norwalk where he is reported to have engaged the sloop 'Huntington,' commanded by Captain Pond. Pond's sloop was probably a modified whaleboat, designed for easy maneuverability. Such boats were common in the Sound during the Revolution as independent warring vessels. The usual ferry to Long Island run by the Raymonds of Norwalk had been interrupted by the presence in that area of the British twelve gun brig 'Halifax,' commanded by Captain Quarme.

"They set sail for Huntington Bay. Two hours before dawn he landed at Great Neck (Eaton's Neck) on the east side of the harbor at a point known as the 'Cedars,' the farm of James Fleet. He was gone about two weeks; when taken, exact drawings of the works of the enemy, with descriptions and notes in Latin were found secreted in the soles of his shoes. He must have learned that New York had fallen to the British on the 15th, and that the defeated Americans had been crowded back to the heights above Harlem.

"Hale had actually entered the main Royal encampment since arriving on Long Island wearing a red ribbon or strip of red flannel attached to his hat as a sign of his loyalty to the British. He again reached the 'Cedars,' passing through the woods around British posts on Long Island on his return journey. Believing himself secure, his mis-

Notes

sion accomplished, he went to Mother Chich's Tavern (Widow Rachael Chichester, a Loyalist whose house was a rendezvous for all the Loyalists in the region) where he waited several hours, talking with customers. Sometime during the interval a man 'with a familiar face' left the room. Later Mother Chich announced that a boat was coming to the shore; Hale left thinking his boat had arrived, and on the beach encountered a party from the 'Halifax' lying around the point of Lloyd's Neck. Several men with muskets met him with the demand 'Surrender or die!'

"He was taken aboard the 'Halifax' to Captain Quarme, where he was betrayed by a 'countryman, relative, tory and renegade,' stripped and searched, his secret papers found, questioned and sent to New York under guard. Charged with his guilt, Hale confessed to being an American officer and spy. A warrant was sworn out and sealed by the British Commander-in-Chief, General William Howe, and sent to the Royal Provost Marshall to take Hale, that day convicted, into custody and see that he be hanged by the neck until dead 'tomorrow morning at daybreak.'

"He went to his death probably wearing a course white gown and cap trimmed with black. He was forced to kneel on his coffin while men finished digging his grave and preparing the gallows. According to William Hull, who related the incident by means of Captain Montresor's description, Hale was 'calm and bore himself with gentle dignity, the consciousness of rectitude and high intentions.' Provost Marshall Cunningham demanded a dying speech and confession. Hale's reply, 'I regret that I have but one life to lose for my country' enraged Cunningham who ordered that he be swung off.

"Hale's execution was deemed important enough for Washington to be formerly notified. On the evening of September 22nd, the daily orders of the British Commander-in-Chief to his army contained the following note: 'A spy from the enemy (by his own full confession) apprehended last night, was this day executed in front of the Artillery Park.'

"Late in the evening of the 22nd Capt. John Montresor of British Engineers serving as aide-de-camp to Howe, appeared under a flag of truce at the American outposts on Harlem Plains. He bore a letter to Washington respecting a change of prisoners. Among those who went to meet him were Israel Putnam, Alexander Hamilton and William Hull. To them Montresor gave the information that Hale had been executed that morning as a spy. He was twenty-one years of age."

4. Wilson, L.W., p. 631. Text follows:

"To the Honorable, the General Assembly of the State of Connecticut, now sitting at Hartford:

"The memorial of us, the subscribers, inhabitants of the town of Norwalk, in said State, humbly sheweth: That the principal place of rendezvous for the enemy's shipping that cruise in the sound, is in Huntington Bay, on Long Island shore, where they have ever since took possession of New York and Long Island, been almost constantly stationed for the purpose of cruising in the sound, and for annoying, distressing, and plundering the inhabitants that live near the shores in the western towns in this State; that the shores easterly and westerly in said Norwalk, are so extensive, and there are so many points and necks of land that put out into the sound, that it is impossible for his town to furnish a sufficient number of men to guard every part thereof from the ravages of the enemy; that Huntington Bay is not more than eight or nine miles southerly from the island's points and shores in said Norwalk, and that the enemy frequently, just at night, cross the sound, and come upon us and take away our stock, and plunder us, notwithstanding the utmost care to prevent it; and that the enemy have in some instances taken off part of our guards, and they very often of late, come hovering about our shores, and anchor about our islands with small armed sloops, and boats come within our harbor, and in two instances, have come in the night up our harbors and fired upon our houses, which causes frequent alarms, and creates great uneasiness among the women and children, who expect to be taken prisoners, or be robbed, plundered and deprived of their whole subsistence and comforts of life; and that as we have no

Rowayton on the half shell

armed force on the water, we have it not in our power to prevent the enemy's small sloops and boats coming into our harbors and distressing us. But your Honors' memorialists humbly conceive it would be otherwise, in case there would be an armed sloop, of about six or eight guns, to cruise in the sound along the western shores in this State, from the experience that the inhabitants had of Captain Hawley's cruising in the sound last summer—as a vessel of such force would be sufficient to encounter and repel the enemy's small craft, and prevent them from coming within our harbors, and landing on our points, necks of land, and shores, and thereby relieve us in a great measure from alarms, distresses, and danger. Whereupon your Honors' memorialists humbly pray your Honors to take their matter into consideration, and order that a well fitted vessel of about six or eight guns be purchased, to cruise in the sound, at the public expense, for the protection of the western shores in this State, and the relief of the inhabitants thereof from the distress and danger they are in from the enemy; or in such other way grant relief in the premises, as your Honors in your great wisdom shall judge best, and your Honors' memorialists, as in duty bound, shall ever pray.
"Dated at Norwalk, the 14th day of October, A.D. 1777."

5. For the burning of Norwalk British General William Tryon had some 2600 troops, July 11, 1779. American General Parsons reported damages as follows: 130 houses, 87 barns, 22 stores, 17 shops, 4 mills, 1 church, 1 meetinghouse.

6. Lossing, Benson J., *Pictorial Field Book of the Revolution*, Harper Brothers, New York, N.Y., 1851. Lossing interviewed Nathaniel Raymond in 1848, who was then aged ninety-five, and had always lived at the "Old Well" (then West Norwalk Wharf, now South Norwalk). He remembered Tryon's raid and seeing Grumman's hill "red with British." A corporal, he took his mother and father to safety three miles away (Rowayton area?), then returned and fought the British.

7. Massachusetts Historical Collection:

"Middlesex
August 30, 1780

To Colonel John Mead:

On the night before the 29th instant a party of the enemy from Long Island in a hostile violent manner entered the house of Jesse Raymond of sd Middlesex, and robbed and plundered him to the value of L150 in silver money besides breaking doors, windows, desks, cases of drawers, and the like, carrying off his best cloaths, striped his house of the greater part of his household utensils, etc; the same night a party of the enemy from Long Island drew near Gorman's Mills, in the sd Middlesex, where they lately had been plundering sundry times, being hailed by the small guard there stationed for the night, the enemy being greatly superior to the guard in numbers, fired upon them, whereby one guard unfortunately was killed by them, and two others of said guard were wounded.
In as much as this particular place is so infested, we desire and request that some way may speedily be devised for our relief, and that a Company may be granted to us as a guard on each side of Five Mile River, which might be a help to each other.
The above request is in behalf of ourselves and the rest of the inhabitants.

Capt. John Bell
Capt. Nathaniel Slason"

8. "Memorial of Jesse Raymond of Norwalk to the General Assembly of the State of Connecticut, at their present session in Hartford, Oct. AD 1780
"That the sd Jesse Raymond on the night before the 29th day of August 1780 being in his own dwelling house in said Norwalk in the peace of God and the country, in the dead of night his sd dwelling house was surrounded, beset, and broken open and entered by a number of the enemy from Long Island, and then and there took from

Notes

your memorialist the several articles mentioned in a certain memorandum to which this memorial is annexed, amounting to the sum of L155.8 money . . . and the same was by said enemy carried off and your memorialist very nearly escaping them who had threatened to burn sd house if they could not find your memorialist who providentially escaped the misfortune of falling into their hands, and prays that the State and other rates and taxes due or that shall become due from your memorialist to the amount of L155.8 as aforesd, may be abated or in some way grant relief to your memorialist, as in wisdom your Honors shall find just and right.

> Men's and women's clothes
> 1 best feather bed
> Dyches English dictionary
> 1 Psalm book Watts   4/Id
> Flavel's Husbandry Spiritualized
> & a number of other books
> Sinch and saddle
> 10 cakes chocolate   35/
> 1 copper coffee pott
> 1 pr. nail cutters   3/
> 1 watch seal   5/
> 1 magnet & box   6/
> 1 case of drawers, mahogany
> front, broke all to slivers   L10

"His claim for losses on August 28, 1780, was reimbursed with a Fire Lands claim in Ohio."

"Connecticut Archives XXI–120 Memorial of Jesse Raymond dated May 16, 1781

"Sometime before the 19th of March 1781 your memorialist lodged in the dwelling house of Joseph Mather (his brother-in-law) of Middlesex Parish to secrete from the enemy, three trunks with goods and effects to considerable value among which were 3 State notes of L10 each . . .

"A party of the enemy from Long Island under the command of Capt. McAlpine were by force of arms violently taken among many other valuable effects and carried off from sd Mather's house."

"State Records of Conn. Vol. II: List of Norwalk men granted abatement of taxes in 1781 for being "plundered and captivated by the enemy" includes the following Rowayton and Brookside families:

	Claims	Sums Abated
Jesse Raymond	L 167	L 10
John Reed	27	—
Isaac Richards	56	6
Eli Reed	69	7
Benjamin Reed	70	8
Nathan Waring & father	103	5
Mary Reed	53	3
Stephen St. John 2nd	171	20 "

9. Thaddeus Bell, Jr., one of the kidnapped prisoners, John Bates, John Dibble, and David Lockwood.

10. September 16, 1781 - Colonel Upham, Commissary of prisoners at Lloyd's Neck to General Parsons: Agrees with Parsons that prisoners would be exchanged "as soon as consistent with public views, we are on each side pursuing; have therefore consented to the exchange of Mr. Hewin and John Bell for Lieutenant Smith; Bell will be sent out as soon as possible - the Reverend Dr. Mather is also to be exchanged for the Rev. Dr. Badoin, the former will be sent with Mmr. Bell. Phinehas Waterbury and Samuel Richards will go at the same time in exchange for Lyon and Hait, now at Hartford.

As to the others now in confinement with us, I beg leave also to refer you to Captain Walker [i.e., Parsons' Aide] for my sentiments and the steps I have taken."

Chapter 5

1. Mather, Frederick, *Refugees of 1776 from Long Island to Connecticut*, p. 222.
2. General Parsons to Gov. Trumbull, October 15, 1781, "Mr. Thaddeus Bell of Middlesex has come from the Provost in New York on his parole for a short time, when he must return to his confinement unless he can effect his exchange for one Conkling Shadden, now in Hartford goal. As there now seems to an inclination on the part of the enemy to drop the matter they have so long contended with the State about, I could wish as many prisoners confined by the enemy might be liberated as we have proper subjects of exchange in our hands."
   (When Darien became a town in 1820, a Thaddeus Bell was their first state representative. Quite possibly our subject.)
3. Colonel Stephen St. John, 2nd to Gen'l Parsons, October 10, 1781, "Dear General: I have to solicit once more a permission for myself and son to return to New York to answer our paroles. We have hitherto been detained" by orders of Colonel Skinner, Commissary of Prisoners, "and the injunction laid on us by your Honor of the 16th of September last, but hope those difficulties that then subsisted are now removed and that we may have your Honor's permission to return to New York again immediately."
4. Dannenberg, pp. 168 and 169.
5. Ibid, p. 148
6. Ray & Stewart, p. 64.
7. Dannenberg, p. 148.
8. Ray & Stewart, p. 67.
   One of Esaias Bouton's sons, Nathan, a teenager and an avowed Tory, fled to Long Island where he joined the British navy. Captured by the patriots while visiting home, he was held by the selectmen in exchange for an American in British hands.

Chapter 6

1. Ray & Stewart, p. 87.
2. Seeley, Alfred, *Ledger for 1825*, Archives, Rowayton Historical Society.
3. Photostatic copy, Archives, Rowayton Historical Society.
4. Ray & Stewart, p. 75; Mills, Oscar S., "History of Rowayton," typed manuscript, Archives, Rowayton Historical Society.
5. Shepard, William R., *The Story of New Amsterdam*, Alfred Knopf, New York, N.Y., 1926, p. 14.
6. Ray & Stewart, p. 89.

Chapter 7

1. Dannenberg, p. 255.
2. *Norwalk Gazette*, issue of January 1, 1869.
3. Crockett, H. L., "Reminiscences, 1948," Archives, Rowayton Historical Society.
4. Dannenberg, p. 261.
5. Hoyt, Mary Lynch, interview, January 1987.

Chapter 8

1. Ray & Stewart, p. 108.
2. Leech, Margaret, *Reveille in Washington*, Harper Bros., New York, N.Y., 1941, p. 217.
3. *Norwalk Hour*, June 8, 1942.
4. Ray & Stewart, pp. 132–133.

Notes

Chapter 9

1. McDonough, James L., *Stones River*, Knoxville, Tenn., 1980, p. 12.
2. Wing, Henry E., *When The President Kissed Me*, Eaton and Mains, New York, N.Y., 1913.
3. Beers, F. W., *Survey of the Town of Norwalk*, Philadelphia, Pa., 1867.
4. Minute Book, Rowayton Gun Committee, Archives, Rowayton Historical Society.
5. Leech, Margaret, *Reveille in Washington*, Harper Bros., New York, N.Y., 1941, p. 217.
6. *Norwalk Hour*, June 8, 1942.
7. Tuttle, Mrs. H. Croswell, nee Cook, Penelope S., "Reminiscences of Rowayton," manuscript, Archives, Rowayton Historical Society.

Chapter 10

1. Kochiss, John M., *Oystering from New York to Boston*, Middletown, Conn., 1974, p. 17 (Hereafter as "Kochiss").
2. Ingersoll, Ernest, *The Oyster Industry*, Department of the Interior, Washington, D.C. 1881, p. 90 (Hereafter as "Ingersoll").
3. Kochiss, pp. 5, 6, and 7.
4. Ibid, p. 11.
5. Ibid, pp. 18, 19.
6. Ingersoll, p. 90.
7. Ibid, p. 90.
8. Kochiss, pp. 131–132.
9. *Encyclopedia of Biography*.
10. "Fourth Report," Shell Fish Commission, State of Connecticut, 1885, p. 14.
11. "Annual List of Merchant Vessels of the United States," 28th issue, U.S. Government Printing Office, Washington, D.C., 1896.
12. Kochiss, pp. 132–133.
13. Ibid, p. 155.
14. Kellogg, James L., *Shell Fish Industries*, Henry Holt & Co., New York, N.Y., 1910, p. 124.
15. Collins, J. W., "Notes on the Oyster Fisheries of Connecticut," Bulletin U.S. Fisheries Commission, U.S. Government Printing Office, Washington, D.C., 1891. Also see Dannenberg, p. 356.
16. Kochiss, p. 21.
17. Mills, Oscar S., Manuscript, 1929, p. 21, Archives, Rowayton Historical Society.
18. Kochiss, p. 157.

Chapter 11

1. Mead, Stanley S., "Roton Point," New Canaan Historical Society Annual, New Canaan, Conn., June 1956.
2. Ibid.
3. Ibid.
4. Ray & Stewart, p. 112.
5. *The Sentinel*, November 12, 1933, South Norwalk, Conn.
6. Raymond, Barbara J., manuscript, 1942, Archives, Rowayton Historical Society.
7. Ibid.
8. Ibid.
9. Ibid.
10. Mead, Stanley S., "Roton Point," New Canaan Historical Society, New Canaan, Conn., 1956.
11. Witnessed by the author.
12. Raymond, Barbara J., manuscript, Archives, Rowayton Historical Society.
13. Ray & Stewart, p. 190.
14. Raymond, Barbara J., manuscript, Archives, Rowayton Historical Society.

15. Ray & Stewart, p. 160.
16. Ibid, p. 160.
17. Mead, p. 96.
18. Ibid, p. 100.
19. Ibid, p. 96.
20. Ibid, p. 96.

Chapter 12

1. Tuttle, Mrs. H. Croswell, "Reminiscences of Rowayton," manuscript, Archives, Rowayton Historical Society.
2. Original minute book, "The Lyceum Library Association," Archives, Rowayton Historical Society.
3. Original minute book of The Association of the Free Library and Reading Room of Rowayton, Inc., Rowayton Library Archives.

Chapter 13

1. Ray & Stewart, p. 159.
2. Ibid, p. 161.
3. Bossone, Mauro, interview, February 7, 1989, a Traendly employee for over twenty years, as were his father and his grandfather.
4. Friend, Doris S. & Benziger, Helen L., *A Point In Time, Wilson Point, A History*, The Wilson Point Association, 1987 (Hereafter Friend & Benziger).

Chapter 14

1. Street, Harry S., interview, December 1985.
2. Dwyer, John W., interview, June 1980.
3. Sixth Taxing District, Rowayton, Conn., Archives.
4. Ibid.

Chapter 15

1. Bond, Newton F., interview, January 1989.
2. Carson, Gerald H., "Who Put the Borax in Dr. Wiley's Butter?" *American Heritage Magazine*, August 1956 issue, pp. 60–63.
3. Soybel, Myra, interview, February 27, 1989.
4. DeLuca, Mrs. Leonard, Fairfield County Savings Bank, interview, February 1989.

Chapter 16

1. Friend & Benziger, p. 16.
2. Hickson, John M., interview, March 1989.
3. Hoyt, Dudley D., interview, March 1989.
4. Hoyt, Mary Lynch, interview, October 1987.
5. Cheh, Joseph W., interview, March 1989.

Chapter 17

1. Contract, City of South Norwalk Water Department to Dudley E. Hoyt for extension of mains to Roton Point, November 11, 1901. Records, Second District Water Department, Water Street, Norwalk, Conn.
2. Kilbourn, Joseph A., "Rowayton Hose Company No. 1," 75th Anniversary Program, 1977, Rowayton Hose Company Archives.

Notes

Boat Builders And Boat Yards

Name	Rowayton Avenue Address
Richards Brothers★	#171
John O. Smith★	195
John & Charles Thomes★	121–125
Dexter Cole★	110 Five Mile River Road
Moses B. Hart★	122
Joseph Fowler★	63
Daniel Wicks	73
Andrew S. Mills	75–79
Harry S. Oberlander★	61–65 Five Mile River Rd.
Joseph Klinefelter	121–124
Rowayton Marine Works, Inc.	
Ferdinand Hartog	103–107
Stadel & Jenkins★	
George Stadel, Wm. P. Jenkins	95–99
William P. Jenkins Boatyard★	95–99 & 135–139
Charles Paight	139
Norge Boats, Inc.★	
Bjarne B. Nilsen	75
Bounty & Smith	
Arthur Bounty, D. Lester Smith	125–135
Johnson's Boatyard	
Henry L. Johnson	99
Five Mile River Marina	
George K. Johnson	75–77
The Boatworks, Inc.★	
R. Grovenor Ely & Sons	95–97
White Bridge Marina	
Leslie Johnson	169
Bait Shop, Inc.,	
Herbert VanSciver	99
Cavanaugh Marina	
Willis Cavanaugh	79–87
Hartog Rowayton Marina, Inc.	115–117
Five Mile River Works, Inc.	115–117

★Builder

Rowayton on the half shell

Taken from a list of vessels licensed to work on Connecticut natural oyster beds, Connecticut Shellfish Commissioners records, Hartford. License fee for vessels under five tons, $2.00. 50 cents per ton additional in excess of five.

License Number	Name of Vessel	Name of Captain (usually owner)	Sailing Port	Fee
18	Thistle	Wm. W. Young	Rowayton	$2.00
20	Harp	Robert J. Utz	Rowayton	6.00
26	Tillie C.	John Jarvis	Rowayton	2.00
27	Lottie	Martin M. Knowlton	Rowayton	2.00
29	Rambler	Charles Newton Raymond	Rowayton	2.00
33	Lillian	Alfred S. Crockett	Rowayton	2.00
34	Lida May	George A. Wicks	Rowayton	3.00
35	Martha	Hans Gager	Rowayton	2.00
45	Gracie	John H. Plander	Rowayton	2.00
46	Ethlene	Frank Hollins	Rowayton	2.00
53	Nancy Hanks	John Jarvis	Rowayton	2.00
54	Viola L.	George H. Ackerly	Rowayton	2.00
56	Henry R.	H. E. Walker	Rowayton	2.50
70	Flying Dutchman	Clifford Cutbill	Rowayton	2.00
74	Willis B.	Peter Boerum	Rowayton	2.00
115	Leo	Daniel H. Wicks	Rowayton	2.00
118	If	Harry W. Wells	Rowayton	2.00
119	Edwin Forrest	John H. Monsell	Rowayton	2.00
124	Mabelle	Henry L. Case	Rowayton	3.00
130	Sneak	Andrew S. Mills	Rowayton	2.00
132	Tiger	Grant B. Rackett	Rowayton	2.00
152	Amy B. Cole	Hickson W. Cole	Rowayton	2.00
163	Wanda	John S. L'Hommedieu	Rowayton	2.00
183	Jennie L.	Theron Lockwood	Rowayton	2.00
186	Flight	George Griffin	Rowayton	2.00
199	Myrtle	Charles E. Stevens	Rowayton	2.00
201	Gene	Oliver Cook	Rowayton	2.00
209	Hattie	Walter Thompson	Rowayton	2.00
218	Mosetta	Preston M. Hart	Rowayton	3.00
232	Minnie B.	Judson H. Williamson	Rowayton	2.00
242	Calista R.	F. O. White	Rowayton	2.00
257	Addie R.	John H. DeWaters★	Norwalk	4.50
266	Ivy Point	Isaac Payne	Rowayton	2.00
297	Wild Duck	Earle P. Stevens	Rowayton	2.00
313	Emma Elleron	Charles E. Stevens	Rowayton	2.50
322	Mary Underhill	Samuel Mott, Jr.	Rowayton	2.50
325	Ruby	Judson H. Williamson	Rowayton	2.50
335	Leslie	Francis A. Jarvis	Rowayton	2.00
349	Kelpie	Soloman D. Woods	Rowayton	2.00

★Resided at 15 Pennoyer Street, Rowayton

Civil War Veterans.

The following lists which were researched by the author during August 1963, are based on three sources: 1. Headstones in the Rowayton Union Cemetery; 2. the National Archives in Washington, D.C.; and 3. The 28th Anniversary Roster of Norwalk's Buckingham Post No. 12, G.A.R., 1908. The 17th Connecticut Volunteer Infantry Regiment was recruited from, and known as, the Fairfield County Regiment.

Known to have resided in Rowayton prior to enlistment:

Crockett, William Gardiner	8th Conn. Vol. Inf. Reg.
Dingee, George	Co. C. 28th Conn. Vol. Inf. Reg.
Grant, Jacob	Co. H 8th Conn. Vol. Inf. Reg.
Mills, William E.	Co. B 17th Conn. Vol. Inf. Reg.
★Tuttle, George O.	Co. A 17th Conn. Vol. Inf. Reg.

★Missing in action, May 2, 1863, Chancellersville, Va. Believed killed.

Known to have lived in Rowayton after discharge:

Baker, Henry	Co. G 3rd Conn. Vol. Inf. Reg.
Boomer, Hiram H.	Co. C 21st Conn. Vol. Inf. Reg.
Clock, Charles H.	Co. G 10th Conn. Vol. Inf. Reg.
Cowperthwaite, Wm. W.	Co. 22nd N.J. Vol. Inf. Reg.
Cushman, William H.	United States Navy
Fairweather, George	Co. H 8th Conn. Vol. Inf. Reg.
Ferris, Stephen H.	Co. H 8th Conn. Vol. Inf. Reg.
Ferris, William H., Jr.	Unit unknown
Finch, Lyman S.	Co. G 10th Conn. Vol. Inf. Reg.
Gregory, James	Co. K 48th N.Y. Vol. Inf. Reg.
Homan, William H.	Co. C 10th Conn. Vol. Inf. Reg.
Hoyt, George H.	Co. H 8th Conn. Vol. Inf. Reg.
Hoyt, John	Co. F 3rd Conn. Vol. Inf. Reg.
Hyler, William	Co. K 9th N.Y. Vol. Inf. Reg.
Ives, Charles	16th N.Y. Vol. Inf. Reg.
Johnston, Elias	Co. B 17th Conn. Vol. Inf. Reg.
Lockwood, William H.	Co. B 28th Conn. Vol. Inf. Reg.
McGraw, John	Co. I 82nd N.Y. Vol. Inf. Reg.
Meeker, Seth	Co. G 10th Conn. Vol. Inf. Reg.
Morton, Fred O.	Co. H 10th Mass. Vol. Inf. Reg.
Raymond, Horace H.	Co. G 15th Conn. Vol. Inf. Reg.
St. John, Benjamin	Co. H 23rd Conn. Vol. Inf. Reg.
Scofield, David C.	Co. B 28th Conn. Vol. Inf. Reg.
Smith, Henry T.	Co. A 17th Conn. Vol. Inf. Reg.
Stevens, James E.	Co. F 17th Conn. Vol. Inf. Reg.
Vincent, Gilbert	Co. G 10th Conn. Vol. Inf. Reg.
Webb, Henry I.	Co. F 17th Conn. Vol. Inf. Reg.
Webb, Henry L.	Co. G 10th Conn. Vol. Inf. Reg.
Whitney, James	Co. F 17th Conn. Vol. Inf. Reg.
Wilkins, William W.	Co. H 8th Conn. Vol. Inf. Reg.
Wing, Henry E.	Co. C 27th Conn. Vol. Inf. Reg.
Winus, John	Co. I 10th Conn. Vol. Inf. Reg.

The Sixth Taxing District was organized in 1923, and elected three Commissioners, one to serve a term of two years, one to serve four years, and one to serve six years. In 1925 and biennially thereafter, one to be elected to serve for a six-year term.

Year	Elected	Succeeded
1923	Samuel G. Adams, six years	
	William F. Jennings, four years	
	Carleton Meuborn, two years	
1925	Clarence E. Crofoot	Meuborn
1927	Frederick P. Stabell	Jennings
1929	Arthur M. Billard	Adams
1931	Oliver I. Clark	Stabell
1933	Clarence E. Crofoot	
1935	William H. Rusch	Billard
1937	Oliver I. Clark	
1939	Clarence E. Crofoot	
1941	William F. Breidenbach	Rusch
1943	Edgar L. Raymond, Jr.	Clark
1945	Clarence E. Crofoot	
1947	William E. LaFontaine	Breidenbach
1949	Edgar L. Raymond, Jr.	
1951	Franklin I. Smith	Crofoot
1953	Joseph R. Taylor	LaFontaine
1955	Jasper J. Harding	Raymond
1957	J. A. Davis Banks	Smith
1959	John A. Pattee	Taylor
1961	Frank E. Raymond	Harding
1963	J. A. Davis Banks	
1965	John A. Pattee	
1967	John E. Amon (appointed)	Pattee (resigned)
1967	Frank E. Raymond	
1969	Robert J. Pettus	Banks
1971	Alfred Alk	Amon
1973	Lester C. Gilman, Jr.	Raymond
1975	Robert J. Pettus	
1977	S. Peter Law	Alk
1979	Lester C. Gilman, Jr.	
1981	Robert J. Pettus	
1983	Richard M. Miner (appointed)	Pettus (resigned)
1983	Grace W. Lichtenstein	Law
1985	Donald F. McLeod	Gilman
1987	Richard M. Miner	
1989	Jonathan B. Kellogg (appointed)	McLeod (resigned)

Alberta Coal Company	See East Norwalk Coal Company.
Allen's Drug Store	159 Rowayton Avenue, c. 1925–1935. See Ritter's Drug Store.
Ancient Sycamore	Tree near corner Soundview Avenue and Fern Street. Remnants date back to Revolution. Later used by oystermen as a range to locate oyster bed boundaries.
Association of the Free Library and Reading Room of Rowayton, Inc.	Organized 1903. See Rowayton Library.
Bait Shop, Inc.	99 Rowayton Avenue, c. 1971, Bert VanSciver, prop.
Ballast Reef	Reef of rocks approx. 100 yards SW of Bayley Beach. Bare at low tide.
Ballast Reef Club	Beach and tennis club west of Bayley Beach at Price's Rocks, c. 1929–1949.
Baptist Parsonage	235 Rowayton Avenue, c. 1914–1967.
Barclay's Estate	123–135 Rowayton Avenue, c. 1890–1950. Formerly of John & Charles Thomes (boatyard), George Palmer Putnam, LePlace family.
Barn Alley	Localese for Westmere Avenue, Bell Island; also formerly West Avenue.
Bartlett's Drug Store	"Main Street" (Rowayton Avenue), Charles W. Bartlett, prop., c. 1900.
Battistone's Store	21 Jacob Street at White Bridge, John Battistone, prop. c. 1925. See: Chuck's Diner.
Bay Avenue	Former name of Pond Street, c. 1900.
Bayley Beach	Bathing beach on Long Island Sound between Roton Point Club west to Wee Burn Beach Club.
Bayley Beach Park	Park on Long Island Sound between Roton Point Club west to Wee Burn Beach Club, owned by Sixth Taxing District, named for former owner, c. 1942.
Bee Hive Corner	Ninety degree turn in Rowayton Avenue near #204 (United Church).
Belden's Point	Now Wilson Point. aka Belden's Neck.
Andrew Bell Estate	All land west of Rowayton Avenue from river north to Jacob Street, divided by Church Street, now Cudlipp Street.
Bell Island	Land south of bridge on Bluff Avenue, named for Harman H. Bell who purchased it in 1852. Formerly Raymond's Island.
Bell Island Bridge	Foot of Bluff Avenue, crossing Farm Creek at Wilson Cove.

Rowayton on the half shell

Bell's Dock	99 Rowayton Avenue, Charles W. Bell Oyster Co., owner. See: Bait Shop.
Charles W. Bell Oyster Company	99 Rowayton Avenue, c. 1885–1925. Later site of John Johnson & Son, Lobsters, and of Henry Johnson Boatyard, c. 1950s.
Bell's Pond	Opposite 105 Rowayton Avenue. Drained swamp area Wilson Avenue to Pond Street. Filled in during early 1930s.
Benny's Store (Variety)	114 Rowayton Avenue, Benjamin A. Mangels, prop., c. 1930–1936. See Rowayton News Store.
Benton's Art Studio	West end of Topping Lane. Harry Stacey Benton, prop.
Blacksmith & Horseshoer	Main Street, Arthur B. Griffin, prop., c. 1900.
Boats to Let	Rowayton Avenue opp. Guider's Store, Theron Lockwood, prop., c. 1900.
The Boatworks, Inc.	95 Rowayton Avenue & 67–71 Rowayton Avenue, formerly Wm. P. Jenkins Boatyard and Stadel & Jenkins Boatyard.
Bora Real Estate	164 Rowayton Avenue, Douglas A. Bora, prop. 1950–1983, built 154–164 Rowayton Avenue, c. 1955.
Boye Park	Park in Bell Island at East Beach.
Old Boston Post Road	Basically present Old King's Highway in Darien and Flax Hill Road in Norwalk.
Bounty-Smith Boatyard	125–133 Rowayton Avenue, Arthur Bounty and D. Lester Smith props., c. 1957–1967.
Bouton-Hoyt Cemetery	Private family cemetery north side Witch Lane east of Memory Lane. Dates back to American Revolution.
Boylston Carriage Factory	293–299 Rowayton Avenue, Francis Boylston, prop. Mfg. baby and doll carriages and invalid chairs, c. 1870–1915.
Brenner's Barber Shop	5 Railroad Place (now Belmont Pl.), Carl Brenner, prop., c. 1920s).
Broadway Ice Company	22 Crockett Street, John Broadway, prop., c. 1900–1925.
Brooker Block	112–114 Rowayton Avenue & McKinley Street. Four stores, F. T. Brooker, prop., c. 1930s.
Brookside Cemetery	Rowayton Avenue at Keeler Brook, pre-Revolution. Grave of Rev. Moses Mather, prominent patriot.
Brookside Lake Ice Company	78 Wilson Avenue, Jacob B. Raymond, prop., c. 1895–1935.
Brookside School	#1 west side Flax Hill Road north of Rowayton Avenue. Converted to residence. Built by Middle Five Mile River School District. #2 382 Highland Avenue.

Some Old Rowayton Place Names

Brown's Store (Groceries)	#1 267 Rowayton Avenue, c. 1918–1925. See Ogden's Store. #2 286 Tokeneke Road at White Bridge, Adolph Brown, prop., c. 1925–1940.
Burchard's Pond	North of Witch Lane east of Trolley Way. Ice cut for domestic use, c. 1890–1918.
Burchard's Woods	Densely wooded area east of Highland Avenue, north and west of Wilson Avenue to railroad.
Brundage's Pond	South side Wilson Avenue, opp. #7, rear present post office. Ice skating only.
Butler's Store (Grocery)	112 Rowayton Avenue, James Butler & Co., prop., c. 1927–1940(?). Successor to People's Grocery Co. (Needle's Store).
Butler's Island	Large island of high ground west side Five Mile River at mouth.
Butler's Island Creek	Tidal inlet north of Butler's Island, west side Five Mile River. aka Tokeneke Creek.
Canfield Springs	Natural springs west of Highland Avenue, north of Devil's Garden Road. aka "The Springy Place."
The Cannon	Veterans monument erected 1901 on land donated by Elias Pennoyer, corner Rowayton and Wilson avenues.
Cape Horn	Neck of land jutting into Farm Creek east of Sammis Street Bridge.
Carolyn Court Bridge	Wooden bridge across Five Mile River south of Chasmer's Pond dam.
Castle Hart	34 Sammis Street, Edward Hart, owner. Field stone mansion built c. 1907 by Theophileus Euphart. Destroyed by fire January 7, 1980. aka Castle Venice.
Castle Venice	See Castle Hart.
Cedar Street	Former name for Jacob Street.
Central Market (Meat Market)	112 Rowayton Avenue, c. 1930s.
Chasmer's Pond	Rear 310 Rowayton Avenue. Caused when NY & NH Railroad dammed Five Mile River to provide water for steam engines. Popular skating pond prior to World War II.
Chuck's Luncheonette	2 Jacob Street, Scott Albrecht, prop., c. early 1920s.
Cinderella Beauty Shop	143 Rowayton Avenue, c. 1940s. Formerly John Vincent's Saloon, John J. Newman & Sons Plumbing Shop.
Church Street	Former name for Cudlipp Street.
Cinque Hardware	1 McKinley Street, Herman Cinque, prop., c. 1933.
Coalpits Lots	Area west of Highland Avenue north of RR tracks. Timber was burned here to produce charcoal for the RR.

Rowayton on the half shell

Cole Oyster Company	51 Rowayton Avenue, c. 1890–1915(?), Hickson Cole & Dexter Cole, props.	
Collender's Point	Point of land west of Scott's Cove jutting into Long Island Sound. aka Long Neck Point.	
Columbia Grove	Copse of trees on bluff east side Five Mile River at mouth. aka Columbus Grove & Raymond's Point.	
Columbus Grove Beach	Mouth of Five Mile River east to Price's Rocks. aka Columbia Grove Beach and Rowayton Beach.	
Community Beach	59–63 Rowayton Avenue. Gift of John Sherman Hoyt for public use 1923. Principal swimming beach for Rowayton 1923–1942.	
Community Center	33 Highland Avenue. Public library, meeting rooms, paddle tennis courts, park land. Purchased by 6th District, 1967.	
Comstock Taxi Company	149 Rowayton Avenue, James Comstock, prop., c. 1930s.	
Contentment Island	West of Butler's Island, north of Fish Islands, Darien.	
Continental Can Corporation	40 Highland Avenue, Corporate World Headquarters, c. 1973.	
Cottage Avenue	Former name of Parkview Avenue, Bell Island.	
Craw's Hall	101 Rowayton Avenue, 2nd floor public meeting room, c. 1875–1920, William H. Craw, owner.	
Craw & L'Hommedieu Oyster Company	57 Rowayton Avenue, c. 1890s. Wm. H. Craw & John L'Hommedieu. Present residence converted from oyster house c. 1920 by Capt. Theodore Smith.	
Craw's Woods	South of Crockett Street between Craw & Roton avenues to Richmond Road.	
The Creek	Localese for Five Mile River Harbor. Pronounced "Krick."	
Crescent Beach Road	Western end of South Beach Drive.	
Cross Street	Former name of Hunt Street and Witch Lane east to Wilson Avenue.	
Darien Avenue	Former name of Nearwater Road.	
DeKlyn's Estate	Pine Point south of Gull Road to the Sound. B.F. DeKlyn, owner, c. 1885–1923.	
Devil's Garden Road	Soundview Avenue west of Highland to Rowayton Avenue. So named as it transversed a remote rocky and hilly area especially forbidding at night.	
Dibble Estate	177 Rowayton Avenue, c. 1820. Same family ownership for 5 generations, 150 years. 1. Alfred Seeley; 2. Alphonso Dibble; 3. S. Edward Dibble; 4. Gertrude Dibble Pinkney; 5. Wm. Pinkney, Jr., – 6th Taxing District.	

Some Old Rowayton Place Names

Dibble's Store (Meats and Grocery)	157 Rowayton Avenue. Oldest store in Rowayton. See: Rowayton Market for list of proprietors.
Douglas Houseboat Studio	65 Rowayton Avenue. 110' World War I submarine chaser moored at "Lower Dock" c. 1925–1930. Home & Studio of marine artist Harold Douglas, named "Elizabeth Ann."
Down the Street	Generally all that area of Rowayton south of Witch Lane. A friendly (?) rivalry persisted with residents living north of Witch Lane.
The Draw	Location of watering troughs west of Rowayton RR station. Trains scooped water into their boilers without stopping. Water supplied from Chasmer's Pond.
The Duck Pond	Small pond east of Vanderbilt Avenue south of Devil's Garden Road.
The Dump	Local depositories for garbage and refuse prior to municipal collections; i.e., McKinley Street & Roton Avenue, East side Highland Avenue and railroad cut, river bank at Crockett Street, Logan Place, McKinley Street, Bell's Pond, etc.
East Beach	Bell Island, east of Central Avenue overlooking Wilson Cove.
East Norwalk Coal Company	Rowayton Avenue corner of Belmont Place. Charcoal, aka Alberta's Coal Co., c. 1940s.
Elm Grove Street	Former name of Soundview Avenue.
The Elm Grove	Early stand of elm trees at corner Flax Hill Road and Soundview Avenue.
Ely's Boatyards	95 Rowayton Avenue & 67–71 Rowayton Avenue. See: Boatworks, Inc., & Jenkins Boatyard.
Ely's Brook	Brook draining area east of Roton Hill emptying into Wilson Cove. Believed by some historians, possibly erroneously, to have been "Pampasashanke Brook" named in Indian deeds.
Ely's Neck	Former name of Wilson Point. See: Belden's Neck/Point.
Ely's Neck Creek	Former name of Wilson Cove. aka Ely's Neck Cove.
Theophileus Euphart	Residence Main Street north of West Street. Early real estate agent and developer, c. 1900. Builder of Castle Hart, 33 Sammis Street, Shirley Manor, 37 Wilson Avenue & 260 Rowayton Avenue.
Excursions Boats	Large passenger boats (usually steam) that made daylight trips to coastal amusement parks, including Roton Point Park. See appendices for partial list.
Farm Creek	Tidal inlet with headwaters north of RR tracks draining west side of Highland Avenue area.

Rowayton on the half shell

	Named for St. John farm 1678–1816, of 75 acres. Later Raymond's Farm.
Farrell Estate	Wilson Avenue from Highland to Bluff Avenue, south to approx. 100 yds. north of McKinley Street and six acres west of Highland north of McKinley Street. James A. Farrell, owner, c. 1912–1947, called "Rockledge." Presently Hewitt Associates & 6th Taxing District owners.
First National Stores (Grocery)	101 Rowayton Avenue, c. 1930–1931. 114 Rowayton Avenue, c. 1931–1950s. Successor to James Butler & Co.
Fish Islands	Group of three islands south of Contentment Island, Darien.
Five Mile Landing Marina	71 Rowayton Avenue, c. 1960s. George K. Johnson, prop.
Five Mile River Landing	East side of Five Mile River south of White Bridge used by packet boats, c. 1826–1896. aka Five Mile Landing.
Five Mile River Road	Darien. Skirts west bank of river from south of Tokeneke Road to dead end. Formerly River Road and West Side Avenue.
Five Mile River Station	Proposed name for Rowayton RR Station, c. 1868. See: Grantville.
"The Float"	59 Rowayton Avenue. Docking facility, formerly bathing beach, c. 1923–1942. See: Community Beach.
Forty Second Street	Localese for Roton Avenue.
Foster Bros. Summer Resorts	Bell Island developers and real estate agents, c. 1900.
Fowler's Houseboat	Ex-oyster sloop *Lida May* (Geo. Wicks) converted by Joseph Fowler, c. 1920. Later owned and occupied by Herbert Trenchard, c. 1934–1958(?). See: Trenchard's Houseboat.
Fox Hollow	Upper Ely's Brook and Flax Hill Road, east of Roton Hill.
The Gables	Five Mile River Road at White Bridge gas station & restaurant. Built by Abraham Modney in 1927. Other props. through 1945: John Wallace, Howard Banta, Harry Derman, Albert Beres, and Roland Roberts.
Gainey's Bridge	Highland Avenue bridge over RR. Believed named for an Irish laborer. Many such camped nearby during building of RR or when new cut was made for widening to four tracks in 1894.
Garden Road	Former name of Devil's Garden Road, c. 1900.

Some Old Rowayton Place Names

"The Gas Station"	105 Rowayton Avenue, Ferdinand Hartog, Sr., prop., c. 1923–1930. Rowayton's first. Later Rowayton Marine Works.
Gene's Lobster Pound	117 Rowayton Avenue, Eugene Peffers, prop., c. 1950–1960(?).
Getner's Brook	North of Rowayton Avenue to Connecticut Avenue. See: Keeler's Brook.
Grantville	Name replaced Five Mile River Landing and Rowayton 1868 to honor donor of property for RR station, Jacob Grant. Renamed Rowayton, c. 1890.
Griffith's Store (Grocery)	167 Rowayton Avenue, c. 1930–1965, George Griffith, prop. See: Ogden's Store.
Guider's Corner	Intersection of Rowayton Avenue and McKinley Street.
Guider's Blacksmith Shop	3 McKinley Street, Charles H. Guider, prop. c. 1868–1910. Currently Velloti's Real Estate.
Guider's Real Estate	See above, c. 1900. One of Rowayton's first. C. H. Guider, prop.
Guider's Hall	112 Rowayton Avenue, 2nd floor, meeting room with stage, c. 1870–1925.
Guider's Store (Hardware and Ship Chandlery)	112 Rowayton Avenue, Charles H. Guider, prop. 1868–1910.
Hadik Park	North side Southview Avenue. 1/3 mile east of Highland Avenue near Hadik Parkway. Airplane field c. 1922. Later athletic field, c. 1930. aka Hadik Field.
Hart Estate	34 Sammis Street. Built 1907. Home of Edward Hart family since 1917. See: Castle Hart - Castle Venice.
Hartog's Boatyard	105 Rowayton Avenue. See: Rowayton Marine Works, Inc.
Head of the Salt	Near White Bridge where salt water from Long Island Sound meets flow of fresh water from Five Mile River.
Cap't. Henry's Restaurant	87 Rowayton Avenue, c. 1965–
Hewitt Associates	40 Highland Avenue, c. 1980. See: Farrell Estate.
Hickory Bluff	Rocky elevation west side Wilson Cove south to Farm Creek.
Hickory Bluff Store (Variety)	77 Bluff Avenue, c. 1885–1986. Props.: 1. George Schlichting, 2. William & Grace Valentine. See: Rowayton Yacht Club.
Higgin's Restaurant	148 Rowayton Avenue, c. 1970–1986. Henry F.B. Higgins, prop. Presently Five Mile River Grill.
Hillside Street	Former name of Crest Road from Pennoyer Street north to Witch Lane. See: Maplewood Road.

Rowayton on the half shell

Hither Islands	Terms used on early deeds for Pine Point and Roton Points.
Hoffman's Store (Grocery)	58 Roton Avenue, c. 1910s. Later Stone's Store, c. 1920s. See: Steinwald's Store.
Holmes Avenue	Former name for upper Nearwater Road, north of Kainer Road to Pine Point Road.
Hoof and Horn Creek	Foot of Ely Brook at head of Wilson Cove. British raiders from Long Island butchered cattle here during Revolution.
Hose Company Hall	151 Rowayton Avenue, 2nd floor meeting room with stage, 1903–1956. Rowayton Hose Company, No. 1.
Hoyt's Island	Wooded island east of Wilson Point south of Village Creek.
Huffington's Houseboat and Studio	Five Mile River Road, 200 yds. south of White Bridge, c. 1918–1928(?). John Huffington, artist.
Indian Field	Both sides of Highland Avenue north to approx. RR, from Witch Lane, totalling 60 acres, sequestered for Indians in 1687. aka The Old Field.
Iron Steamboat Company	Operators of excursion boats from New York City to Roton Point Park c. 1890–1929(?). Many of their vessels were coal burning steamers with walking beams and side wheels.
Ivy Point	Neck of land west side Five Mile River where river broadens and Five Mile River Road makes right angle turn. Site of Oberlander's Boatyard, c. 1900.
Jarvis Clams & Lobsters	12 Crockett Street, John Jarvis, prop., 1890s–1940s. George Jarvis, prop., 1940s–1970s.
Jenkins' Boatyard	95 Rowayton Avenue, Wm. P. Jenkins, prop., 1943–1971. Successors to Stadel & Jenkins, 1941–1943.
Joe's Barber Shop	155 Rowayton Avenue, Joseph Vitago, prop., c. 1927–1947(?). See: Rowayton Barber Shop.
Johnson's Boatyard	99 Rowayton Avenue, Henry Johnson, prop., c. 1950s.
The Junction	Localese for trolley switch Highland Avenue south of McKinley Street. Routed cars from Roton Point line east to Norwalk or west to Stamford line.
The Jungle	Area near RR tracks and Farm Creek headwaters. Frequent hangout and campsite for hoboes, c. 1920s.
Kaplan Musical String Company	Rear 104 Highland Avenue, Stanislaus Kaplan & Sons (Stanley and Otto), props., 1920–1975. Mfg. gut and metal strings for musical instruments.
Keeler's Ice House	Large wooden structure for ice storage north side Keeler Avenue west of Flax Hill Road. c.

Some Old Rowayton Place Names

	1890–1930. See: Brookside Lake Ice Company, Keeler's Pond.
Keeler's Pond	Large pond north of Keeler Avenue between Flax Hill Road and Boston Post Road. Ice cut for domestic use. See: Brookside Lake Ice Company.
Kiggin's Coal & Fuel Oil Company	21 Jacob Street, Walter F. Kiggins, prop., c. 1945– . See: Rowayton Fuel Co., Inc.
Kiggins Taxi & Trucking Company	Rowayton RR Station, c. 1916–1929; 21 Jacob Street, 1929–1940s. Walter F. Kiggins, prop.
Knickerbocker Grove	Copse of trees northwest corner Bayley Beach Park, Roton Avenue and Pine Point Road. A separate island in early times.
Klein's Estate	33 Wilson Avenue. Charles Klein, c. 1905–1915, author & playwright, *The Lion and the Mouse*. Mansion built for Edward White, c. 1895 (?). Owned by Dr. Anson Hurd, c. 1918–1938.
Klinefelter's Boatyard	121 Rowayton Avenue. Shorefront used for boat storage & self-service repairs, c. 1900–1930s. Joseph Klinefelter, prop.
Klinefelter's Plumbing Shop	157 Rowayton Avenue (Dibble's Store basement). Joseph H. Klinefelter, Jr., prop., c. 1910.
Klinefelter's Store (Meat and Vegetables)	155 Rowayton Avenue, J. H. Klinefelter, Sr., prop., c. 1910–1923. Successor to Alphonso Dibble.
The Knob Club	Private beach and tennis club east side Wilson Point, c. 1879–1930s.
Ladrigan's Livery Stable	1. Rear 315 Rowayton Avenue; 2. Carolyn Court; 3. rear 11 Hunt Street, Edward Ladrigan, Sr., prop., c. 1885–1915. Expressman and truckman.
Lenox Lot	East side Highland Avenue north of Lenox Avenue to Soundview Avenue.
Library Hall	145 Rowayton Avenue, second floor public meeting room, c. 1927–1967. See: Reliance Hall.
Lighthouse Liquors	1. McKinley Street, props. 1. Richard Smith; 2. Charles Draper; 3. Raymond Humiston, c. 1950–1970s.
Lincoln Avenue	Former name for McKinley Street.
Loading Rock	Large rock on west bank of Five Mile River rear 125 Five Mile River Road, used as landing by packet boats.
Lockwood's Taxi	11 Hunt Street, c. 1922–1928, Frank Lockwood, prop. (one 4 door Model T Ford). Successor to Edward Ladrigan's Livery.
The Log Cabins	55 Wilson Avenue. Group of five cabins built for a movie set about Abraham Lincoln, c. 1918. Razed c. 1930.
The Loop	Horseshoe shaped road east from Farm Creek Road, partially incorporated in Topsail Road.

Rowayton on the half shell

The Long Island	aka Sheffield Island. See: Smith's Island.
Long Neck Point	Darien. Land jutting into Long Island Sound west of Scott's Cove. See: Collender's Point.
Louie's Store (Variety)	114 Rowayton Avenue, Louis Rovegno, prop., c. 1947–1967. See: Benny's Store.
The Lower Dock	61–71 Rowayton Avenue, long north-south pier, Stevens Oyster Co., prop., c. 1880–1920. Bayliss Oyster Co., Oyster Bay, N.Y., prop., c. 1920–1935.
Lowndes Oyster Company	77–79 Rowayton Avenue, John H. Lowndes, prop., c. 1870–1910. 81–85 Rowayton Avenue, Stanley Lowndes, prop. moved business to Northport, N.Y., c. 1910.
Main Street	Former name of Rowayton Avenue.
Manresa Island	East of Wilson Point, west side Norwalk Harbor. Formerly Bouton's, Raymond's, Comstock's, and Keyser's Island.
Maple Street	Former name of Pennoyer Street.
Maplewood Road	Former name of Crest Road (Wilson Avenue to Pennoyer). See Hillside Street.
McKendry's Store (Variety)	275 Rowayton Avenue, Frank McKendry, prop., c. 1925–1930 (?).
McKinley Place	Former name of Harstrom Place.
Mead Bros. Store (General Merchandise)	167 Rowayton Avenue, Samuel & Frederick B. Mead, props., 1879–1929. Destroyed by fire Dec. 18, 1934. Location of first telephone in Rowayton.
Methodist Parsonage	7 Pennoyer Street, c. 1875 (?).
Middle Five Mile River School District	Included both sides of river in Brookside area. School converted to residence stands west side of Flax Hill Road north of Rowayton Avenue.
Miller Dress Shop	135 Rowayton Avenue, Lydia Miller, prop., c. 1929–1934 (?). Small one room building now rear 16 Pine Point Road. Also used as nursery school, c. 1892, and shoe repair shop, c. 1930s and '40s.
Mill's Boatyard	77–79 Rowayton Avenue, Andrew Mills, prop., c. 1912–1940. Slipway and storage shed. Rowayton's first gas dock, "Socony" products.
Mills' Hill	Both sides of Highland Avenue approx. 100 yds. north of Wilson Avenue to approx. 100 yeds. north of Englewood Road. A number of Mills families were first to build and reside in the vicinity.
Mills' Gas Dock	79 Rowayton Avenue, Rowayton's first dispenser of gas and oil for boats, c. 1912–1941. See: Mills' Boatyard.
Modern Grocery Store	101 Rowayton Avenue, c. 1927–1930.
Monsell Oyster Company	87 Rowayton Avenue, John Monsell, prop. (formerly partner of Wm. Craw), c. 1890s. Now Cap't Henry's Restaurant.

Some Old Rowayton Place Names

Montgomery House	166 Rowayton Avenue. Early name for Winthrop House, c. 1900.
Mount Misery	Rocky ridge north from RR tracks to Devil's Garden Road east of Rowayton Avenue. From early deeds.
The Movie Lot	55 Wilson Avenue. Location of movie set for picture about Abraham Lincoln, never finished, c. 1918. See: Log Cabins.
Mud Ocean	Localese for swamp land north of Wilson Avenue east of Indian Spring Road to Witch Lane.
Nash's (Nash Engineering Co.)	310 Wilson Avenue, South Norwalk. Mfg. of industrial pumps. Employer of many Rowayton residents.
Natural Growth Oyster Beds	State owned oyster ground off Rowayton from Noroton Point (Bell Island) to Fish Islands, restricted to sailing vessels.
Nelson's Clams & Lobsters	101 Rowayton Avenue, Hjalmar Nilsen (Jim Nelson) prop., c. 1927–1947.
Newman's Plumbing Shop	143 Rowayton Avenue, John J. Newman and Sons, prop., c. 1918–1938.
Noewanton	An Indian name for Rowayton and West Norwalk. Given as west boundary of Norwalk in Partrick deed of 1640.
Norge Boat Works, Inc.	75 Rowayton Avenue, Bjarne B. Nilsen, prop., Edward Webber, partner, c. 1947–1958. Importers of Scandinavian yachts.
Noroton Point	Southernmost tip of Bell Island. aka Bell Island Point.
Norroaton Point	See Noroton Point.
North Five Mile River School District	Included both sides of Five Mile River in West Norwalk. Schoolhouse on West Norwalk Road, c. 1860–1913.
North Street	Former name of western Wilson Avenue from Rowayton Avenue to Roton Avenue.
Norwalk Avenue	Former name of lower Pine Point Road.
Norwalk Long Island	aka The Long Island, Smith's Island and Sheffield Island.
Norwalk Yacht Club	59 Bluff Avenue, c. 1894–1965; Nathan Hale Road, Wilson Point, 1965– .
Oberlander's Boatyard	Five Mile River Road, Darien, at Ivy Point, John Oberlander, prop., c. 1890s. Builders of early powered launches.
Oberlander's Point	See: Ivy Point.
Ogden's Store (Grocery)	167 Rowayton Avenue, Mortimer Ogden, prop., c. 1895–1918, aka later: Brown's, Nardi's, Hertz's, Eagen's (Meats), Arnold's & Griffith's.
Oil Factory	Building on Noroton Point, Bell Island, for pressing fish oil from menhaden, aka bonies or bunker. On survey map of 1867.

Rowayton on the half shell

Paight Marine Repairs	143 Rowayton Avenue, Charles Paight, prop., c. 1940–1950.
Pampaskeshanke	Indian name for western boundary of Norwalk in Runckingheage deed of 1651. Believed by some historians to have been Rhoton or Ely's Brook. Recent studies place it at Good Wives' River, Darien, or Pine Brook. See: Ely's Brook.
The Old Field	See: Indian Field.
People's Grocery Company	112 Rowayton Avenue, Pincus M. Needle, prop., c. 1912–1928, successor to Marshall Thatcher. aka Needle's Store.
Pickle's Deli	163 Rowayton Avenue, current, successor to Wagner's Delicatessen.
Pine Brook	Darien, aka Good Wives' River. See: Pampaskeshanke Brook.
Pine Point	Land between South or Crescent Beach to the east and Roton Point Beach to the west to Farm Creek.
Pine Point Beach	Western part of South, or Crescent, Beach.
Pink Needle's Store	See: People's Grocery Company
Price's Rocks	Point of rocks jutting into Long Island Sound, separating Rowayton Beach on the west, and Wee Burn Beach to the east.
Pump House	West side Chasmer's Road Dam. Pumped water into tank and troughs for trains, c. 1880s–1912. See: The Draw. aka The Pumping Station.
Quarter Mile Hill	50 Witch Lane west to intersection of Hunt Street and Steeple Top Road. Favorite hill for sledding.
Railroad Avenue	Former name of Belmont Place. aka Railroad Place.
Raymond Avenue	Former name of Craw Avenue.
Raymond Cemetery	Private family cemetery, Rowayton Avenue at Cudlipp Street. First Burial 1783.
J. B. Raymond Dock Building & Pile Driving	78 Wilson Avenue, Jacob B. Raymond, prop., c. 1890–1915 (?).
Jake Raymond's corner	Wilson and Highland avenues.
Raymond's Farm	South of Wilson Avenue between Roton Avenue and Wilson Cove to Long Island Sound. Formerly St. John's Farm. See: Farm Creek.
Raymond Heights	West bank of Five Mile River north of Tokeneke Road.
Raymond's Ice House	South of dam opposite 20 Roton Avenue. Razed c. 1930.
Raymond's Island	Former name of Bell Island, and also Manresa Island.
Raymond's Lower Fields	Term in colonial deed for area south of stone wall at 136 Rowayton Avenue east to Roton

Some Old Rowayton Place Names

	Avenue to approximately Crockett Street.
Raymond's Lumber Yard	Rowayton Avenue foot of Wilson Avenue. Samuel Raymond, prop., c. 1880s.
Raymond's Point	High bluff east side of Five Mile River at mouth. aka Columbus and/or Columbia Grove.
Raymond's Pond	Roton Avenue north of McKinley Street. Dammed for domestic ice, c. 1880 (?). Skaters favorite since electric refrigeration. aka School Pond.
Raymond's Store	Elm Grove, Flax Hill Road & Soundview Avenue. Robert Raymond, prop., c. 1890–1930.
Raymond Street & Son	Tokeneke and Five Mile River Roads, Harry S. Street, prop., c. 1920s–1970s. Gas station and auto repair.
Raymond's Upper Fields	Term in Colonial deeds for area north of stone wall at 136 Rowayton Avenue between Rowayton and Roton Avenues to Witch Lane.
Reid Coalyard	Railroad Avenue east of station. William A. Reid, prop., c. 1920s–1930s.
Reliance Hall	145 Rowayton Avenue, second floor meeting room, c. 1905–1927. See: Library Hall.
Reliance Hook & Ladder Company	145 Rowayton Avenue. Volunteer Fire Company, c. 1903–1923. Building built 1905. Frank R. Stevens, chief.
Remington Rand, Inc.	40 Highland Avenue, c. 1950s; 33 Highland Avenue, 1950–1960s. Developers of "Univac," early computer, here.
Rhotan Brook	See: Ely's Brook & Pampaskeshanke Brook.
Richard's Shipyard	171 Rowayton Avenue, Samuel & James Richards, prop., c. 1700, making it by far Rowayton's earliest.
The Riding Light	87 Rowayton Avenue, book store, c. 1940s.
Ritter's Confectionary Store	159 Rowayton Avenue, c. early 1920s; later Bank's, Allen's, Andus', Peck's, Soybel's Drug Store, and Rowayton Pharmacy.
Riverview Drug Co.	161 Rowayton Avenue, current, successor to Rowayton Drug Company.
The Rock	South side Dibble Street, near Hill Top Homes. Huge glacial boulder.
The Rocks	Giant stone monolith east of 10–14 Harstrom Place. Levelled by Pond Ridge developers in 1987.
Roller Coaster Beach	West of Roton Point to Price's Rocks, including Bayley and Wee Burn beaches.
Roton Hill	Elevated ridge extending entire length of Highland Avenue. Also spelled in early Norwalk records as Rooten, Roarten, Rhoaton, Rhoton and Roaton.
Roton Islands	Various uplands at Bayley Beach, Roton Point, Rowayton Beach, Pine Point, Bell Island.

Rowayton on the half shell

Roton Neck	All of Rowayton south of Witch Lane (Norwalk Land Rcords, 1713).	
Roton Point	Rocky bluff jutting into Long Island Sound west of Pine Point and east of Price's Rocks, heavily wooded & variously spelled. See: Roton Hill.	
Roton Point Beach Club	Bathing, tennis, and sailing club on eastern area of former Roton Point Park.	
Roton Point Park	Large amusement park complex c. 1875–1942. Partial list of Park operators: Mike & Joe Jacobs; Conn. Lighting and Railway Company; The Connecticut Company; The Roton Point Improvement Co.; Roton Point Park, Inc., Neville Bayley, President and CEO. (1928–1942).	

Partial list of attractions:

Airplane Swings	On east end of the mid-way in rear of Roton Point Hotel.
Band stand	Still standing on rocks southeast of hotel.
Beach	West of Pine Point to breakwater.
The Bug	Speedy ride revolving around center post in cars attached to undulating track.
Dance pavilion	Built on spiles and rocks southwest of hotel, one of the earliest buildings, c. 1880–1942. Razed, c. 1950.
Dock	Seaward from tip of Pine Point. Pier for excursion and sight-seeing boats.
Hotel	Large 3-story structure in center of park, c. 1890 (?). Restaurant and hotel facilities.
Merry-go-round	1. East of hotel behind bath houses, c. 1880–1900. 2. West of hotel at water's edge near Roller Coaster Beach, c. 1900–1942.
Penny arcade	On mid-way rear of hotel. Transported by barge to foot of First Street, East Norwalk, c. 1946 for restaurant.
Skee-ball	Game of skill west side of hotel near Merry-go-round. c. 1928–1942.
Skooter	Electric bumper cars on steel floor, west end of mid-way behind hotel.
Shooting gallery	Test of skill with 22 caliber rifles against moving targets, clay pipes on wheels and moving ducks.
Roller coaster	1. Fast, undulating ride in open cars along present Bayley and Wee Burn beaches, c. 1900–1925. 2. Shorter, steeper, faster ride along Bayley Beach only, c. 1925–1942.
The Whip	A level ride in seats attached to spokes of a rapidly rotating wheel with a snapping effect. On mid-way.

Some Old Rowayton Place Names

Roton Road	Former name of South Beach Drive and Crescent Beach Road, Bell Island.
Roton Point Road	Formerly Wilson Avenue from Witch Lane south and west to present Roton Avenue, south to end, c. 1900.
Rowayton	Southwestern/Norwalk south of Devil's Garden Road and west of Wilson Cove to Five Mile River.
Rowayton Arts Center	145 Rowayton Avenue, est. c. 1970. See: Reliance Hook & Ladder Co.
Rowayton Athletic Club	275 Rowayton Avenue, c. 1927. Arthur H. Billard, director.
Rowayton Baptist Church	11 Cudlipp Street, c. 1859–1905. 212 Rowayton Avenue, c. 1905–1967.
Rowayton Barber Shop	155 Rowayton Avenue, c. 1927–1941. See: Joe's Barber Shop.
Rowayton Beach	Bathing beach east of Five Mile River to Price's Rocks. aka Columbia Beach and Columbus Beach.
Rowayton Beach	Residential area south of 50 Rowayton Avenue to Long Island Sound east to Roton Avenue.
Rowayton Drug Store	164 Rowayton Avenue. See: Riverview Drug.
Rowayton Fire Department	136 Rowayton Avenue. See: Rowayton Hose Co., Reliance Hook & Ladder Company.
Rowayton Flower Club	Joint effort by two churches. Locally grown flowers collected and shipped by messenger to an orphan's home in Brooklyn regularly. Mrs. John Sherman Hoyt, sponsor; Henry Cutbill, courier, c. 1910.
Rowayton Fuel and Oil Co., Inc.	21 Jacob Street. Successor to Kiggins Coal & Fuel Company.
Rowayton Garage	105 Rowayton Avenue. See: The Gas Station.
Rowayton Greenhouses	Brookside, c. 1900s–1950s: 1. George H. Traendly; 2. Frank H. Traendly, props. Growers of roses and orchids. Had extensive greenhouses upper Raymond Street, Darien.
Rowayton Hardware	140 Rowayton Avenue, Jasper Harding, prop., 1949–1973; Louis Froelich, prop., 1973– . Successor to Harding Hardware.
Rowayton Hose Company No. 1, Inc.	Volunteer Fire Company, Est. 1902. Located: 1. 6 Logan Place (Wm. Cushman barn); 2. 169 Rowayton Avenue, 1903 (Charles Klein boathouse); 3. 151 Rowayton Avenue, 1905; 4. 136 Rowayton Avenue, 1956.
Rowayton Hotel	166 Rowayton Avenue, erected c. 1848 by Chas. L. Raymond, aka Fairview Hotel, C. H. Schmit, prop., c. 1900; Rowayton Inn, c. 1933; Winthrop House since 1950 (?), Robert Bassler, prop.

Rowayton on the half shell

The Rowayton House	363 Rowayton Avenue, William T. Raymond residence, c. 1880. Converted to summer hotel operated by Galt family 1910–1920.
Rowayton Library	Organized December 1903. Locations: 1. 87 Rowayton Avenue, 1903–1907; 2. 101 Rowayton Avenue, 1907–1927; 3. 145 Rowayton Avenue, 1927–1963; 4. 33 Highland Avenue, 1966–. Corporate title: The Association of The Free Library and Reading Room of Rowayton, Inc.
Rowayton Liquor Store	165 Rowayton Avenue, Daniel Lefkoff, prop., 1950s; Donald Craig, prop., 1970s.
Rowayton Lobster Pound	93 Rowayton Avenue, est. c. 1980, Kevin Conroy, prop. Seafood market.
Rowayton Lyceum	157 Rowayton Avenue (basement room Dibble's Store), c. 1867–1881. Rowayton's first lending library.
Rowayton Marine Works, Inc.	105 Rowayton Avenue, c. 1930–1985. Ferdinand Hartog, Sr., prop.
Rowayton Market	157 Rowayton Avenue. Rowayton's oldest store, since 1753. Partial list of operators: James Richards, Gershom Richards, Alfred Seeley, Alphonso Dibble, S. Edward Dibble, Joseph Klinefelter, Frank Ritter, Stephanak Bros., Stanizewski Bros., Rocco Luppino. aka Flynn's Market.
Rowayton Methodist Episcopal Church	Organized 1868 as Third M.E. Church, 1–5 Pennoyer Street. aka Rowayton Methodist Church.
Rowayton News Store (Variety)	114 Rowayton Avenue, props.: Benjamin A. Mangels, 1929–1935; George Thornhill, 1935–(?); Russell Hartwright; Howard Banta; Louis Rovegno. aka Louis' Store.
Rowayton Pharmacy	159 Rowayton Avenue, 1948–1960; 161 Rowayton Avenue, 1960–1984. George Soybel, prop., 1939–1952. Successor to Andrus Drug Store. aka Soybel's Drug Store. Now Riverview Drug Store.
Rowayton Post Office	Est. 1867. Locations: 1. RR Station - 1890; 2. 286 Rowayton Avenue, 1890–1914; 3. 291 Rowayton Avenue, 1914–1927; 4. 153 Rowayton Avenue, 1927–1947; 5. 1 McKinley St., 1949; 6. 144 Rowayton Avenue, 1949–.
Rowayton Radio & Television	John Geriak, prop., 1. 112 Rowayton Avenue, 1952–1964 (?); 2. 158 Rowayton Avenue, 1964–1978.
Rowayton School	Locations: 1. 11 Hunt Street, 1820–1848; 2. 1–3 Cudlipp Street, 1848–1894; 3. 192 Rowayton Avenue, 1894–1940; 4. 1 Roton Avenue, 1940–. See: South Five Mile River School District.

Some Old Rowayton Place Names

Rowayton Shoe Repair — 137 Rowayton Avenue, Frank L. Waters, prop., c. 1933; Joseph Troiano, 1940s. There were a number of other props. through the years.

Rowayton Union Cemetery — Organized 1849. West side Rowayton Avenue south of Devil's Garden Road. Rowayton's principal burial ground.

Rowayton Woods — West side Highland Avenue north of RR bridge. Area's first condominium development, c. 1971.

Rowayton Yacht Club — 1. 169 Rowayton Avenue, c. 1900–1915; 2. 77 Bluff Avenue, organized 1987–.

Rowland's Store (Confectionary) — Rear of 24 Crockett Street, Ida Rowland, prop., c. 1928–1935.

Runckinheage — Indian name for Rowayton area used in deed of February 15, 1651, after local Sachem.

St. John Avenue — Former name for Thomes Street.

The Salting Place — Area south of Witch Lane where Wilson Cove meets Wilson Avenue.

Sammis Avenue — Former name for Sammis Street.

Sammis Street — Former name for Milton Place. See: Sammis Avenue.

Sammis Street Bridge — Wooden bridge over Farm Creek west end of Sammis Street near Roton Avenue.

The Sand Bank — Sand and gravel pit at Highland Park and Flax Hill Road, Geofrey Shaw, prop.

Sandy Bottom — Swimming hole north end of Chasmer's Pond at confluence of Five Mile River and Keeler's Brook.

The Saw Mill Pond — Five Mile River northwest side Jacob Street, just north of White Bridge.

School Districts — aka School societies, often crossed town lines, and each financed district school and set curriculum. Norwalk once had 12 districts. See: North, Middle & South Five Mile River School Districts.

School Hill — Steep ridge behind school at 192 Rowayton Avenue (1894–1939). Favorite sledding site.

School Lot — 192 Rowayton Avenue, corner Witch Lane, site of 3rd Rowayton School, 1894–1939. Building razed 1940.

School Pond — See: Raymond's Pond.

Scott's Cove — Darien. Tidal cove west of Fish and Contentment Islands. aka Scotch Cove.

Shaw's Gravel Bank — See: Sand Bank.

Shaw's Woods — Area north of Flax Hill Road in vicinity of Westview Lane.

Sheep Lots — Area west of Highland Avenue, south of Flax Hill Road to Devil's Garden Road.

Sheffield Island — Westernmost of Norwalk Islands, aka Smith's

	Island, The Long Island, Norwalk Long Island, Little Long Island.
The Shell Path	Foot and wagon path north edge of Wilson Point from Wilson Avenue east to opposite Hoyt's Island, paved with oyster shells.
The Shipping Board	Federal maritime authority during WW I, 1917–1918. Operated ship outfitting facility at Wilson Point dock 1918–1922. Present site of Norwalk Yacht Club.
The Shipyard	175 Rowayton Avenue, c. 1700; See: Richard's Shipyard.
Shirley Manor	33 Wilson Avenue, Estate of Charles Klein (1900–1915). See: Klein Estate.
Sixth Taxing District	Area east of Wilson Cove to Five Mile River south of irregular line from Rowayton Union Cemetery to Wilson Avenue. Resident electors therein created a body-politic with limited powers by legislature in 1921.
The Smith Lots	East side of Highland Avenue north of RR to south of Brien McMahon High School.
Captain Smith's Boatyard	131 Rowayton Avenue, D. Lester Smith, prop., c. 1950s. Successor to Bounty-Smith, Inc.
Smith's Island	See: Sheffield Island.
South Beach	Bell Island, south end Yarmouth Road west to Pine Point Beach.
South Five Mile River School District	Included both sides of river south of Brookside. c. 1820–1913.
Spangle Marina	124 Wilson Avenue (head of Wilson Cove), Russell J. Spangle, prop., c. 1950–1965. Now site of Wilson Cove Marina and Wilson Cove Yacht Club.
Spangle Marine Contractors	124 Wilson Avenue, R. J. Spangle, prop., 1950–1965. Dock building and dredging. Successor to Daniel Toomey.
The Springy Place	See: Canfield Springs.
Stadel & Jenkins Boatyard	95 Rowayton Avenue, c. 1941–1946; See: Jenkins Boatyard.
The Stage Stop	South side Flax Hill Road at Richards Avenue, Brookside. George Washington said to have stopped (and/or slept) here.
Stamford Avenue	Former name of Ensign Road.
Standard Oil Company of New York	Operators of tank farm and distribution center, Wilson and Ely avenues, and docks at Wilson Point, c. 1920–1950. Employers of many Rowayton residents.
Steinwald Confectionary Store	58 Roton Avenue, Charles Steinwald, prop., c. 1900(?). See: Hoffman's Store.
Stevens Clams & Lobsters	111 Rowayton Avenue. Aaron & George Stevens, props., c. 1890–1940.

Some Old Rowayton Place Names

Stevens Oyster Company	61–71 Rowayton Avenue and 121–125 Rowayton Avenue, Captain William Isaac (Ike) Stevens, prop., 1860–1920. Rowayton's largest oystering operation.
Stewart's Gut	Water course from Five Mile River eastward; skirted southern edge of Craw's Woods emptying into Farm Creek opposite foot of Richmond Road prior to 1923.
Stewart's Meadow	Salt meadow in vicinity of Meridian Road. Granted to Robert Stewart in 1699.
Street's Pond	Domestic ice pond south side Tokeneke Road ¼ mile west of White Bridge. A favorite skating pond for Rowaytonites.
Sunk Rock	Approximately ½ mile south of Tokeneke Beach and ¼ mile east of outermost Fish Island. Falls bare at low tide.
Summit Avenue	Former name of Yarmouth Road.
The Sunk Swamp	East of Rowayton Avenue, north of Devil's Garden Road.
The Switch	Double trolley tracks north side Cudlipp Street opposite #3–5 to allow cars to pass each other.
The Giant Sycamore	See: Ancient Sycamore.
Tavern Island	West side Norwalk Harbor off Wilson Point. aka Oysterman's Island, Pilot's Island, Billy Rose's Island, Hill's Island, etc.
Marshall Thatcher's Store	112 Rowayton Avenue, c. 1910–1912, successor to Charles Guider.
Third Methodist Episcopal Church	See: Rowayton M.E. Church. So named as being third in Town of Norwalk.
Thomas' Hill	Steep incline in Wilson Avenue at head of Wilson Cove. Conn. Highway Route 136.
Thomas School	Est. 1922, Mabel Thomas, prop. Sites: 1. 100 Wilson Avenue, 1922–1927; 2. 11 Bluff Avenue, 1927–1964; 3. 40 Highland Avenue, 1964–1969. Now Low-Haywood Thomas School, Stamford, Connecticut.
Thomes Boatyard	121–135 Rowayton Avenue, John & Charles Thomes, props., c. 1870s. Boat builders.
Thomes' Coalyard	Rowayton Avenue, foot of Crockett Street. Ephriam Thomes, prop., c. 1880s.
Thomes' Store	147–149 Rowayton Avenue, Charles Thomes, prop., 1880–1901. Destroyed by fire resulting in organization of Fire Department.
Tokeneke Club	Darien. Private bathing and tennis club between Butler's and Contentment Islands.
Tokeneke Beach	Private beach on Long Island Sound between Butler's and Contentment Islands. See: Tokeneke Club.
Tokeneke Tower	Water tower which reached high above the trees

Rowayton on the half shell

	north of Scott's Cove, widely used as range for determining oyster ground boundaries.
The Toll House	56 Wilson Avenue (intersection of Roton Avenue). Toll charged in early times for access to salt meadows for pasturage.
The Toll Road	Roton Avenue south from Wilson Avenue. See: Toll House.
Tolles Pond	South of Devil's Garden Road at Erin Court, between Timberline Road and Deepwood Lane.
Toomey Marine Contractors	124 Wilson Avenue, c. 1935–1950 (?), Daniel Toomey, prop. Dock building and dredging. See: Spangle Marine.
Tory Hole	Shallow rocky cave in Tokeneke, refuge said to have been used by Loyalists during Revolutionary War.
Traendly's Greenhouses	See: Rowayton Greenhouses; aka Traendly The Florist.
Cap't. Trenchard's Houseboat	Rowayton Avenue next to Community Beach, Herbert Trenchard, owner, c. 1930–1950s. See: Fowler's Houseboat.
Trolley Trestles	1. Bridge from foot of Highland Avenue south across Farm Creek to Pine Point causeway, c. 1894–1934. 2. Bridge at west end of Cudlipp Street across Five Mile River south of White Bridge to Tokeneke Road, c. 1917–1934.
Twin Rocks	Two closely placed boulders approx. 100 feet south of Roton Point. Fall bare at low water.
United Church of Rowayton	210 Rowayton Avenue. Est. 1950. Combined congregations of Rowayton Baptist and Methodist churches. Erected 1965.
The Upper Dock	123–125 Rowayton Avenue, c. 1870–1920, long wooden pier of Stevens Oyster Company. Robert S. Barclay estate 1920–1945.
"Up the Street"	Localese for that area of Rowayton north of Witch Lane.
"Uptown"	Localese for South Norwalk. To South Norwalk residents it meant Norwalk.
Valentine's Barber Shop	Village center, c. 1900. Henry Valentine, prop. Possibly Rowayton's first.
Village Creek	Tidal inlet northeast of Wilson Point east of Wilson Avenue and southeast of Meadow Street.
Vincent's Livery Stable	134 Rowayton Avenue, John Vincent, prop., c. 1880–1910.
Vincent's Saloon	143 Rowayton Avenue, John Vincent, prop., 1880–1910(?), later John J. Newman & Sons, Plumbing; Jenkins Boatyard Marine Hardware; Cinderella Beauty Salon.
Vosburg's Coalyard	Rowayton Avenue, foot of Crockett Street, successor to Ephriam Thomes; c. 1900(?).

Some Old Rowayton Place Names

Wagner's Delicatessen	163 Rowayton Avenue, c. 1950s. Donald and Jeanne Wagner, props.
Wallie's Store (Meat Market)	157 Rowayton Avenue, Stephanak Bros., props., c. 1920–1950s. Wallace Stephanak, Mgr. See: Rowayton Market.
Waring's Field	West side Rowayton Avenue south of Jacob Street. See: Andrew Bell Estate. Norwalk Town Records 1744.
Waring's Swamp	West of Rhoton Hill Road, now Highland Avenue, north of RR tracks. c. 1737.
The Watering Place	Five Mile River at west end of Carolyn Court, c. 1851.
Wee Burn Beach Club	Foot of Roton Avenue from Bayley Beach west to Price's Rocks. Successors to Ballast Reef Beach Club.
Charles H. Wells Dockbuilding	18 McKinley Street, c. 1915–1925, successor to J. B. Raymond.
H. W. Wells Bridge & Dock Builders	Lincoln Avenue (McKinley Street) c. 1880s.
West Avenue	Former name of Westmere Avenue.
West Side Avenue	Former name of Five Mile River Road, Darien.
Whistleville	Southwestern South Norwalk between Highland Avenue RR bridge and South Norwalk RR station. Bend in track caused trains to blow whistles.
White Bridge	West end Cudlipp Street across Five Mile River to Tokeneke Road. Conn. Route 136. Bridges have been built here since first settlement.
White's Farms	Ed. White, prop., c. 1885–1910(?). 1. 33 Wilson Avenue north to stone wall end of Bryan Road between Crest and Indian Springs Roads. See Klein Estate. 2. 204–214 Rowayton Avenue. Both farms operated simultaneously.
Daniel Wicks Oysters	75 Rowayton Avenue, c. 1890–1925. Oyster opening house and boatyard.
The Weir	Tidal creek north of Wilson Point South and rear of Nash Engineering. Site of early pottery and fish weir for smelt. aka Village Creek.
The Winthrop House	166 Rowayton Avenue, apartments. Robert Bassler, prop. See: Rowayton Hotel.
Harry Williams Clam Dealer	2 McKinley Street, c. 1920–1930; also 135 Rowayton Avenue, c. 1930–1955.
Wilson Cove Marina	124 Wilson Avenue, c. 1965. See: Wilson Cove Yacht Club, Spangle Marina.
Wilson Cove Yacht Club	124 Wilson Avenue, yacht club operated in conjunction with Wilson Cove Marina, primarily for marina customers, c. 1965–.
Wilson Point Dock	Long pier on southwest end of Wilson Point built c. 1890 by New England RR. During WWI used by U. S. Shipping Board as ship outfitting yard. Then by Standard Oil Co. of New

	York for terminal. Currently owned by Norwalk Yacht Club.
Wilson Point Road	Former name for Wilson Avenue from Witch Lane east to Meadow Street, South Norwalk, Conn. Route 136.
Witch Lane	East-west road from Rowayton Avenue to Wilson Avenue. One of the area's earliest named roads. Said to be named for some women residents speaking a strange tongue. A dozen French speaking Arcadians were billeted in Norwalk during the French and Indian War 1759. Some may have remained and thought to be witches.
Witch's Woods	Heavily wooded area north of Witch's Lane, east of Little Brook Road and west of Range Road.
Wood's Woods	Area north of Wilson Avenue between Indian Spring Road and Flicker Lane to Witch Lane. Once owned by Wesley Wood.
Ziegler's Cove	Tidal inlet east side Long Neck Point at western end of Scott's Cove, Darien.

Some Old Rowayton Place Names

Sources

Books

Ancient Historical Records, Norwalk, CT. With "A plan of the Ancient Settlement 1847," Compiled by Edwin Hall. *Reprint published for Friends of Lockwood House.* Silvermine Publications, Norwalk, CT. 1973.

Annual List of Merchant Vessels of the United States. U.S. Government Printing Office, Washington, DC. 1896.

Collins, J. W., "Notes on Oyster Fisheries of Connecticut." United States Fisheries Commission, Washington, DC. 1891.

Dannenberg, Elsie P., *The Romance of Norwalk.* The States History Company, New York, NY. 1929.

Encyclopedia of Connecticut Biography. American Publishing Company, New York, NY. 1923.

Friend, Doris S., and Bensinger, Helen L., *A Point in Time.* Wilson Point Property Owners Association, Norwalk, CT. 1987.

Ingersoll, Ernest, *The Oyster Industry.* Department of the Interior, Washington, DC. 1881.

Kellogg, James L., *Shell Fish Industries.* Henry Holt & Co., New York, NY. 1910.

Kochiss, John M., *Oystering From New York to Boston.* Mystic Seaport, Inc., Mystic, CT. 1974.

Leech, Margaret, *Reveille in Washington.* Harper Bros., New York, NY. 1941.

Lossing, Benson J., *Pictorial Field Book of the Revolution.* Harper Bros., New York, NY. 1851.

Mather, Frederick, *Refugees of 1776 From Long Island to Connecticut.* Archives, Darien Historical Society.

McDonough, James L., *Stones River, Bloody Winter in Tennessee.* University of Tennessee Press, Knoxville, TN. 1980.

Mills, Oscar, *Rowayton, Connecticut, Reminiscences of Old Rowayton.* (Typewritten Copy of Manuscript.)

Ray, Deborah, and Stewart, Gloria, *Norwalk, Being an Historical Account of That Connecticut Town.* Norwalk Historical Society, Norwalk, CT. 1979.

Selleck, Charles M., *Norwalk.* Published by author, 1896. Printed by Henry Gardner.

Shephard, William R., *Story of New Amsterdam.* Knopf, New York, NY. 1926.

Survey of Town of Norwalk, Connecticut. F. W. Beers, Philadelphia, PA. 1867.

Wilson, L. W., *History of Fairfield County, Connecticut.* S. J. Clarke Publishing Company, Chicago, IL. 1929.

Wing, Henry E., *When Lincoln Kissed Me, A Story of the Wilderness Campaign.* Eaton & Maims, New York, NY. 1913.

Newspapers and Periodicals

Carson, Gerald H., "Who Put The Borax in Dr. Wiley's Butter?" American Heritage Magazine, August, 1956.

Norwalk Gazette, January 1, 1869.

Norwalk Hour, June 8, 1942.

The Sentinel, November 11, 1933.

Byrne, Leonard, "A Testament of Courage." *New England Galaxy Magazine,* Old Sturbridge Village, Sturbridge, MA. Spring 1975.

Government Reports

Second District Water Department, Norwalk, Connecticut, Records. Contract with Dudley E. Hoyt, 1901.

Shell Fish Commission, State of Connecticut, Hartford, CT. "Fourth Report," 1885.

Shell Fish Commissioners Records, Hartford, CT. 1910.
Sixth Taxing District, City of Norwalk, Records, Rowayton, CT.
United States Bicentennial Commission of Connecticut, Hartford, CT. Report: "The Fundamental Orders of Connecticut," by Mary Jeanne Anderson Jones, 1988.

Minute Books

Lyceum Library Association, Rowayton, CT, original minute book.
"Rowayton Gun Committee," original minute book (in Rowayton Historical Society archives).

Annual Reports

Darien Historical Society Annual, 1976, 1982, 1983–1984 editions.
New Canaan Historical Society Annual, 1956, "Roton Point," by Stanley S. Mead.

Archives

Darien Historical Society, Darien, CT.
Lockwood Museum, Norwalk, CT.
Norwalk Public Library, Norwalk, CT.
Norwalk Town Clerk's Office, Norwalk, CT.
Rowayton Historical Society, Rowayton, CT.
Rowayton Public Library, Rowayton, CT.
Following documents and manuscripts in Rowayton Historical Society archives:
Lynch, William, private collection.
Crockett, H. LeRoy, of New Haven, manuscripts.
Kilbourn, Joseph, "Rowayton Hose Company No. 1, Inc.," a history, 1977.
Raymond, Barbara J., manuscripts, 1942.
Seeley, Alfred, "Ledger for 1825."
Tuttle, Mrs. H. Croswell, "Reminiscences of Rowayton," manuscript.

Interviews

Bond, Newton F., Norwalk, CT, March, 1987.
Bossone, Mauro, Danbury, CT, February, 1989.
Cheh, Joseph W., Rowayton, CT, March, 1989.
DeLuca, Mrs. Leonard, Rowayton, CT, September, 1985.
Dwyer, John, Norwalk, CT, September, 1985.
Hickson, John M., Rowayton, CT, March, 1989.
Hoyt, Dudley D., Rowayton, CT, December, 1988.
Hoyt, Mary L., New Canann, CT, November, 1988.
Hunt, Malcolm, New Milford, CT, March, 1986.
Kiggins, Walter F., Darien, CT, March, 1987.
Soybel, Myra, Rowayton, CT, February 27, 1989.
Street, Harry S., Darien, CT, December, 1985.

Sources

The great majority of the illustrations appearing in this volume came from the archives of the Rowayton Historical Society. Other sources only are noted in the list which follows and the author is deeply grateful to all who provided material for consideration. A special note of thanks is due the distinguished marine artist John Stobart whose painting "Five Mile River, Rowayton, 1920" embellishes the endleaves, and to Rowayton's own Nina Pattesen Craig whose sketches of the local scene appear throughout the book.

Rowayton on the half shell

Illustrations and Credits

INDEX

Index

Index

Rowayton on the half shell

Index

216

Index

Rowayton on the half shell

This book was made possible by the generosity of the
following members of the Rowayton Historical Society.

Mrs. Ernest C. Albin
Mr. and Mrs. Alfred L. Alk
Mr. and Mrs. Frederick B. Anderson
Mr. and Mrs. Ralph Arcamone
Mr. and Mrs. Reginald W. Arnold
Mr. and Mrs. John W. Bender
Douglas A. Bora
Mrs. Gordon W. Brown
Mr. and Mrs. John F. Cagnina
Genevieve Cahalan
Mr. and Mrs. George F. Carroll, Jr.
Mr. and Mrs. Renwick E. Case
Mr. and Mrs. L. Peter Clow
Mrs. John H. Coates
Mr. and Mrs. Thomas W. Cohn
Mr. and Mrs. George E. Cronk
Mrs. Barbara J. Currie
Mr. and Mrs. Robert G. Duckworth
Mr. and Mrs. Lester Fairchild, Jr.
June & Ernest Faulkner
Mr. and Mrs. Frank T. Gauthier
Mr. and Mrs. Walter H. Glass
Mr. and Mrs. Henry J. Gloetzner
Mr. and Mrs. Richard F. Goennel
Mr. and Mrs. Ehrick Haight
Mr. and Mrs. William H. Hain
Nancy Hennen
Mrs. Norma A. Hishon
Mr. and Mrs. Henry F. B. Higgins
Mr. and Mrs. Richard A. Hopkins
Mr. and Mrs. Dudley D. Hoyt
Mr. and Mrs. W. Bradford Hoyt
Mr. and Mrs. Harold B. Hubbell
Mr. and Mrs. Brian L. Huson
Mr. and Mrs. Thomas C. Jackson
Dorothy E. Johnson
Claire Jones
Mrs. Alvah B. Kellogg
Midge & Bill Kennedy
Mr. and Mrs. W. Adriance Kipp, Jr.
Karin E. Klink

Mr. and Mrs. Arthur J. Ladrigan
Mr. and Mrs. Philip C. Langdon
Susan & Peter Lawrence
Mr. and Mrs. William D. LeMoult
Mrs. Grace W. Lichtenstein
Joseph & Molly MacCabe
Ann & Bill Martin
Mr. and Mrs. John M. Maury
Mr. and Mrs. Allan McKissock, Jr.
Mrs. Horace McMahon
Sandy & John Meagher
Mr. and Mrs. A. Middleton
Jocelyn K. Moreland
Mr. and Mrs. Bjarne B. Nilsen
Mr. and Mrs. Harold A. Osgood
Betty & Ken Otis
Mr. and Mrs. Robert J. Pettus
Mr. and Mrs. Walter N. Plaut
Mr. and Mrs. Douglas M. Pratt
The Rambusch Family
Mr. and Mrs. Edgar L. Raymond
Mr. and Mrs. Frank E. Raymond
Mr. and Mrs. Lunsford Richardson, Jr.
Willard & Nina Richardson
Mr. and Mrs. Kenneth W. Ritt
Mr. and Mrs. William J. Robinson
Mr. and Mrs. Andrew A. Rooney
Mrs. Gordon S. Rowland
Mr. and Mrs. Nick J. Seitz
Mrs. Josephine H. Slocomb
Mr. and Mrs. D. Lester Smith
Mrs. J. Douglas Smith
Mrs. William D. Stewart
Mr. and Mrs. Raymond D. Street
Mr. and Mrs. William H. Sullivan, Jr.
William Tims
Mr. and Mrs. Peter J. VanSlyck
Richard H. Walker
Carl T. Westhelle
Mr. and Mrs. Robert W. White
Mr. and Mrs. Richard N. Williams

Designed by A. L. Morris
the text of this volume was composed in Bem
and printed by Knowlton & McLeary
in Farmington, Maine
on Mohawk Vellum Text.
The jacket and endleaves were printed
on Strathmore Grandee Text,
and the binding in James River Graphics Kivar
was executed by New Hampshire Bindery
in Concord, New Hampshire.

Rowayton on the half shell

has been published in a first edition
of three thousand copies
of which one hundred and fifty
have been numbered and signed
by the author.
This is copy number

and is here signed.